THE PUBLIC INTEREST ON CRIME AND PUNISHMENT

EDITED BY NATHAN GLAZER

UNIVERSITY PRESS OF AMERICA,   INC.

LANHAM • NEW YORK • LONDON

University Press of America,™ Inc.

4720 Boston Way
Lanham, MD 20706

3 Henrietta Street
London WC2E 8LU England

Library of Congress Cataloging in Publication Data
Main entry under title:

The Public interest on crime and punishment.

Reprint. Originally published: Cambridge, Mass. :
Abt Books, c1984.
Essays originally published in the Public interest
since 1974.
1. Crime and criminals—United States—Addresses,
essays, lectures. 2. Punishment—United States—Addresses,
essays, lectures. I. Glazer, Nathan. II. Public interest.
NV6789.P82   1984b   364'.973   84-17372
ISBN 0-8191-4138-0
ISBN 0-8191-4139-9 (pbk.)

Reprinted by arrangement with
Abt Books.

Contents

Acknowledgements

"What Works—Questions and Answers About Prison Reform", No. 35, Spring 1974.

"Methadone: The Forlorn Hope", No. 36, Summer 1974.

"How Many Games in Town? The Pros and Cons of Legalized Gambling", No. 36, Summer 1974.

"Does Punishment Deter Crime?", No. 36, Summer 1974.

"Crime and Punishment in England", No. 43, Spring 1976.

"Learning About Crime—The Japanese Experience", No. 44, Summer 1976.

"The Rehabilitation of Punishment", No. 44, Summer 1976.

"The Great American Gun War", No. 45, Fall 1976.

"Age, Crime, and Punishment", No. 51, Spring 1978.

"Fact, Fancy, and Organized Crime", No. 53, Fall 1978.

"On Subway Graffiti in New York", No. 54, Winter 1979.

"Crime in American Public Schools", No. 58, Winter 1980.

"Torture and Plea Bargaining", No. 58, Winter 1980.

"To Serve and Protect: Learning from Police History", No. 70, Winter 1983.

Introduction

IT is not news that the United States is afflicted with more crime than any other major industrial society: *why*, is a perpetual concern of social scientists, and what can be done about it a perpetual issue of public policy analysts and elected officials. *The Public Interest* has addressed questions of crime and punishment many times, and the following selection of thirteen articles drawn from issues of the past ten years—and still directly relevant to current issues in crime and public safety—has been put together to serve as an introduction to policy issues in this area, treated by some of the ablest analysts in the field. Robert Martinson addresses the major question whether prison rehabilitates. His skepticism by now is the ground from which discussion of prison reform begins. Drug addiction and drug dealing is a major source of American crime, and Edward Jay Epstein describes one major effort to deal with this source at the root. Gambling is another major source of crime: Jess Marcum and Henry Rowen consider whether legalized gambling can reduce the crime that feeds off gambling when it is illegal. Organized crime in particular seems to base itself on drugs and gambling: Peter Reuter and Jonathan B. Rubenstein analyze what we actually know about the role of organized crime. The issue of the role of punishment has long agitated analysts of crime: Gordon Tullock, Marc Plattner, and Barbara Bolan and James Q. Wilson analyze the questions raised by punishment as a deterrent to crime, as a necessary form of teaching of decent behavior, and as a means of incapacitation of criminals. B. Bruce-Briggs considers one proposed approach to the reduction of crime, gun control. Jackson Toby deals with the troubling problem of crime in American schools, and Nathan Glazer discusses a minor crime that has succeeded in placing its mark—visually, at least—on the environment of New York City, and has resisted all efforts at eradication. David Bayley asks whether we can learn anything from Japan, which maintains by far the lowest level of crime of any major nation. And Mark H. Moore and George L. Kelling present a new view, based on history and research, of what we may expect from policing in our efforts to control crime.

Nathan Glazer

What works?
—questions and answers
about
prison reform

ROBERT MARTINSON

I N THE past several years, Ameri-
can prisons have gone through one of their recurrent periods of
strikes, riots, and other disturbances. Simultaneously, and in consequence, the articulate public has entered another one of its sporadic
fits of attentiveness to the condition of our prisons and to the perennial questions they pose about the nature of crime and the uses of
punishment. The result has been a widespread call for "prison reform," i.e., for "reformed" prisons which will produce "reformed" convicts. Such calls are a familiar feature of American prison history.
American prisons, perhaps more than those of any other country,
have stood or fallen in public esteem according to their ability to
fulfill their promise of rehabilitation.

One of the problems in the constant debate over "prison reform"
is that we have been able to draw very little on any systematic empirical knowledge about the success or failure that we have met
when we *have* tried to rehabilitate offenders, with various treatments
and in various institutional and non-institutional settings. The field
of penology has produced a voluminous research literature on this
subject, but until recently there has been no comprehensive review
of this literature and no attempt to bring its findings to bear, in a

useful way, on the general question of "What works?". My purpose in this essay is to sketch an answer to that question.

The travails of a study

In 1966, the New York State Governor's Special Committee on Criminal Offenders recognized their need for such an answer. The Committee was organized on the premise that prisons could rehabilitate, that the prisons of New York were not in fact making a serious effort at rehabilitation, and that New York's prisons should be converted from their existing custodial basis to a new rehabilitative one. The problem for the Committee was that there was no available guidance on the question of what had been shown to be the most effective means of rehabilitation. My colleagues and I were hired by the committee to remedy this defect in our knowledge; our job was to undertake a comprehensive survey of what was known about rehabilitation.

In 1968, in order to qualify for federal funds under the Omnibus Crime Control and Safe Streets Act, the state established a planning organization, which acquired from the Governor's Committee the responsibility for our report. But by 1970, when the project was formally completed, the state had changed its mind about the worth and proper use of the information we had gathered. The Governor's Committee had begun by thinking that such information was a necessary basis for any reforms that might be undertaken; the state planning agency ended by viewing the study as a document whose disturbing conclusions posed a serious threat to the programs which, in the meantime, they had determined to carry forward. By the spring of 1972—fully a year after I had re-edited the study for final publication—the state had not only failed to publish it, but had also refused to give me permission to publish it on my own. The document itself would still not be available to me or to the public today had not Joseph Alan Kaplon, an attorney, subpoenaed it from the state for use as evidence in a case before the Bronx Supreme Court.[1]

During the time of my efforts to get the study released, reports of it began to be widely circulated, and it acquired something of an underground reputation. But this article is the first published account, albeit a brief one, of the findings contained in that 1,400-page manuscript.

What we set out to do in this study was fairly simple, though it

---

[1] Following this case, the state finally did give its permission to have the work published; it will appear in its complete form in a forthcoming book by Praeger.

turned into a massive task. First we undertook a six-month search of the literature for any available reports published in the English language on attempts at rehabilitation that had been made in our corrections systems and those of other countries from 1945 through 1967. We then picked from that literature all those studies whose findings were interpretable—that is, whose design and execution met the conventional standards of social science research. Our criteria were rigorous but hardly esoteric: A study had to be an evaluation of a treatment method, it had to employ an independent measure of the improvement secured by that method, and it had to use some control group, some untreated individuals with whom the treated ones could be compared. We excluded studies only for methodological reasons: They presented insufficient data, they were only preliminary, they presented only a summary of findings and did not allow a reader to evaluate those findings, their results were confounded by extraneous factors, they used unreliable measures, one could not understand their descriptions of the treatment in question, they drew spurious conclusions from their data, their samples were undescribed or too small or provided no true comparability between treated and untreated groups, or they had used inappropriate statistical tests and did not provide enough information for the reader to recompute the data. Using these standards, we drew from the total number of studies 231 acceptable ones, which we not only analyzed ourselves but summarized in detail so that a reader of our analysis would be able to compare it with his independent conclusions.

These treatment studies use various measures of offender improvement: recidivism rates (that is, the rates at which offenders return to crime), adjustment to prison life, vocational success, educational achievement, personality and attitude change, and general adjustment to the outside community. We included all of these in our study; but in these pages I will deal only with the effects of rehabilitative treatment on recidivism, the phenomenon which reflects most directly how well our present treatment programs are performing the task of rehabilitation. The use of even this one measure brings with it enough methodological complications to make a clear reporting of the findings most difficult. The groups that are studied, for instance, are exceedingly disparate, so that it is hard to tell whether what "works" for one kind of offender also works for others. In addition, there has been little attempt to replicate studies; therefore one cannot be certain how stable and reliable the various findings are. Just as important, when the various studies use the term "recidivism rate," they may in fact be talking about somewhat different measures of offender behavior—i.e., "failure" measures such as arrest rates or parole violation rates, or "success" measures such as favorable discharge from parole or probation. And not all of these measures correlate very highly with one another. These difficulties will become apparent again and again in the course of this discussion.

With these caveats, it is possible to give a rather bald summary of our findings: *With few and isolated exceptions, the rehabilitative efforts that have been reported so far have had no appreciable effect on recidivism.* Studies that have been done since our survey was completed do not present any major grounds for altering that original conclusion. What follows is an attempt to answer the questions and challenges that might be posed to such an unqualified statement.

Education and vocational training

1. *Isn't it true that a correctional facility running a truly rehabilitative program—one that prepares inmates for life on the outside through education and vocational training—will turn out more successful individuals than will a prison which merely leaves its inmates to rot?*

If this *is* true, the fact remains that there is very little empirical evidence to support it. Skill development and education programs are in fact quite common in correctional facilities, and one might begin by examining their effects on young males, those who might be thought most amenable to such efforts. A study by New York State (1964)[2] found that for young males as a whole, the degree of success achieved in the regular prison academic education program, as measured by changes in grade achievement levels, made no significant difference in recidivism rates. The only exception was the relative improvement, compared with the sample as a whole, that greater progress made in the top seven per cent of the participating population—those who had high I.Q.'s, had made good records in previous schooling, and who also made good records of academic progress in the institution. And a study by Glaser (1964) found that while it was true that, when one controlled for sentence length, more attendance in regular prison academic programs slightly decreased the subsequent chances of parole violation, this improvement was not large enough to outweigh the associated disadvantage for the "long-attenders": Those who attended prison school the longest also turned out to be those who were in prison the longest. Presumably,

---

[2] All studies cited in the text are referenced in the bibliography which appears at the conclusion of this article.

those getting the most education were also the worst parole risks in the first place.[3]

Studies of special education programs aimed at vocational or social skill development, as opposed to conventional academic education programs, report similarly discouraging results and reveal additional problems in the field of correctional research. Jacobson (1965) studied a program of "skill re-education" for institutionalized young males, consisting of 10 weeks of daily discussions aimed at developing problem-solving skills. The discussions were led by an adult who was thought capable of serving as a role model for the boys, and they were encouraged to follow the example that he set. Jacobson found that over all, the program produced no improvement in recidivism rates. There was only one special subgroup which provided an exception to this pessimistic finding: If boys in the experimental program decided afterwards to go on to take three or more regular prison courses, they did better upon release than "control" boys who had done the same. (Of course, it also seems likely that experimental boys who did *not* take these extra courses did *worse* than their controls.)

Zivan (1966) also reported negative results from a much more ambitious vocational training program at the Children's Village in Dobbs Ferry, New York. Boys in his special program were prepared for their return to the community in a wide variety of ways. First of all, they were given, in sequence, three types of vocational guidance: "assessment counseling," "development counseling," and "preplacement counseling." In addition, they participated in an "occupational orientation," consisting of role-playing, presentations via audio-visual aids, field trips, and talks by practitioners in various fields of work. Furthermore, the boys were prepared for work by participating in the Auxiliary Maintenance Corps, which performed various chores in the institution; a boy might be promoted from the Corps to the Work Activity Program, which "hired" him, for a small fee, to perform various artisans' tasks. And finally, after release from Children's Village, a boy in the special program received supportive after-care and job placement aid.

None of this made any difference in recidivism rates. Nevertheless, one must add that it is impossible to tell whether this failure lay in the program itself or in the conditions under which it was administered. For one thing, the education department of the institution

---

[3] The net result was that those who received *less* prison education—because their sentences were shorter or because they were probably better risks—ended up having better parole chances than those who received more prison education.

itself was hostile to the program; they believed instead in the efficacy of academic education. This staff therefore tended to place in the pool from which experimental subjects were randomly selected mainly "multi-problem" boys. This by itself would not have invalidated the experiment as a test of vocational training for this particular type of youth, but staff hostility did not end there; it exerted subtle pressures of disapproval throughout the life of the program. Moreover, the program's "after-care" phase also ran into difficulties; boys who were sent back to school before getting a job often received advice that conflicted with the program's counseling, and boys actually looking for jobs met with the frustrating fact that the program's personnel, despite concerted efforts, simply could not get businesses to hire the boys.

We do not know whether these constraints, so often found in penal institutions, were responsible for the program's failure; it might have failed anyway. All one can say is that this research failed to show the effectiveness of special vocational training for young males.

The only clearly positive report in this area comes from a study by Sullivan (1967) of a program that combined academic education with special training in the use of IBM equipment. Recidivism rates after one year were only 48 per cent for experimentals, as compared with 66 per cent for controls. But when one examines the data, it appears that this difference emerged only between the controls and those who had successfully *completed* the training. When one compares the control group with all those who had been *enrolled* in the program, the difference disappears. Moreover, during this study the random assignment procedure between experimental and control groups seems to have broken down, so that towards the end, better risks had a greater chance of being assigned to the special program.

In sum, many of these studies of young males are extremely hard to interpret because of flaws in research design. But it can safely be said that they provide us with no clear evidence that education or skill development programs have been successful.

Training adult inmates

When one turns to adult male inmates, as opposed to young ones, the results are even more discouraging. There have been six studies of this type; three of them report that their programs, which ranged from academic to prison work experience, produced no significant differences in recidivism rates, and one—by Glaser (1964)—is almost impossible to interpret because of the risk differentials of the prisoners participating in the various programs.

Two studies—by Schnur (1948) and by Saden (1962)—*do* report a positive difference from skill development programs. In one of them, the Saden study, it is questionable whether the experimental and control groups were truly comparable. But what is more interesting is that both these "positive" studies dealt with inmates incarcerated prior to or during World War II. Perhaps the rise in our educational standards as a whole since then has lessened the differences that prison education or training can make. The only other interesting possibility emerges from a study by Gearhart (1967). His study was one of those that reported vocational education to be non-significant in affecting recidivism rates. He did note, however, that when a trainee succeeded in finding a job related to his area of training, he had a slightly higher chance of becoming a successful parolee. It is possible, then, that skill development programs fail because what they teach bears so little relationship to an offender's subsequent life outside the prison.

One other study of adults, this one with fairly clear implications, has been performed with women rather than men. An experimental group of institutionalized women in Milwaukee was given an extremely comprehensive special education program, accompanied by group counseling. Their training was both academic and practical; it included reading, writing, spelling, business filing, child care, and grooming. Kettering (1965) found that the program made no difference in the women's rates of recidivism.

Two things should be noted about these studies. One is the difficulty of interpreting them as a whole. The disparity in the programs that were tried, in the populations that were affected, and in the institutional settings that surrounded these projects make it hard to be sure that one is observing the same category of treatment in each case. But the second point is that despite this difficulty, one can be reasonably sure that, so far, educational and vocational programs have not worked. We don't know why they have failed. We don't know whether the programs themselves are flawed, or whether they are incapable of overcoming the effects of prison life in general. The difficulty may be that they lack applicability to the world the inmate will face outside of prison. Or perhaps the type of educational and skill improvement they produce simply doesn't have very much to do with an individual's propensity to commit a crime. What we do know is that, to date, education and skill development have not reduced recidivism by rehabilitating criminals.

The effects of individual counseling

2. *But when we speak of a rehabilitative prison, aren't we refer-ring to more than education and skill development alone? Isn't what's needed some way of counseling inmates, or helping them with the deeper problems that have caused their maladjustment?*

This, too, is a reasonable hypothesis; but when one examines the programs of this type that have been tried, it's hard to find any more grounds for enthusiasm than we found with skill development and education. One method that's been tried—though so far, there have been acceptable reports only of its application to young offenders—has been individual psychotherapy. For young males, we found seven such reported studies. One study, by Guttman (1963) at the Nelles School, found such treatment to be ineffective in reducing recidivism rates; another, by Rudoff (1960), found it unrelated to *institutional* violation rates, which were themselves related to parole success. It must be pointed out that Rudoff used only this indirect measure of association, and the study therefore cannot rule out the possibility of a treatment effect. A third, also by Guttman (1963) but at another institution, found that such treatment was actually related to a slightly *higher* parole violation rate; and a study by Adams (1959b and 1961b) also found a lack of improvement in parole revocation and first suspension rates.

There were two studies at variance with this pattern. One by Persons (1967) said that if a boy was judged to be "successfully" treated—as opposed to simply being subjected to the treatment ex-perience—he did tend to do better. And there was one finding both hopeful and cautionary: At the Deuel School (Adams, 1961a), the experimental boys were first divided into two groups, those rated as "amenable" to treatment and those rated "non-amenable." Amenable boys who got the treatment did better than non-treated boys. On the other hand, "non-amenable" boys who were treated actually did *worse* than they would have done if they had received no treatment at all. It must be pointed out that Guttman (1963), dealing with younger boys in his Nelles School study, did not find such an "amen-ability" effect, either to the detriment of the non-amenables who were treated *or* to the benefit of the amenables who were treated. But the Deuel School study (Adams, 1961a) suggests both that there is something to be hoped for in treating properly selected amenable subjects and that if these subjects are *not* properly selected, one may not only wind up doing no good but may actually produce harm.

There have been two studies of the effects of individual psychotherapy on young incarcerated *female* offenders, and both of them (Adams 1959a, Adams 1961b) report no significant effects from the therapy. But one of the Adams studies (1959a) does contain a suggestive, although not clearly interpretable, finding: If this individual therapy was administered by a psychiatrist or a psychologist, the resulting parole suspension rate was almost two-and-a-half times *higher* than if it was administered by a social worker without this specialized training.

There has also been a much smaller number of studies of two other types of individual therapy: counseling, which is directed towards a prisoner's gaining new insight into his own problems, and casework, which aims at helping a prisoner cope with his more pragmatic immediate needs. These types of therapy both rely heavily on the empathetic relationship that is to be developed between the professional and the client. It was noted above that the Adams study (1961b) of therapy administered to girls, referred to in the discussion of individual psychotherapy, found that social workers seemed better at the job than psychologists or psychiatrists. This difference seems to suggest a favorable outlook for these alternative forms of individual therapy. But other studies of such therapy have produced ambiguous results. Bernsten (1961) reported a Danish experiment that showed that socio-psychological counseling combined with comprehensive welfare measures—job and residence placement, clothing, union and health insurance membership, and financial aid —produced an improvement among some short-term male offenders, though not those in either the highest-risk or the lowest-risk categories. On the other hand, Hood, in Britain (1966), reported generally non-significant results with a program of counseling for young males. (Interestingly enough, this experiment *did* point to a mechanism capable of changing recidivism rates. When boys were released from institutional care and entered the army directly, "poor risk" boys among both experimentals *and* controls did better than expected. "Good risks" did worse.)

So these foreign data are sparse and not in agreement; the American data are just as sparse. The only American study which provides a direct measure of the effects of individual counseling—a study of California's Intensive Treatment Program (California, 1958a), which was "psychodynamically" oriented—found no improvement in recidivism rates.

It was this finding of the failure of the Intensive Treatment Program which contributed to the decision in California to de-emphasize individual counseling in its penal system in favor of group methods. And indeed one might suspect that the preceding reports reveal not the inadequacy of counseling as a whole but only the failure of one *type* of counseling, the individual type. *Group* counseling methods, in which offenders are permitted to aid and compare experiences with one another, might be thought to have a better chance of success. So it is important to ask what results these alternative methods have actually produced.

Group counseling

Group counseling has indeed been tried in correctional institutions, both with and without a specifically psychotherapeutic orientation. There has been one study of "pragmatic," problem-oriented counseling on *young* institutionalized males, by Seckel (1965). This type of counseling had no significant effect. For adult males, there have been three such studies of the "pragmatic" and "insight" methods. Two (Kassebaum, 1971; Harrison, 1964) report no long-lasting significant effects. (One of these two did report a real but short-term effect that wore off as the program became institutionalized and as offenders were at liberty longer.) The third study of adults, by Shelley (1961), dealt with a "pragmatic" casework program, directed towards the educational and vocational needs of institutionalized young adult males in a Michigan prison camp. The treatment lasted for six months and at the end of that time Shelley found an improvement in attitudes; the possession of "good" attitudes was independently found by Shelley to correlate with parole success. Unfortunately, though, Shelley was not able to measure the *direct* impact of the counseling on recidivism rates. His two separate correlations are suggestive, but they fall short of being able to tell us that it really is the counseling that has a direct effect on recidivism.

With regard to more professional group *psychotherapy*, the reports are also conflicting. We have two studies of group psychotherapy on young males. One, by Persons (1966), says that this treatment did in fact reduce recidivism. The improved recidivism rate stems from the improved performance only of those who were clinically judged to have been "successfully" treated; still, the overall result of the treatment was to improve recidivism rates for the experimental group as a whole. On the other hand, a study by Craft (1964) of young males designated "psychopaths," comparing "self-government" group psychotherapy with "authoritarian" individual counseling, found that the "group therapy" boys afterwards committed *twice* as many new offenses as the individually treated ones. Perhaps some forms of group psychotherapy work for some types of offenders but not others; a reader must draw his own conclusions, on the basis of sparse evidence.

With regard to young females, the results are just as equivocal. Adams, in his study of females (1959a), found that there was no improvement to be gained from treating girls by group rather than individual methods. A study by Taylor of borstal (reformatory) girls in New Zealand (1967) found a similar lack of any great improvement for group therapy as opposed to individual therapy or even to no therapy at all. But the Taylor study does offer one real, positive finding: When the "group therapy" girls *did* commit new offenses, these offenses were less serious than the ones for which they had originally been incarcerated.

There is a third study that does report an overall positive finding as opposed to a partial one. Truax (1966) found that girls subjected to group psychotherapy and then released were likely to spend less time reincarcerated in the future. But what is most interesting about this improvement is the very special and important circumstance under which it occurred. The therapists chosen for this program did not merely have to have the proper analytic training; they were specially chosen for their "empathy" and "non-possessive warmth." In other words, it may well have been the therapists' special personal gifts rather than the fact of treatment itself which produced the favorable result. This possibility will emerge again when we examine the effects of other types of rehabilitative treatment later in this article.

As with the question of skill development, it is hard to summarize these results. The programs administered were various; the groups to which they were administered varied not only by sex but by age as well; there were also variations in the length of time for which the programs were carried on, the frequency of contact during that time, and the period for which the subjects were followed up. Still, one must say that the burden of the evidence is not encouraging. These programs seem to work best when they are new, when their subjects are amenable to treatment in the first place, and when the counselors are not only trained people but "good" people as well. Such findings, which would not be much of a surprise to a student of organization or personality, are hardly encouraging for a policy planner, who must adopt measures that are generally applicable, that are capable of being successfully institutionalized, and that must rely for personnel on something other than the exceptional individual.

Transforming the institutional environment

3. *But maybe the reason these counseling programs don't seem to work is not that they are ineffective per se, but that the institutional environment outside the program is unwholesome enough to undo any good work that the counseling does. Isn't a truly successful rehabilitative institution the one where the inmate's whole environment is directed towards true correction rather than towards custody or punishment?*

This argument has not only been made, it has been embodied in several institutional programs that go by the name of "milieu therapy." They are designed to make every element of the inmate's environment a part of his treatment, to reduce the distinctions between the custodial staff and the treatment staff, to create a supportive, non-authoritarian, and non-regimented atmosphere, and to enlist peer influence in the formation of constructive values. These programs are especially hard to summarize because of their variety; they differ, for example, in how "supportive" or "permissive" they are designed to be, in the extent to which they are combined with other treatment methods such as individual therapy, group counseling, or skill development, and in how completely the program is able to control all the relevant aspects of the institutional environment.

One might well begin with two studies that have been done of institutionalized adults, in regular prisons, who have been subjected to such treatment; this is the category whose results are the most clearly discouraging. One study of such a program, by Robison (1967), found that the therapy did seem to reduce recidivism after one year. After two years, however, this effect disappeared, and the treated convicts did no better than the untreated. Another study by Kassebaum, Ward, and Wilner (1971), dealt with a program which had been able to effect an exceptionally extensive and experimentally rigorous transformation of the institutional environment. This sophisticated study had a follow-up period of 36 months, and it found that the program had no significant effect on parole failure or success rates.

The results of the studies of youth are more equivocal. As for young females, one study by Adams (1966) of such a program found that it had no significant effect on recidivism; another study, by Goldberg and Adams (1964), found that such a program *did* have a positive effect. This effect declined when the program began to deal with girls who were judged beforehand to be worse risks.

As for young males, the studies may conveniently be divided into

those dealing with juveniles (under 16) and those dealing with
youths. There have been five studies of milieu therapy administered
to juveniles. Two of them—by Laulicht (1962) and by Jesness (1965)
—report clearly that the program in question either had no significant effect or had a short-term effect that wore off with passing time.
Jesness does report that when his experimental juveniles did commit
new offenses, the offenses were less serious than those committed by
controls. A third study of juveniles, by McCord (1953) at the Wilt-
wyck School, reports mixed results. Using two measures of performance, a "success" rate and a "failure" rate, McCord found that his
experimental group achieved both less failure *and* less success than
the controls did. There have been two positive reports on milieu
therapy programs for male juveniles; both of them have come out of
the Highfields program, the milieu therapy experiment which has
become the most famous and widely quoted example of "success"
via this method. A group of boys was confined for a relatively short
time to the unrestrictive, supportive environment of Highfields; and
at a follow-up of six months, Freeman (1956) found that the group
did indeed show a lower recidivism rate (as measured by parole
revocation) than a similar group spending a longer time in the regular reformatory. McCorkle (1958) also reported positive findings
from Highfields. But in fact, the McCorkle data show, this improvement was not so clear: The Highfields boys had lower recidivism
rates at 12 and 36 months in the follow-up period, but not at 24 and
60 months. The length of follow-up, these data remind us, may have
large implications for a study's conclusions. But more important were
other flaws in the Highfields experiment: The populations were not
fully comparable (they differed according to risk level and time of
admission); different organizations—the probation agency for the
Highfield boys, the parole agency for the others—were making the
revocation decisions for each group; more of the Highfields boys
were discharged early from supervision, and thus removed from any
risk of revocation. In short, not even from the celebrated Highfields
case may we take clear assurance that milieu therapy works.

    In the case of male youths, as opposed to male juveniles, the find-
ings are just as equivocal, and hardly more encouraging. One such
study by Empey (1966) in a residential context did not produce
significant results. A study by Seckel (1967) described California's
Fremont Program, in which institutionalized youths participated in
a combination of therapy, work projects, field trips, and community
meetings. Seckel found that the youths subjected to this treatment
committed *more* violations of law than did their non-treated counter-

parts. This difference could have occurred by chance; still, there was certainly no evidence of relative improvement. Another study, by Levinson (1962-1964), also found a lack of improvement in recidivism rates—but Levinson noted the encouraging fact that the treated group spent somewhat more time in the community before recidivating, and committed less serious offenses. And a study by the State of California (1967) also shows a partially positive finding. This was a study of the Marshall Program, similar to California's Fremont Program but different in several ways. The Marshall Program was shorter and more tightly organized than its Fremont counterpart. In the Marshall Program, as opposed to the Fremont Program, a youth could be ejected from the group and sent back to regular institutions before the completion of the program. Also, the Marshall Program offered some additional benefits: the teaching of "social survival skills" (i.e., getting and holding a job), group counseling of parents, and an occasional opportunity for boys to visit home. When youthful offenders were released to the Marshall Program, either directly or after spending some time in a regular institution, they did no better than a comparable regularly institutionalized population, though both Marshall youth and youth in regular institutions did better than those who were directly released by the court and given no special treatment.

So the youth in these milieu therapy programs at least do no worse than their counterparts in regular institutions and the special programs may cost less. One may therefore be encouraged—not on grounds of rehabilitation but on grounds of cost-effectiveness.

What about medical treatment?

4. *Isn't there anything you can do in an institutional setting that will reduce recidivism, for instance, through strictly medical treatment?*

A number of studies deal with the results of efforts to change the behavior of offenders through drugs and surgery. As for surgery, the one experimental study of a plastic surgery program—by Mandell (1967)—had negative results. For non-addicts who received plastic surgery, Mandell purported to find improvement in performance on parole; but when one reanalyzes his data, it appears that surgery alone did not in fact make a significant difference.

One type of surgery does seem to be highly successful in reducing recidivism. A twenty-year Danish study of sex offenders, by Stuerup (1960), found that while those who had been treated with hormones and therapy continued to commit both sex crimes (29.6 per cent of them did so) and non-sex crimes (21.0 per cent), those who had been castrated had rates of only 3.5 per cent (not, interestingly enough, a rate of zero; where there's a will, apparently there's a way) and 9.2 per cent. One hopes that the policy implications of this study will be found to be distinctly limited.

As for drugs, the major report on such a program—involving tranquilization—was made by Adams (1961b). The tranquilizers were administered to male and female institutionalized youths. With boys, there was only a slight improvement in their subsequent behavior; this improvement disappeared within a year. With girls, the tranquilization produced worse results than when the girls were given no treatment at all.

The effects of sentencing

5. *Well, at least it may be possible to manipulate certain gross features of the existing, conventional prison system—such as length of sentence and degree of security—in order to affect these recidivism rates. Isn't this the case?*

At this point, it's still impossible to say that this is the case. As for the degree of security in an institution, Glaser's (1964) work reported that, for both youth and adults, a less restrictive "custody grading" in American federal prisons was related to success on parole; but this is hardly surprising, since those assigned to more restrictive custody are likely to be worse risks in the first place. More to the point, an American study by Fox (1950) discovered that for "older youths" who were deemed to be good risks for the future, a minimum security institution produced better results than a maximum security one. On the other hand, the data we have on youths under 16—from a study by McClintock (1961), done in Great Britain—indicate that so-called Borstals, in which boys are totally confined, are more effective than a less restrictive regime of partial physical custody. In short, we know very little about the recidivism effects of various degrees of security in existing institutions; and our problems in finding out will be compounded by the probability that these effects will vary widely according to the particular *type* of offender that we're dealing with.

The same problems of mixed results and lack of comparable populations have plagued attempts to study the effects of sentence length. A number of studies—by Narloch (1959), by Bernsten (1965), and by the State of California (1956)—suggest that those who are released earlier from institutions than their scheduled parole date, or those who serve short sentences of under three months rather than longer sentences of eight months or more, either do better on parole or at least do no worse.[4] The implication here is quite clear and important: Even if early releases and short sentences produce no improvement in recidivism rates, one could at least maintain the same rates while lowering the cost of maintaining the offender and lessening his own burden of imprisonment. Of course, this implication carries with it its concomitant danger: the danger that though shorter sentences cause no worsening of the recidivism rate, they may increase the total amount of crime in the community by increasing the absolute number of potential recidivists at large.

On the other hand, Glaser's (1964) data show not a consistent linear relationship between the shortness of the sentence and the rate of parole success, but a curvilinear one. Of his subjects, those who served less than a year had a 73 per cent success rate, those who served up to two years were only 65 per cent successful, and those who served up to three years fell to a rate of 56 per cent. But among those who served sentences of *more* than three years, the success rate rose again—to 60 per cent. These findings should be viewed with some caution since Glaser did not control for the pre-existing degree of risk associated with each of his categories of offenders. But the data do suggest that the relationship between sentence length and recidivism may not be a simple linear one.

More important, the effect of sentence length seems to vary widely according to type of offender. In a British study (1963), for instance, Hammond found that for a group of "hard-core recidivists," shortening the sentence caused no improvement in the recidivism rate. In Denmark, Bernsten (1965) discovered a similar phenomenon: That the beneficial effect of three-month sentences as against eight-month ones disappeared in the case of these "hard-core recidivists." Garrity found another such distinction in his 1956 study. He divided his offenders into three categories: "pro-social," "anti-social," and "manip-ulative." "Pro-social" offenders he found to have low recidivism rates regardless of the length of their sentence; "anti-social" offenders did better with short sentences; the "manipulative" did better with long ones. Two studies from Britain made yet another division

---

[4] A similar phenomenon has been measured indirectly by studies that have dealt with the effect of various parole policies on recidivism rates. Where parole decisions have been liberalized so that an offender could be released with only the "reasonable assurance" of a job rather than with a definite job already developed by a parole officer (Stanton, 1963), this liberal release policy has produced no worsening of recidivism rates.

of the offender population, and found yet other variations. One (Great Britain, 1964) found that previous offenders—but not first offenders—did better with *longer* sentences, while the other (Cambridge, 1952) found the *reverse* to be true with juveniles. To add to the problem of interpretation, these studies deal not only with different types and categorizations of offenders but with different types of institutions as well. No more than in the case of institution type can we say that length of sentence has a clear relationship to recidivism.

Decarcerating the convict

6. *All of this seems to suggest that there's not much we know how to do to rehabilitate an offender when he's in an institution. Doesn't this lead to the clear possibility that the way to rehabilitate offenders is to deal with them* outside *an institutional setting?*

This is indeed an important possibility, and it is suggested by other pieces of information as well. For instance, Miner (1967) reported on a milieu therapy program in Massachusetts called Outward Bound. It took youths 15½ and over; it was oriented toward the development of skills in the out-of-doors and conducted in a wilderness atmosphere very different from that of most existing institutions. The culmination of the 26-day program was a final 24 hours in which each youth had to survive alone in the wilderness. And Miner found that the program did indeed work in reducing recidivism rates.

But by and large, when one takes the programs that have been administered in institutions and applies them in a non-institutional setting, the results do not grow to encouraging proportions. With casework and individual counseling in the community, for instance, there have been three studies; they dealt with counseling methods from psycho-social and vocational counseling to "operant conditioning," in which an offender was rewarded first simply for coming to counseling sessions and then, gradually, for performing other types of approved acts. Two of them report that the community-counseled offenders did no better than their institutional controls, while the third notes that although community counseling produced fewer arrests per person, it did not ultimately reduce the offender's chance of returning to a reformatory.

The one study of a non-institutional skill development program, by Kovacs (1967), described the New Start Program in Denver, in which offenders participated in vocational training, role playing, programmed instruction, group counseling, college class attendance, and trips to art galleries and museums. After all this, Kovacs found no significant improvement over incarceration.

There have also been studies of milieu therapy programs conducted with youthful male probationers not in actual physical custody. One of them found no significant improvement at all. One, by Empey (1966), did say that after a follow-up of six months, a boy who was judged to have "successfully" completed the milieu program was less likely to recidivate afterwards than was a "successful" regular probationer. Empey's "successes" came out of an extraordinary program in Provo, Utah, which aimed to rehabilitate by subjecting offenders to a non-supportive milieu. The staff of this program operated on the principle that they were *not* to go out of their way to interact and be empathetic with the boys. Indeed, a boy who misbehaved was to be met with "role dispossession": He was to be excluded from meetings of his peer group, and he was not to be given answers to his questions as to why he had been excluded or what his ultimate fate might be. This peer group and its meetings were designed to be the major force for reform at Provo; they were intended to develop, and indeed did develop, strong and controlling norms for the behavior of individual members. For one thing, group members were not to associate with delinquent boys outside the program; for another, individuals were to submit to a group review of all their actions and problems; and they were to be completely honest and open with the group about their attitudes, their states of mind, their personal failings. The group was granted quite a few sanctions with which to enforce these norms: They could practice derision or temporary ostracism, or they could lock up an aberrant member for a weekend, refuse to release him from the program, or send him away to the regular reformatory.

One might be tempted to forgive these methods because of the success that Empey reports, except for one thing. If one judges the program not only by its "successful" boys but by all the boys who were subjected to it—those who succeeded and those who, not surprisingly, failed—the totals show *no* significant improvement in recidivism rates compared with boys on regular probation. Empey did find that both the Provo boys and those on regular probation did better than those in regular reformatories—in contradiction, it may be recalled, to the finding from the residential Marshall Program, in which the direct releases given no special treatment did *worse* than boys in regular institutions.

The third such study of non-residential milieu therapy, by McCravey (1967), found not only that there was no significant improvement, but that the longer a boy participated in the treatment, the *worse* he was likely to do afterwards.

Psychotherapy in community settings

There is some indication that individual psychotherapy may "work" in a community setting. Massimo (1963) reported on one such program, using what might be termed a "pragmatic" psychotherapeutic approach, including "insight" therapy and a focus on vocational problems. The program was marked by its small size and by its use of therapists who were personally enthusiastic about the project; Massimo found that there was indeed a decline in recidivism rates. Adamson (1956), on the other hand, found no significant difference produced by another program of individual therapy (though he did note that arrest rates among the experimental boys declined with what he called "intensity of treatment"). And Schwitzgebel (1963, 1964), studying other, different kinds of therapy programs, found that the programs *did* produce improvements in the attitudes of his boys—but, unfortunately, not in their rates of recidivism.

And with *group* therapy administered in the community, we find yet another set of equivocal results. The results from studies of pragmatic group counseling are only mildly optimistic. Adams (1965) did report that a form of group therapy, "guided group interaction," when administered to juvenile gangs, did somewhat reduce the percentage that were to be found in custody six years later. On the other hand, in a study of juveniles, Adams (1964) found that while such a program did reduce the number of contacts that an experimental youth had with police, it made no ultimate difference in the detention rate. And the attitudes of the counseled youth showed no improvement. Finally, when O'Brien (1961) examined a community-based program of group psychotherapy, he found not only that the program produced no improvement in the recidivism rate, but that the experimental boys actually did worse than their controls on a series of psychological tests.

Probation or parole versus prison

But by far the most extensive and important work that has been done on the effect of community-based treatments has been done in the areas of probation and parole. This work sets out to answer the question of whether it makes any difference how you supervise and treat an offender once he has been released from prison or has come under state surveillance in lieu of prison. This is the work that has provided the main basis to date for the claim that we do indeed have the means at our disposal for rehabilitating the offender or at least decarcerating him safely.

One group of these studies has compared the use of probation with other dispositions for offenders; these provide some slight evidence that, at least under some circumstances, probation may make an offender's future chances better than if he had been sent to prison. Or, at least, probation may not worsen those chances.[5] A British study, by Wilkins (1958), reported that when probation was granted more frequently, recidivism rates among probationers did not increase significantly. And another such study by the state of Michigan in 1963 reported that an expansion in the use of probation actually improved recidivism rates—though there are serious problems of comparability in the groups and systems that were studied.

One experiment—by Babst (1965)—compared a group of parolees, drawn from adult male felony offenders in Wisconsin, and excluding murderers and sex criminals, with a similar group that had been put on probation; it found that the probationers committed fewer violations if they had been first offenders, and did no worse if they were recidivists. The problem in interpreting this experiment, though, is that the behavior of those groups was being measured by separate organizations, by probation officers for the probationers, and by parole officers for the parolees; it is not clear that the definition of "violation" was the same in each case, or that other types of uniform standards were being applied. Also, it is not clear what the results would have been if subjects had been released directly to the parole organization without having experienced prison first. Another such study, done in Israel by Shoham (1964), must be interpreted cautiously because his experimental and control groups had slightly different characteristics. But Shoham found that when one compared a suspended sentence plus probation for first offenders with a one-year prison sentence, only first offenders under 20 years of age did better on probation; those from 21 to 45 actually did *worse*. And Shoham's findings also differ from Babst's in another way. Babst had found that parole rather than prison brought no improvement for recidivists, but Shoham reported that for recidivists with four or more prior offenses, a suspended sentence was actually *better*—though the improvement was much less when the recidivist had committed a crime of violence.

---

[5] It will be recalled that Empey's report on the Provo program made such a finding.

But both the Babst and the Shoham studies, even while they suggest the possible value of suspended sentences, probation, or parole for some offenders (though they contradict each other in telling us *which* offenders), also indicate a pessimistic general conclusion concerning the limits of the effectiveness of treatment programs. For they found that the personal characteristics of offenders—first-offender status, or age, or type of offense—were more important than the form of treatment in determining future recidivism. An offender with a "favorable" prognosis will do better than one without, it seems, no matter how you distribute "good" or "bad," "enlightened" or "regressive" treatments among them.

Quite a large group of studies deals not with probation as compared to other dispositions, but instead with the type of treatment that an offender receives once he is *on* probation or parole. These are the studies that have provided the most encouraging reports on rehabilitative treatment and that have also raised the most serious questions about the nature of the research that has been going on in the corrections field.

Five of these studies have dealt with youthful probationers from 13 to 18 who were assigned to probation officers with small caseloads or provided with other ways of receiving more intensive supervision (Adams, 1966—two reports; Feistman, 1966; Kawaguchi, 1967; Pilnick, 1967). These studies report that, by and large, intensive supervision does work—that the specially treated youngsters do better according to some measure of recidivism. Yet these studies left some important questions unanswered. For instance, was this improved performance a function merely of the number of contacts a youngster had with his probation officer? Did it also depend on the length of time in treatment? Or was it the quality of supervision that was making the difference, rather than the quantity?

Intensive supervision: the Warren studies

The widely-reported Warren studies (1966a, 1966b, 1967) in California constitute an extremely ambitious attempt to answer these questions. In this project, a control group of youths, drawn from a pool of candidates ready for first admission to a California Youth Authority institution, was assigned to regular detention, usually for eight to nine months, and then released to regular supervision. The experimental group received considerably more elaborate treatment. They were released directly to probation status and assigned to 12-man caseloads. To decide what special treatment was appropriate within these caseloads, the youths were divided according to their "interpersonal maturity level classification," by use of a scale developed by Grant and Grant. And each level dictated its own special type of therapy. For instance, a youth might be judged to occupy the lowest maturity level; this would be a youth, according to the scale, primarily concerned with "demands that the world take care of him. . . . He behaves impulsively, unaware of anything except the grossest effects of his behavior on others." A youth like this would be placed in a supportive environment such as a foster home; the goals of his therapy would be to meet his dependency needs and help him gain more accurate perceptions about his relationship to others. At the other end of the three-tier classification, a youth might exhibit high maturity. This would be a youth who had internalized "a set of standards by which he judges his and others' behavior. . . . He shows some ability to understand reasons for behavior, some ability to relate to people emotionally and on a long-term basis." These high-maturity youths could come in several varieties—a "neurotic acting out," for instance, a "neurotic anxious," a "situational emotional reactor," or a "cultural identifier." But the appropriate treatment for these youths was individual psychotherapy, or family or group therapy for the purpose of reducing internal conflicts and increasing the youths' awareness of personal and family dynamics.

"Success" in this experiment was defined as favorable discharge by the Youth Authority; "failure" was unfavorable discharge, revocation, or recommitment by a court. Warren reported an encouraging finding: Among all but one of the "subtypes," the experimentals had a significantly lower failure rate than the controls. The experiment did have certain problems: The experimentals might have been performing better because of the enthusiasm of the staff and the attention lavished on them; none of the controls had been *directly* released to their regular supervision programs instead of being detained first; and it was impossible to separate the effects of the experimentals' small caseloads from their specially designed treatments, since no experimental youths had been assigned to a small caseload with "inappropriate" treatment, or with no treatment at all. Still, none of these problems were serious enough to vitiate the encouraging prospect that this finding presented for successful treatment of probationers.

This encouraging finding was, however, accompanied by a rather more disturbing clue. As has been mentioned before, the experimental subjects, when measured, had a lower *failure* rate than the controls. But the experimentals also had a lower *success* rate. That is, fewer of the experimentals as compared with the controls had been judged to have successfully completed their program of supervision and to be suitable for favorable release. When my colleagues and I undertook a rather laborious reanalysis of the Warren data, it became clear why this discrepancy had appeared. It turned out that fewer experimentals were "successful" because the experimentals were actually committing more offenses than their controls. The reason that the experimentals' relatively large number of offenses was not being reflected in their failure rates was simply that the experimentals' probation officers were using a more lenient revocation policy. In other words, the controls had a higher failure rate because the controls were being revoked for less serious offenses.

So it seems that what Warren was reporting in her "failure" rates was not merely the treatment effect of her small caseloads and special programs. Instead, what Warren was finding was not so much a change in the behavior of the experimental youths as a change in the behavior of the experimental *probation officers,* who knew the "special" status of their charges and who had evidently decided to revoke probation status at a lower than normal rate. The experimentals continued to commit offenses; what was different was that when they committed these offenses, they were permitted to remain on probation.

The experimenters claimed that this low revocation policy, and the greater number of offenses committed by the special treatment youth, were *not* an indication that these youth were behaving specially badly and that policy makers were simply letting them get away with it. Instead, it was claimed, the higher reported offense rate was primarily an artifact of the more intense surveillance that the experimental youth received. But the data show that this is not a sufficient explanation of the low failure rate among experimental youth; the difference in "tolerance" of offenses between experimental officials and control officials was much greater than the difference in the rates at which these two systems detected youths committing new offenses. Needless to say, this reinterpretation of the data presents a much bleaker picture of the possibilities of intensive supervision with special treatment.

"Treatment effects" vs. "policy effects"

This same problem of experimenter bias may also be present in the predecessors of the Warren study, the ones which had also found positive results from intensive supervision on probation; indeed, this

disturbing question can be raised about many of the previously discussed reports of positive "treatment effects."

This possibility of a "policy effect" rather than a "treatment effect"
applies, for instance, to the previously discussed studies of the effects
of intensive supervision on juvenile and youthful probationers. These
were the studies, it will be recalled, which found lower recidivism
rates for the intensively supervised.[6]

One opportunity to make a further check on the effects of this
problem is provided, in a slightly different context, by Johnson
(1962a). Johnson was measuring the effects of intensive supervision
on youthful *parolees* (as distinct from probationers). There have
been several such studies of the effects on youths of intensive parole
supervision plus special counseling, and their findings are on the
whole less encouraging than the probation studies; they are difficult
to interpret because of experimental problems, but studies by Boston
University in 1966, and by Van Couvering in 1966, report no significant effects and possibly some bad effects from such special programs. But Johnson's studies were unique for the chance they provide
to measure both treatment effects and the effect of agency policy.

Johnson, like Warren, assigned experimental subjects to small caseloads and his experiment had the virtue of being performed with two
separate populations and at two different times. But in contrast with
the Warren case, the Johnson experiment did not engage in a large
continuing attempt to choose the experimental counselors specially,
to train them specially, and to keep them informed about the progress
and importance of the experiment. The first time the experiment was
performed, the experimental youths had a slightly lower revocation
rate than the controls at six months. But the second time, the experimentals did *not* do better than their controls; indeed, they did slightly
worse. And with the experimentals from the first group—those who
had shown an improvement after six months—this effect wore off at
18 months. In the Johnson study, my colleagues and I found, "intensive" supervision did *not* increase the experimental youths' risk of
detection. Instead, what was happening in the Johnson experiment
was that the first time it had been performed—just as in the Warren
study—the experimentals were simply revoked less often per number
of offenses committed, and they were revoked for offenses more
serious than those which prompted revocation among the controls.
The second time around, this "policy" discrepancy disappeared; and

---

[6] But one of these reports, by Kawaguchi (1967), also found that an intensively supervised juvenile, by the time he finally "failed," had had more previous *detentions* while under supervision than a control juvenile had
experienced.

when it did, the "improved" performance of the experimentals disappeared as well. The enthusiasm guiding the project had simply worn off in the absence of reinforcement.

One must conclude that the "benefits" of intensive supervision for youthful offenders may stem not so much from a "treatment" effect as from a "policy" effect—that such supervision, so far as we now know, results not in rehabilitation but in a decision to look the other way when an offense is committed. But there is one major modification to be added to this conclusion. Johnson performed a further measurement (1962b) in his parole experiment: He rated all the supervising agents according to the "adequacy" of the supervision they gave. And he found that an "adequate" agent, whether he was working in a small *or* a large caseload, produced a relative improvement in his charges. The converse was not true: An *in*adequate agent was more likely to produce youthful "failures" when he was given a *small* caseload to supervise. One can't much help a "good" agent, it seems, by reducing his caseload size; such reduction can only do further harm to those youths who fall into the hands of "bad" agents.

So with youthful offenders, Johnson found, intensive supervision does not seem to provide the rehabilitative benefits claimed for it; the only such benefits may flow not from intensive supervision itself but from contact with one of the "good people" who are frequently in such short supply.

Intensive supervision of adults

The results are similarly ambiguous when one applies this intensive supervision to adult offenders. There have been several studies of the effects of intensive supervision on adult parolees. Some of these are hard to interpret because of problems of comparability between experimental and control groups (general risk ratings, for instance, or distribution of narcotics offenders, or policy changes that took place between various phases of the experiments), but two of them (California, 1966; Stanton, 1964) do not seem to give evidence of the benefits of intensive supervision. By far the most extensive work, though, on the effects of intensive supervision of adult parolees has been a series of studies of California's Special Intensive Parole Unit (SIPU), a 10-year-long experiment designed to test the treatment possibilities of various special parole programs. Three of the four "phases" of this experiment produced "negative results." The first phase tested the effect of a reduced caseload size; no lasting effect was found. The second phase slightly increased the size of the small caseloads and provided for a longer time in treatment; again there was no evidence of a treatment effect. In the fourth phase, caseload sizes and time in treatment were again varied, and treatments were simultaneously varied in a sophisticated way according to personality characteristics of the parolees; once again, significant results did not appear.

The only phase of this experiment for which positive results were reported was Phase Three. Here, it was indeed found that a smaller caseload improved one's chances of parole success. There is, however, an important caveat that attaches to this finding: When my colleagues and I divided the whole population of subjects into two groups—those receiving supervision in the North of the state and those in the South—we found that the "improvement" of the experimentals' success rates was taking place primarily in the North. The North differed from the South in one important aspect: Its agents practiced a policy of returning both "experimental" and "control" violators to prison at relatively high rates. And it was the North that produced the higher success rate among its experimentals. So this improvement in experimentals' performance was taking place only when accompanied by a "realistic threat" of severe sanctions. It is interesting to compare this situation with that of the Warren studies. In the Warren studies, experimental subjects were being revoked at a relatively *low* rate. These experimentals "failed" less, but they also committed more new offenses than their controls. By contrast, in the Northern region of the SIPU experiment, there was a policy of *high* rate of return to prison for experimentals; and here, the special program *did* seem to produce a real improvement in the behavior of offenders. What this suggests is that when intensive supervision *does* produce an improvement in offenders' behavior, it does so not through the mechanism of "treatment" or "rehabilitation," but instead through a mechanism that our studies have almost totally ignored—the mechanism of *deterrence*. And a similar mechanism is suggested by Lohman's study (1967) of intensive supervision of probationers. In this study intensive supervision led to higher total violation rates. But one also notes that intensive supervision combined the highest rate of technical violations with the lowest rate for *new* offenses.

The effects of community treatment

In sum, even in the case of treatment programs administered outside penal institutions, we simply cannot say that this treatment in itself has an appreciable effect on offender behavior. On the other hand, there is one encouraging set of findings that emerges from these studies. For from many of them there flows the strong suggestion that even if we can't "treat" offenders so as to make them do better, a great many of the programs designed to rehabilitate them at least did not make them do *worse*. And if these programs did not show the advantages of actually rehabilitating, some of them did have the advantage of being less onerous to the offender himself without seeming to pose increased danger to the community. And some of these programs—especially those involving less restrictive custody, minimal supervision, and early release—simply cost fewer dollars to administer. The information on the dollar costs of these programs is just beginning to be developed but the implication is clear: *that if we can't do more for (and to) offenders, at least we can safely do less.*

There is, however, one important caveat even to this note of optimism: In order to calculate the true costs of these programs, one must in each case include not only their administrative cost but also the cost of maintaining in the community an offender population increased in size. This population might well not be committing new offenses at any greater rate; but the offender population might, under some of these plans, be larger in absolute *numbers*. So the total number of offenses committed might rise, and our chances of victimization might therefore rise too. We need to be able to make a judgment about the size and probable duration of this effect; as of now, we simply do not know.

Does nothing work?

7. *Do all of these studies lead us irrevocably to the conclusion that nothing works, that we haven't the faintest clue about how to rehabilitate offenders and reduce recidivism? And if so, what shall we do?*

We tried to exclude from our survey those studies which were so poorly done that they simply could not be interpreted. But despite our efforts, a pattern has run through much of this discussion—of studies which "found" effects without making any truly rigorous attempt to exclude competing hypotheses, of extraneous factors permitted to intrude upon the measurements, of recidivism measures which are not all measuring the same thing, of "follow-up" periods which vary enormously and rarely extend beyond the period of legal supervision, of experiments never replicated, of "system effects" not taken into account, of categories drawn up without any theory to guide the enterprise. It is just possible that some of our treatment programs *are* working to some extent, but that our research is so bad that it is incapable of telling.

Having entered this very serious caveat, I am bound to say that these data, involving over two hundred studies and hundreds of thousands of individuals as they do, are the best available and give us very little reason to hope that we have in fact found a sure way of reducing recidivism through rehabilitation. This is not to say that we found no instances of success or partial success; it is only to say that these instances have been isolated, producing no clear pattern to indicate the efficacy of any particular method of treatment. And neither is this to say that factors *outside* the realm of rehabilitation may not be working to reduce recidivism—factors such as the tendency for recidivism to be lower in offenders over the age of 30; it is only to say that such factors seem to have little connection with any of the treatment methods now at our disposal.

From this probability, one may draw any of several conclusions. It may be simply that our programs aren't yet good enough—that the education we provide to inmates is still poor education, that the therapy we administer is not administered skillfully enough, that our intensive supervision and counseling do not yet provide enough personal support for the offenders who are subjected to them. If one wishes to believe this, then what our correctional system needs is simply a more full-hearted commitment to the strategy of treatment.

It may be, on the other hand, that there is a more radical flaw in our present strategies—that education at its best, or that psychotherapy at its best, cannot overcome, or even appreciably reduce, the powerful tendency for offenders to continue in criminal behavior. Our present treatment programs are based on a theory of crime as a "disease"—that is to say, as something foreign and abnormal in the individual which can presumably be cured. This theory may well be flawed, in that it overlooks—indeed, denies—both the normality of crime in society and the personal normality of a very large proportion of offenders, criminals who are merely responding to the facts and conditions of our society.

This opposing theory of "crime as a social phenomenon" directs our attention away from a "rehabilitative" strategy, away from the notion that we may best insure public safety through a series of "treatments" to be imposed forcibly on convicted offenders. These treatments have on occasion become, and have the potential for becoming, so draconian as to offend the moral order of a democratic society; and the theory of crime as a social phenomenon suggests that such treatments may be not only offensive but ineffective as well. This theory points, instead, to decarceration for low-risk offenders—and, presumably, to keeping high-risk offenders in prisons which are nothing more (and aim to be nothing more) than custodial institutions.

But this approach has its own problems. To begin with, there is the moral dimension of crime and punishment. Many low-risk offenders have committed serious crimes (murder, sometimes) and even if one is reasonably sure they will never commit another crime, it violates our sense of justice that they should experience no significant retribution for their actions. A middle-class banker who kills his adulterous wife in a moment of passion is a "low-risk" criminal; a juvenile delinquent in the ghetto who commits armed robbery has, statistically, a much higher probabilty of committing another crime. Are we going to put the first on probation and sentence the latter to a long-term in prison?

Besides, one cannot ignore the fact that the punishment of offenders is the major means we have for *deterring* incipient offenders. We know almost nothing about the "deterrent effect," largely because "treatment" theories have so dominated our research, and "deterrence" theories have been relegated to the status of a historical curiosity. Since we have almost no idea of the deterrent functions that our present system performs or that future strategies might be made to perform, it is possible that there is indeed something that works— that to some extent is working right now in front of our noses, and that might be made to work better—something that deters rather than cures, something that does not so much reform convicted offenders as prevent criminal behavior in the first place. But whether that is the case and, if it is, what strategies will be found to make our deterrence system work better than it does now, are questions we will not be able to answer with data until a new family of studies has been brought into existence. As we begin to learn the facts, we will be in a better position than we are now to judge to what degree the prison has become an anachronism and can be replaced by more effective means of social control.

BIBLIOGRAPHY OF STUDIES REFERRED TO BY NAME

Adams, Stuart. "Effectiveness of the Youth Authority Special Treatment Program: First Interim Report." Research Report No. 5. California Youth Authority, March 6, 1959. (Mimeographed.)

Adams, Stuart. "Assessment of the Psychiatric Treatment Program: Second Interim Report." Research Report No. 15. California Youth Authority, December 13, 1959. (Mimeographed.)

Adams, Stuart. "Effectiveness of Interview Therapy with Older Youth Authority Wards: An Interim Evaluation of the PICO Project." Research Report No. 20. California Youth Authority, January 20, 1961. (Mimeographed.)

Adams, Stuart. "Assessment of the Psychiatric Treatment Program, Phase I:

Third Interim Report." Research Report No. 21. California Youth Authority, January 31, 1961. (Mimeographed.)

Adams, Stuart. "An Experimental Assessment of Group Counseling with Juvenile Probationers." Paper presented at the 18th Convention of the California State Psychological Association, Los Angeles, December 12, 1964. (Mimeographed.)

Adams, Stuart, Rice, Rogert E., and Olive, Borden. "A Cost Analysis of the Effectiveness of the Group Guidance Program." Research Memorandum 65-3. Los Angeles County Probation Department, January 1965. (Mimeographed.)

Adams, Stuart. "Development of a Program Research Service in Probation." Research Report No. 27 (Final Report, NIMH Project MH007 18.) Los Angeles County Probation Department, January 1966. (Processed.)

Adamson, LeMay, and Dunham, H. Warren. "Clinical Treatment Of Male Delinquents. A Case Study in Effort and Result," American Sociological Review, XXI, 3 (1956), 312-320.

Babst, Dean V., and Mannering, John W. "Probation versus Imprisonment for Similar Types of Offenders: A Comparision by Subsequent Violations," Journal of Research in Crime and Delinquency, II, 2 (1965), 60-71.

Bernsten, Karen, and Christiansen, Karl O. "A Resocialization Experiment with Short-term Offenders," Scandinavian Studies in Criminology, I (1965), 35-54.

California, Adult Authority, Division of Adult Paroles. "Special Intensive Parole Unit, Phase I: Fifteen Man Caseload Study." Prepared by Walter I. Stone. Sacramento, Calif., November 1956. (Mimeographed.)

California, Department of Corrections. "Intensive Treatment Program: Second Annual Report." Prepared by Harold B. Bradley and Jack D. Williams. Sacramento, Calif., December 1, 1958. (Mimeographed.)

California, Department of Corrections. "Special Intensive Parole Unit, Phase II: Thirty Man Caseload Study." Prepared by Ernest Reimer and Martin Warren. Sacramento, Calif., December 1958. (Mimeographed.)

California, Department of Corrections. "Parole Work Unit Program: An Evaluative Report." A memorandum to the California Joint Legislative Budget Committee, December 30, 1966. (Mimeographed.)

California, Department of the Youth Authority. "James Marshall Treatment Program: Progress Report." January 1967. (Processed.)

Cambridge University, Department of Criminal Science. Detention in Remard Homes. London: Macmillan, 1952.

Craft, Michael, Stephenson, Geoffrey, and Granger, Clive. "A Controlled Trial of Authoritarian and Self-Governing Regimes with Adolescent Psychopaths," American Journal of Orthopsychiatry, XXXIV, 3 (1964), 543-554.

Empey, LeMar T. "The Provo Experiment: A Brief Review." Los Angeles: Youth Studies Center, University of Southern California. 1966. (Processed.)

Feistman, Eugene G. "Comparative Analysis of the Willow-Brook-Harbor Intensive Services Program, March 1, 1965 through February 28, 1966." Research Report No. 28. Los Angeles County Probation Department, June 1966. (Processed.)

Forman, B. "The Effects of Differential Treatment on Attitudes, Personality Traits, and Behavior of Adult Parolees." Unpublished Ph.D. dissertation, University of Southern California, 1960.

Fox, Vernon. "Michigan's Experiment in Minimum Security Penology," Journal of Criminal Law, Criminology, and Police Science, XLI, 2 (1950), 150-166.

Freeman, Howard E., and Weeks, H. Ashley. "Analysis of a Program of Treatment of Delinquent Boys," American Journal of Sociology, LXII, 1 (1956), 56-61.

Garrity, Donald Lee. "The Effects of Length of Incarceration upon Parole Adjustment and Estimation of Optimum Sentence: Washington State Correctional Institutions." Unpublished Ph.D. dissertation, University of Washington, 1956.

Gearhart, J. Walter, Keith, Harold L., and Clemmons, Gloria. "An Analysis of the Vocational Training Program in the Washington State Adult Correctional Institutions." Research Review No. 23. State of Washington, Department of Institutions, May 1967. (Processed.)

Glaser, Daniel. *The Effectiveness of a Prison and Parole System.* New York: Bobbs-Merrill, 1964.

Goldberg, Lisbeth, and Adams, Stuart. "An Experimental Evaluation of the Lathrop Hall Program." Los Angeles County Probation Department, December 1964. (Summarized in: Adams, Stuart. "Development of a Program Research Service in Probation," pp. 19-22.)

Great Britain. Home Office. *The Sentence of the Court: A Handbook for Courts on the Treatment of Offenders.* London: Her Majesty's Stationery Office, 1964.

Guttman, Evelyn S. "Effects of Short-Term Psychiatric Treatment on Boys in Two California Youth Authority Institutions." Research Report No. 36. California Youth Authority, December 1963. (Processed.)

Hammond, W. H., and Chayen, E. *Persistent Criminals: A Home Office Research Unit Report.* London: Her Majesty's Stationery Office, 1963.

Harrison, Robert M., and Mueller, Paul F. C. "Clue Hunting About Group Counseling and Parole Outcome." Research Report No. 11. California Department of Corrections, May 1964. (Mimeographed.)

Havel, Joan, and Sulka, Elaine. "Special Intensive Parole Unit: Phase Three." Research Report No. 3. California Department of Corrections, March 1962. (Processed.)

Havel, Joan. "A Synopsis of Research Report No. 10, SIPU Phase IV—The High Base Expectancy Study." Administrative Abstract No. 10. California Department of Corrections, June 1963. (Processed.)

Havel, Joan. "Special Intensive Parole Unit—Phase Four: 'The Parole Outcome Study.'" Research Report No. 13. California Department of Corrections, September 1965. (Processed.)

Hood, Roger. Homeless Borstal Boys: *A Study of Their After-Care and After-Conduct.* Occasional Papers on Social Administration No. 18. London: G. Bell & Sons, 1966.

Jacobson, Frank, and McGee, Eugene. "Englewood Project: Re-education: A Radical Correction of Incarcerated Delinquents." Englewood, Colo.: July 1965. (Mimeographed.)

Jesness, Carl F. "The Fricot Ranch Study: Outcomes with Small versus Large Living Groups in the Rehabilitation of Delinquents." Research Report No. 47. California Youth Authority, October 1, 1965. (Processed.)

Johnson, Bertram. "Parole Performance of the First Year's Releases, Parole Research Project: Evaluation of Reduced Caseloads." Research Report No. 27. California Youth Authority, January 31, 1962. (Mimeographed.)

Johnson, Bertram. "An Analysis of Predictions of Parole Performance and of Judgments of Supervision in the Parole Research Project," Research Report No. 32. California Youth Authority, December 31, 1962. (Mimeographed.)

Kassebaum, Gene, Ward, David, and Wilnet, Daniel. *Prison Treatment and Parole Survival: An Empirical Assessment.* New York: Wiley, 1971.

Kawaguchi, Ray M., and Siff, Leon, M. "An Analysis of Intensive Probation Services—Phase II." Research Report No. 29. Los Angeles County Probation Department, April 1967. (Processed.)

Kettering, Marvin E. "Rehabilitation of Women in the Milwaukee County Jail: An Exploration Experiment." Unpublished Master's Thesis, Colorado State College, 1965.

Kovacs, Frank W. "Evaluation and Final Report of the New Start Demonstration Project." Colorado Department of Employment, October 1967. (Processed.)

Lavlicht, Jerome, et al., in *Berkshire Farms Monographs,* I, 1 (1962), 11-48.

Levinson, Robert B., and Kitchenet, Howard L. "Demonstration Counseling Project." 2 vols. Washington, D.C.: National Training School for Boys, 1962-1964. (Mimeographed.)

Lohman, Joseph D., et al., "The Intensive Supervision Caseloads: A Preliminary Evaluation." The San Francisco Project: A Study of Federal Probation and Parole. Research Report No. 11. School of Criminology, Universiy of California, March 1967. (Processed.)

McClintock, F. H. *Attendance Centres*. London. Macmillan, 1961.

McCord, William and Joan. "Two Approaches to the Cure of Delinquents," *Journal of Criminal Law, Criminology, and Police Science*, XLIV, 4 (1953), 442-467.

McCorkle, Lloyd W., Elias, Albert, and Bixby, F. Lovell. *The Highfields Story: An Experimental Treatment Project for Youthful Offenders*. New York: Holt, 1958.

McCravy, Newton, Jr., and Delehanty, Dolores S. "Community Rehabilitation of the Younger Delinquent Boy, Parkland Non-Residential Group Center." Final Report, Kentucky Child Welfare Research Foundation, Inc., September 1, 1967. (Mimeographed.)

Mandell, Wallace, *et al.* "Surgical and Social Rehabilitation of Adult Offenders." Final Report. Montefiore Hospital and Medical Center, With Staten Island Mental Health Society. New York City Department of Correction, 1967. (Processed.)

Massimo, Joseph L., and Shore, Milton F. "The Effectiveness of a Comprehensive Vocationally Oriented Psychotherapeutic Program for Adolescent Delinquent Boys," *American Journal of Orthopsychiatry*, XXXIII, 4 (1963), 634-642.

Minet, Joshua, III, Kelly, Francis J., and Hatch, M. Charles. "Outward Bound Inc.: Juvenile Delinquency Demonstration Project, Year End Report." Massachusetts Division of Youth Service, May 31, 1967.

Narloch, R. P., Adams, Stuart, and Jenkins, Kendall J. "Characteristics and Parole Performance of California Youth Authority Early Releases." Research Report No. 7. California Youth Authority, June 22, 1959. (Mimeographed.)

New York State, Division of Parole, Department of Correction. "Parole Adjustment and Prior Educational Achievement of Male Adolescent Offenders, June 1957-June 1961." September 1964. (Mimeographed.)

O'Brien, William J. "Personality Assessment as a Measure of Change Resulting from Group Psychotherapy with Male Juvenile Delinquents." The Institute for the Study of Crime and Delinquency, and the California Youth Authority, December 1961. (Processed.)

Persons, Roy W. "Psychological and Behavioral Change in Delinquents Following Psychotherapy," *Journal of Clinical Psychology*, XXII, 3 (1966), 337-340.

Persons, Roy W. "Relationship Between Psychotherapy with Institutionalized Boys and Subsequent Community Adjustment," *Journal of Consulting Psychology*, XXXI, 2 (1967), 137-141.

Pilnick, Saul, *et al.* "Collegefields: From Delinquency to Freedom." A Report . . . on Collegefields Group Educational Center. Laboratory for Applied Behavioral Science, Newark State College, February 1967. (Processed.)

Robison, James, and Kevotkian, Marinette. "Intensive Treatment Project: Phase II. Parole Outcome: Interim Report." Research Report No. 27. California Department of Corrections, Youth and Adult Correctional Agency, January 1967. (Mimeographed.)

Rudoff, Alvin. "The Effect of Treatment on Incarcerated Young Adult Delinquents as Measured by Disciplinary History." Unpublished Master's thesis, University of Southern California, 1960.

Saden, S. J. "Correctional Research at Jackson Prison," *Journal of Correctional Education*, XV (October 1962), 22-26.

Schnur, Alfred C. "The Educational Treatment of Prisoners and Recidivism," *American Journal of Sociology*, LIV, 2 (1948), 142-147.

Schwitzgebel, Robert and Ralph. "Therapeutic Research: A Procedure for the Reduction of Adolescent Crime." Paper presented at meetings of the American Psychological Association, Philadelphia, Pa., August 1963.

Schwitzgebel, Robert and Kolb, D. A. "Inducing Behavior Change in Adolescent Delinquents," *Behavior Research Therapy*, I (1964), 297-304.

Seckel, Joachim P. "Experiments in Group Counseling at Two Youth Authority Institutions." Research Report No. 46. California Youth Authority, September 1965. (Processed.)

Seckel, Joachim P. "The Fremont Experiment, Assessment of Residential Treatment at a Youth Authority Reception Center." Research Report No. 50. California Youth Authority, January 1967. (Mimeographed.)

Shelley, Ernest L. V., and Johnson, Walter F., Jr. "Evaluating an Organized Counseling Service for Youthful Offenders," *Journal of Counseling Psychology*, VIII, 4 (1961), 351-354.

Shoham, Shlomo, and Sandberg, Moshe. "Suspended Sentences in Israel: An Evaluation of the Preventive Efficacy of Prospective Imprisonment," *Crime and Delinquency*, X, 1 (1964), 74-83.

Stanton, John M. "Delinquencies and Types of Parole Programs to Which Inmates are Released." New York State Division of Parole, May 15, 1963. (Mimeographed.)

Stanton, John M. "Board Directed Extensive Supervision." New York State Division of Parole, August 3, 1964. (Mimeographed.)

Stuerup, Georg K. "The Treatment of Sexual Offenders," *Bulletin de la societe internationale de criminologie* (1960), pp. 320-329.

Sullivan, Clyde E., Mandell, Wallace. "Restoration of Youth Through Training: A Final Report." Staten Island, New York: Wakoff Research Center, April 1967. (Processed.)

Taylor, A. J. W. "An Evaluation of Group Psychotherapy in a Girls' Borstal," *International Journal of Group Psychotherapy*, XVII, 2 (1967), 168-177.

Truax, Charles B., Wargo, Donald G., and Silber, Leon D. "Effects of Group Psychotherapy with High Adequate Empathy and Nonpossessive Warmth upon Female Institutionalized Delinquents," *Journal of Abnormal Psychology*, LXXI, 4 (1966), 267-274.

Warren, Marguerite. "The Community Treatment Project after Five Years." California Youth Authority, 1966. (Processed.)

Warren, Marguerite, et al. "Community Treatment Project, an Evaluation of Community Treatment for Delinquents: a Fifth Progress Report." C.T.P. Research Report No. 7. California Youth Authority, August 1966. (Processed.)

Warren, Marguerite, et al. "Community Treatment Project, an Evaluation of Community Treatment for Delinquents: Sixth Progress Report." C.T.P. Research Report No. 8. California Youth Authority, September 1967. (Processed.)

Wilkins, Leslie T. "A Small Comparative Study of the Results of Probation," *British Journal of Criminology*, VIII, 3 (1958), 201-209.

Zivan, Morton. "Youth in Trouble: A Vocational Approach." Final Report of a Research and Demonstration Project, May 31, 1961-August 31, 1966. Dobbs Ferry, N.Y., Children's Village, 1966. (Processed.)

Methadone: the forlorn hope

EDWARD JAY EPSTEIN

I N 1898, the Bayer Company of Germany synthesized a white crystallized compound from morphine and marketed it under the trade name of Heroin. The new drug, though three times as powerful a pain-reliever as morphine, was purported to be non-addictive, and was even recommended in authoritative medical journals as a means of treating addiction to morphine and other drugs. Less than 10 years later, the medical profession, confronted with an increasing number of heroin addicts, recognized heroin as a highly addictive and dangerous drug, and by the 1920's the United States government had effectively outlawed heroin. Medical opinion remained divided, however, on the question of how to treat the existing heroin addicts. Some doctors believed that heroin induced a permanent change in the bio-chemistry of its victims, and therefore addicts would have to be maintained on heroin for the rest of their lives. Other doctors held to the theory that heroin itself was the toxic agent in the body, and therefore addicts could be successfully "detoxified" by withdrawing the drug from them.

Although this controversy was never really settled on the basis of medical evidence, the American Medical Association strongly endorsed the view that the only proper treatment for heroin addiction was totally to withdraw the addict from the use of the drug. In 1923, with the full support of the medical establishment, the federal government closed the heroin clinics (which had been set up to maintain addicts on a minimum dosage of heroin after the Harrison Narcotics Control Act of 1914 and subsequent court decisions had illegalized their normal sources of supply) and relentlessly prosecuted doctors who disbursed heroin to their patients for the purpose of maintaining their habit. Up until the late 1960's, detoxification remained the only legal remedy for addiction, and some 5,000 doctors were jailed for dispensing opiates in violation of this policy.

The development of methadone

Methadone was developed by German scientists during World War II as a substitute for heroin and morphine that could be manufactured in domestic laboratories. After the War, the formula for this synthetic drug was given to American drug companies. It was manufactured for "investigative use" by Eli Lilly & Company, who described it as a "synthetic narcotic analgesic with multiple actions quantitatively similar to those of morphine" and "a narcotic with significant potential for abuse with dependence-producing characteristics."

Though somewhat less powerful than heroin, methadone produces virtually the same analgesic and sedative effects, and is no less addictive than natural opiates. Because of its similarity to heroin, methadone initially was used in hospitals for "detoxifying" addicts—a procedure in which addicts are given progressively decreased dosages of a narcotic until they are "drug-free." As a detoxifying agent, methadone has distinct advantages over the natural opiates: It is less expensive than heroin and morphine (which have to be imported into the United States); it can be administered orally rather than by intravenous injection; and since its effects last for up to 24 hours, it need not be given at such frequent intervals.

In the 1960's, however, methadone was proposed for a very different form of treatment: maintenance. Reviving the half-century old controversy, a group of doctors proposed that heroin addicts, rather than being detoxified, should be maintained on a relatively high dosage of methadone dispensed by government-approved clinics. This time the maintenance view prevailed, and by 1973 some 73,000 addicts in the United States were receiving daily dosages of a synthetic opiate. Underlying this radical change in government policy—and in medical perceptions—was the powerful hope that the new drug would not only undercut heroin addiction, but also alleviate the problems of urban crime and unemployment in America.

The "Cinderella drug"

In 1964, under the auspices of the New York Health Research Council, Dr. Vincent P. Dole, a research associate at the Rockefeller Institute, and Dr. Marie E. Nyswander, a psychiatrist, initiated a series of experiments which laid the conceptual groundwork for methadone maintenance. In the original experiment, 22 heroin addicts were hospitalized and were given progressively increased dosages of methadone until they were "stabilized" on it—a state which is achieved when the patient has neither withdrawal symptoms nor a craving for increased dosages of methadone. Once "stabilized," the patients left the hospital and lived at home, returning once a day for their oral dosage of methadone and periodic tests for other drugs and side-effects. (Although drug maintenance technically violated the regulations of the Federal Bureau of Narcotics, the new director of the Bureau decided not to intervene on the grounds that the Dole-Nyswander project was "bona fide" research.) In August 1965, Doctors Dole and Nyswander issued a "progress report" which revealed that "patients who before treatment appeared hopelessly addicted are now engaged in useful occupations and are not using diacetylmorphine (heroin). As measured by social performance, these patients have ceased to be addicts."[1]* Such remarkable results were possible, Dole and Nyswander suggested, because methadone established "a pharmacological block" against the effects of heroin, and therefore protected the patients "against readdiction."[2] While the mechanics of the "blockade" were not then clearly defined, the inference was that methadone somehow prevented heroin from producing its usual effects. Establishing this "blockade" required a daily dosage of from 80 to 150 mgs. of methadone, the dosage previously given to terminal cancer patients.

On the basis of such encouraging findings, the project was vastly expanded, and the following year (August 1966) Dole and Nyswander reported even more conclusive results. Of 120 addicts admitted into the program, only 13 failed to respond adequately to the methadone treatment—a success rate of 89 per cent.[3] Dole and Nyswander reported that "a majority of the patients continuing on the program (71 per cent) are employed in a steady job, going to school, or both."[4] Furthermore, they claimed that "heroin use has been stopped consistently," and "the blockade treatment . . . has virtually eliminated criminal activity" among the patients.[5] Since "before entering the program all patients had been involved in illegal activities," Dole and

---

* All footnotes may be found at the end of this article.

Nyswander estimated that the reduction of crime and addiction which resulted from their program had "already saved the community three million dollars" (or $27,470 per patient treated).[6]

To explain how methadone worked to "virtually" eliminate criminal behavior and heroin addiction, Dole and Nyswander further developed the theory of the "narcotic blockade," which they identified as a "new procedure, not to be confused with giving of narcotic drugs to addicts for self-administration." Rather than describing methadone as a synthetic or narcotic (as it was officially designated), they termed it "an antinarcotic agent" which "blocks the euphorogenic action of heroin and other opiates." Thus, after being "stabilized" on methadone, "blockaded patients lose interest in narcotic drugs and are able to work and live in the city"—presumably without seeking heroin or committing thefts to pay for it.[7]

In a follow-up study in 1968 entitled "Successful Treatment of 750 Criminal Addicts," Dole and Nyswander reported that "a four year trial of methadone blockade has shown 94 per cent success in ending the criminal activity of former heroin addicts."[8] And in 1969, the Methadone Evaluation Unit, which had been set up by the sponsors of the Dole-Nyswander program to provide an independent evaluation of its results, concluded that the methadone program had substantially reduced the "anti-social behavior" of the addicts treated, and that the majority of these remaining in the program had become "productive members of society as measured by schooling and employment records."[9]

The authoritative claim that a new drug—an "antinarcotic agent"— had the power to eliminate heroin addiction and criminal behavior resounded in the press, and stirred the popular imagination. An article in *Look* magazine, for example, depicted methadone as a "Cinderella drug" that induces "miracle change" in heroin addicts, explaining that "a teaspoon of [methadone] medicine taken daily in a cup of orange juice is changing former dope addicts into decent law-abiding men."

Although some controversy persisted about the ethics of substituting one form of addiction for another, the putative advantages of methadone to society at large, reported under such headlines as "Methadone Found To Reduce Crime," were generally accepted as established fact. Amidst the continuing reports of methadone's success, and an increasing public concern about urban crime and heroin addiction, the idea of an easily dispensable chemical solution to urban problems took on new force and plausibility. Within one year after the Methadone Evaluation Unit reported its finding, 64 different offi-

cial and quasi-official groups had moved to set up methadone programs in their respective communities.

Reevaluating the Dole-Nyswander program

But though methadone seemed to readers of the popular press to
be the "magic bullet" that ended addiction, in reality it was only part
of a program of recruiting, rehabilitating, and monitoring addicts.
The successful results of the Dole-Nyswander project could not be
entirely attributed to the chemical properties of the drug. Aside from
the dispensing of dosages of methadone dissolved in fruit juices, the
program included such other elements as the admission criteria for
addicts; the medical, psychiatric, and counseling services rendered to
patients; the incentives provided for remaining in the program; the
rules under which patients were discharged for misconduct; and the
standards and methods by which the program was statistically evaluated. To fully account for the early achievement of the Methadone
Maintenance Treatment Program, as the Dole-Nyswander project was
officially called, it is necessary to examine the other variables in the
program more closely.

Unlike detoxification programs, which admitted almost all the addicts who applied for withdrawal treatment (and some non-voluntary
cases remanded by the courts), the Dole-Nyswander experiment carefully screened the volunteers for methadone maintenance, and admitted only the relatively small proportion of addicts who met their
criteria for treatment. For example, out of 1,233 applicants from the
Morris J. Bernstein Institute—the major source of addict-patients—
only 521 were admitted for methadone maintenance treatment. Those
admitted tended to be older (more than half of the group from the
Bernstein Institute were over 32), "whiter" (there were over twice
as many whites as blacks in the group), and less recently involved in
criminal activities.[10] Moreover, all accepted applicants showed a
strong motivation towards accepting methadone treatment, as demonstrated by the fact that they volunteered and remained on a waiting
list for six months to a year.

The fact that the methadone recipients were considerably older
on the average than street addicts at large was itself an important
predeterminant of the group's subsequent performance. More than
two thirds of the addicts selected by Dole and Nyswander were over
30 (and 17 per cent were over 40), whereas only one third of the addicts listed in New York City's "Narcotic Register" were over 30.[11]
Since criminal behavior (as well as other forms of risk-taking) gen-

erally tends to decline after the age of 30, and since a substantial proportion of addicts begin to "mature out" of heroin use of their own accord when they reach their mid-thirties, one would expect to find declining rates of criminal offenses (which include drug charges) and heroin use among a group of addicts in their thirties and forties, even if they were not given methadone.

The statistical measures of patient success in the Dole-Nyswander project were further inflated by the constant expansion of the treatment program, which grew from 22 patients in 1964 to 1,800 in 1969, to 4,376 in 1970. The influx of new patients, who comprised a large proportion of the total at any given time, gave the program a much higher "retention rate" than it might otherwise have had. In 1969, for example, Dole and Nyswander claimed that 82 per cent of all patients accepted in the program since its inception had remained on methadone treatment—and they defined this "retention rate" as a key index of success.[12] Because of the enormous expansion of the program in 1969, however, most of the patients in the "retained" category had actually been admitted to treatment only six months before. When groups of patients who had been in the program for more than one year are analyzed, a much lower "retention rate" is obtained (though it is still much higher than the retention rates that had previously been achieved in detoxification programs). For example, of the cohort admitted 48 months before the evaluation, only 58 per cent remained in the program; and of the cohort admitted 33 months before the evaluation, only 66 per cent were retained. In other words, the magnitude of the actual rate of attrition was partially masked by the large numbers of newly admitted patients.[13]

Moreover, most of the departing patients were discharged because they were arrested or otherwise failed to conform to the strict rules of the program, which required that patients seek employment, abstain from illicit use of drugs, and not engage in criminal or anti-social behavior. The dropping of a substantial number of unemployed patients, drug-takers, and law-breakers obviously improved the overall statistical performance of the remaining group. Consider, for example, the claim that "the majority of patients have become productive citizens."[14] Some 26 per cent of the men were employed before admission to the methadone treatment program, and, according to the data compiled by Dole and Nyswander, 66 per cent were employed after one year's treatment, and 78 per cent after four years in the program. This employment rate, however, applies only to the patients who remained in the program. If the discharged patients and drop-outs are included, a much lower employment rate is obtained. Of the *total* number of patients who entered the program four years before the evaluation, only 45 per cent were employed (contrasted to 78 per cent of those *retained* in the program).[15]

The methadone program also was not as effective at eliminating drug abuse among the patients as the claims of Dole and Nyswander implied. Indeed, the claim that "heroin use has been stopped consistently" rested on a quite subjective interpretation of what constitutes the usage of heroin. According to studies conducted by Dole and Nyswander themselves, urinalysis samplings revealed that 45 per cent of their patients took heroin (at least once) while receiving methadone, and 15 per cent continued to use heroin repeatedly.[16] (Presumably, this rate of heroin abuse would have been even higher if a substantial number of those who persisted in drug abuse had not been discharged from the program—and thus from the statistical picture as well.) Dole and Nyswander accounted for this apparent contradiction by contending that since methadone works as an "anti-narcotic" by "blockading" the euphoria induced by heroin, those who continued to take heroin were merely "testing" the blockade rather than "using heroin" per se. If, however, "using heroin" is defined simply as ingesting heroin—which can be objectively tested by urinalysis —it cannot be maintained that methadone treatment "stopped" heroin abuse.

The reduction in crime

The most impressive and widely publicized statistics presented by Dole and Nyswander suggested that the criminal behavior of addicts had been "virtually eliminated" through methadone maintenance treatment.[17] They claimed a 98 per cent decrease in incarcerations, a 90 per cent decrease in convictions, and a 94 per cent success rate in ending the criminal activities of patients.[18] Since patients who persisted in criminal activities tended to be dropped very early from the program, and thus were not counted in the statistical appraisal of those in treatment, some decrease in the overall crime rate of the patients was to be expected. But a reduction of more than 90 per cent in incarcerations, convictions, and criminal behavior cannot wholly, or even in large part, be accounted for by attrition from the program.

This does not mean, however, that the treatment itself produced this result, for the measures that give rise to these impressive statistics are questionable. Incarceration, for example, measures not only criminal behavior but also judicial behavior, the sentences that judges mete out for crimes. And in the case of violations of narcotic laws, the most common offense among addicts, a study by the Center for Criminal Justice at the Harvard Law School shows that New York City judges tend to give much less severe sentences to addicts enrolled in a methadone program than to addicts at large.[19] In fact, the study found that an addict at large is four times as likely to be incarcerated for a violation of the same magnitude as an addict in treatment, and that only one out of 20 addicts in treatment was actually sentenced to prison. Since addicts in treatment are less likely to be incarcerated because of the very fact that they are in a treatment program, a lower incarceration rate does not necessarily mean a lower crime rate.

Moreover, the "90 per cent drop in rate of convictions" also drastically overstates the effectiveness of methadone in reducing the number of convictions of those admitted to the program. The "rate of convictions" is based on the total "man-years" of treatment, a figure obtained by multiplying the number of patients under treatment by the time each spent in the program. An addict who remained in the program for four years, for example, would count as 48 man-months or four man-years, while an addict discharged from the program after one month would count for only one man-month. Obviously, such a formula gives much heavier weight to long-term patients than to those discharged from the program (and anyone convicted was automatically discharged); the rate of convictions, then, tends to diminish accordingly when it is presented as a per cent of the total "man-years."[20] As for the claim that the methadone program resulted in 94 per cent of the addicts being arrest-free their first year of treatment, it is undercut by the fact that 80 per cent were *not* arrested during the year *prior* to their admission. The improvement in the arrest-free record was thus only 14 per cent. On the other hand, the fact that 20 per cent of the addicts were arrested the year prior to admission, and only six per cent were arrested after they were in the program three months or longer is certainly significant, and does seem to indicate a real reduction in criminal activity.[21]

Even here, however, the significance of this reduction in crime is somewhat unclear because the overall statistics are not broken down by criminal charges. Because no distinction is made between arrests for narcotics violations (such as possession of heroin) and arrests for crimes against persons and property, it is not possible to ascertain to what extent the decline in arrests of methadone users reflects merely a reduction in illegal heroin purchases (which would be expected with the free distribution of methadone), and to what extent it reflects a reduction of street crime such as theft, robbery, and assault. This is particularly important since methadone is justified in terms of its power to reduce street crime. Dole and Nyswander, for example, opened the Fifth National Conference on Methadone Treatment in Washington in 1973 by asserting: "As a conservative estimate, methadone programs in the New York area . . . are saving the community $1,000,000 per day in prevented crime."

A different assessment—the ARTC program

A quite different picture of the impact of methadone treatment on crime emerges from a study by the Center for Criminal Justice of 416 addicts enrolled in the Addiction Research and Treatment Corporation (ARTC). These addicts, like those in the Dole-Nyswander project, were drawn from the poorer sections of New York City, and were provided with medical, counseling, and psychiatric services as well as a daily dosage of methadone; and also like their counterparts in the Dole-Nyswander project, they showed a marked decline in criminal behavior—a 20 per cent decrease in the *overall* crime index of addicts after one year in the methadone program, measured by their record of police arraignments.

But these ARTC gross crime statistics, unlike the Dole-Nyswander totals, were "decomposed," so that they present a fairly detailed analysis of which sorts of crimes were reduced—and for which age groups: Among the addicts younger than 31, the only reductions in criminal arraignments one year after they had begun methadone treatment (compared with their record one year prior to treatment) occurred in three categories: drug offenses—which was by far the largest component in the total reduction—forgery, and prostitution. In all other categories, the rate of criminal charges filed against younger addicts actually *increased*, even though they were receiving daily dosages of free methadone. Robbery charges quadrupled; assault charges were up by almost 50 per cent; and even burglary and property theft charges increased after one year of methadone treatment. In fact, the only decline in street crime charges occurred in the group over 31, who were mostly in their late thirties and forties (and who would be expected to decrease their crime rate with aging, even if they were not receiving methadone.)[22] Moreover, since many of the patients were remanded to the program by the courts, the year before their entry into the program tended to be the peak year for accumulating criminal charges. If the full period of a patient's addiction is taken as a measure, rather than merely the peak year, the level of criminal charges actually was higher after one year of methadone than it was during an *average* year on heroin.[23]

One possible explanation for the pronounced increase in street crimes committed by younger methadone users is that the substitution of methadone for heroin made the criminally prone members of this group less sedentary, and thus more active and efficient in pursuing their careers in crime. Professor Irving F. Lukoff, the director of the evaluation team monitoring the project, suggests that the crime pattern is better explained in terms of chronological aging than by methadone use: "With or without methadone or heroin, men seem to increase their criminal activity in their twenties, and decrease it in their thirties." In any case, Lukoff came to quite different conclusions than Dole and Nyswander: First, "Arrest rates alone tend to exaggerate the decline of criminal behavior;" second, "The decline in criminal behavior—in fact any conformist behavior—is contingent on increasing chronological age" (and not necessarily methadone use); and, finally, "A large part of the decline in crime is a function of the unusually high rates in the period preceding entrance, and possibly the reason why many enter treatment. The largest part of the decline is attributable to fewer arrests for drug charges." [24]

Explaining the disparity

Why should two methadone programs in New York City, both dealing with criminal addicts, yield such different results? It is true that the addicts in the Dole-Nyswander program were maintained on a much higher daily dosage of methadone than the addicts in the ARTC's program; but a series of "double-blind" experiments, in which neither doctors nor patients know who is receiving high or low dosages, has shown that the higher dosage has almost no effect on criminal behavior and arrests. [25] The differing results would thus seem to stem from different modes of administration and evaluation. Dole and Nyswander employed far stricter criteria for admittance and continuance in the program than the ARTC, and such selection procedures, by excluding or discharging the addicts most likely to continue criminal careers, may have accounted in part for their higher success rate. It is also possible that the Dole-Nyswander project had superior counseling and rehabilitative services (though it is difficult to compare the quality of such services).

To a large extent, however, the differences between the two programs' crime rates seem to be a statistical artifact. Rather than relying entirely on police and official records of criminal behavior, as the ARTC did, Dole and Nyswander depended heavily on their own counsellors in the program (who were mainly ex-addicts themselves) to compile the record of criminal activity by the patients. Lukoff suggests, on the basis of other studies of the problem, that this probably led to a substantial underreporting of criminal charges. And Dole and Nyswander then used measures such as "man years" and "convictions" which tended further to exaggerate the decline in crime.

In any case, the reduction of crime—if any—and other anti-social behavior does not result simply from distributing the drug methadone to addicts. As Dr. Jerome H. Jaffe insightfully pointed out at the time he was directing the Illinois Drug Abuse Program: "It is perhaps unreasonable to infer that methadone by itself produces a change in life style. Changes in criminal activity and gainful employment are more fairly viewed as measures of the efficacy of the rehabilitative system rather than of oral maintenance procedures per se."[26]

The metabolic theory of addiction

Methadone maintenance has been advanced not only as a means of reducing urban crime and unemployment but also as a medical treatment for heroin addicts. The theory which underlies—and medically justifies—this form of treatment holds that heroin abuse, under certain conditions, induces a permanent change in the nervous system that can be compensated for only by the ingestion of heroin or other opiates. Without opiates, addicts with this metabolic disorder are physiologically unable to function, and are medically abnormal. Since the metabolic change produced by heroin abuse cannot be reversed, the only possible medical treatment is to maintain the patient on a less harmful opiate than heroin for the duration of his life. Dr. Dole, who fully developed the metabolic theory of addiction, explains:

> Methadone, when properly prescribed, acts as a normalizer rather than as a narcotic. In this respect the treatment is similar to other maintenance therapies used in medical practice for treatment with patients with chronic metabolic disorders. The medical analogies are numerous—insulin for the diabetic, digitalis for the cardiac patient, cortisone for the arthritic, diphenylhydantoin for the epileptic, etc. Patients with these chronic diseases are dependent on their medication for their normal functioning. The methadone patient, who is also dependent on the daily dose of his medication for his normal functioning, is in the same medical status."[27]

But unlike diabetes, heart disorders, arthritis, and epilepsy, which are associated with readily discernable physiological symptoms, the putative metabolic disorder caused by heroin does not have physiological manifestations detectable by any medical tests. If addicts are receiving a sufficient daily amount of opiates, the metabolic change presumably is fully compensated for; and, if addicts suffering this disorder are withdrawn from opiates completely, the only symptom is a desire or "craving" for opiates (that cannot be measured by medical instruments).

An immediate problem with the metabolic theory of addiction is that it does not explain a large proportion of the cases. Consider, for example, the Army's experience with addiction in Vietnam. An estimated 35 per cent of the enlisted personnel in Vietnam used heroin at least once, and 20 per cent—or about 100,000 soldiers—considered themselves to be "addicted" at one time. Even after urine testing was instituted in 1971, some 12 per cent of soldiers scheduled to return to the United States failed the test, and were detained in Vietnam. As Dr. Jerome Jaffe noted, "This group was not only experimenting with heroin, but they were apparently using it so heavily that they couldn't stop even when they knew they would be delayed in going home."[28] Yet, after they withdrew or were "detoxified," more than 90 per cent did not relapse into using heroin, and did not experience a continued "craving" for the drug or any other disability.[29]

Follow-up studies showed that "fewer than one in 10 of these soldiers had developed an addiction problem at home eight to 12 months after their return."[30] Dr. Jaffe explained that "we are learning that you can be addicted in one environment, and that if your environment changes enough, or your peers change enough—and if the addiction is not the kind that comes with hardline, intravenous injection—it may be possible to stop using [heroin]."[31] In other words, the Army found that in at least 93 per cent of the cases, heroin addiction was the result not of a permanent metabolic disorder, but of environmental factors such as the availability of heroin or peer group influences.

Similarly, hard-core addicts serving prison terms have been found to function after "detoxification" without any of the disabilities or drug-craving behavior predicted by the metabolic theory. (Once they are released from prison, and heroin is again available, the ex-addicts may become readdicted, but this is perfectly consistent with the environmental theory of addiction.) And since it is estimated (though the data on this question is very limited) that a large segment of all heroin addicts "mature out" of addiction on their own after the age of 35,[32] the theory of a permanent metabolic change could, at best, apply to only a small fraction of even the hard-core addicts. Furthermore, the Dole theory provides no diagnostic method of determining whether a given case of addiction stems from a meta-bolic disorder or from environmental or psychological reasons. Doctors dispensing methadone therefore would have no way of knowing whether they are medically treating a metabolic disorder or simply prolonging an addiction. The fact that doctors, including Dole and Nyswander, generally feel justified in denying methadone to patients who fail to conform to the rules of the program (by discharging them) suggests that not even proponents of the metabolic theory take the analogy with diabetes seriously. (Certainly, a doctor would not feel justified in denying insulin to a diabetic.) The theoretical under-pinnings of the view that methadone is a "normalizing" medicine thus remain highly questionable.

The "blockade" theory

Even if the metabolic theory has only limited application, however, methadone could still be considered a medicine if it prevented or "blockaded" an addict from using other more harmful drugs (in the same sense that gamma globulin acts as a preventive medicine in protecting someone against hepatitis). The "blockade" theory, it will be recalled, holds that a high dosage of methadone acts as an "anti-narcotic" by preventing addicts from receiving any euphoria or other positive reinforcement from heroin. This claim of a "blockade" effect is problematic at best: Methadone neither prevents the heroin from reaching the receptors in the brain (which is usually what a "block-ade" infers), nor cuts the addict off from the sedative and pain-killing effects of heroin. Instead, according to the Dole-Nyswander theory, high dosages of methadone build up the addict's "tolerance" for opiates to the point where he will no longer receive a euphoric feeling from taking a standard-size dose of heroin. This form of "blockade" is analogous to feeding a "strawberry ice cream addict" a sufficient number of gallons of vanilla ice cream to prevent him from receiving pleasure from additional quantities of strawberry (assuming that there is as much "cross-tolerance" between ice creams as there is between opiates.) Since the euphoria-"blockade" is difficult to measure ob-jectively—patients are either asked about the euphoria or observed by ex-addicts employed by the program—and since addicts, especially older ones, commonly take heroin for its sedative and pain-killing effects, there is simply no way of proving or disproving the euphoria-"blockade" theory.

Doctors Dole and Nyswander predicated this "blockade" theory on the early results achieved in their program and on the reports of

the ex-addicts serving as counsellors to the methadone patients.
Other researchers subsequently found, however, through daily urinalyses of methadone maintenance patients that they continued, and
even increased, their usage of narcotics while receiving high dosages
of methadone. In extensive month-long examinations of a sample of
patients drawn from a maintenance program in Philadelphia, Carl D.
Chambers and W. J. Russell Taylor found (through urinalyses) a
remarkably high pattern of "cheating." Some 77 per cent (all of whom
had been in the program six months or longer) were still using heroin,
30 per cent were using barbiturates, and 25 per cent amphetamines.
(During the same period, the counsellors on the program reported
that only 40 per cent were using heroin, 7.5 per cent barbiturates, and
five per cent amphetamines—indicating that they heavily under-
reported drug usage).[33]

Nine months later the same sample was again tested for a month-
long period. This time 92.3 per cent of the methadone patients were
found to be using heroin, 43.6 per cent barbiturates, 69.2 per cent
amphetamines, and 43.6 per cent cocaine.[34] Moreover, nearly two
thirds of the patients had "dirty urine" (i.e., evidence of drug abuse)
half the time they were tested. Chambers and Taylor concluded:

> . . . [E]ven after a year on relatively high dosages of methadone, neither
> a narcotic blockade had occurred nor had drug craving significantly
> diminished. These findings must also be viewed within the context that
> neither the patients themselves nor the program within which they were
> being treated are significantly different from most other methadone pro-
> grams or patients.[35]

And similar patterns of "cheating" have become apparent with the
application of more sophisticated urinalysis techniques to a wide
variety of other methadone programs.

The new justification: methadone as chemical parole

By the time that the Fourth National Conference on Methadone
Treatment was convened in 1971, there was little support for either
the "metabolic disease" or the "blockade" theories. Indeed, almost
all the empirical evidence presented at the conference tended to
undercut them, and even the strongest proponents of methadone
expressed doubts about the original medical justifications for its use.
Dr. Avram Goldstein, the highly respected director of the Addiction
Research Laboratory at Stanford, demonstrated through data drawn
from his California methadone programs that "the dose of methadone
is largely irrelevant." Finding no empirical basis for the "metabolic

disorder" theory, and rejecting the "blockade" theory as "confusing," he concluded:

> Methadone cannot magically prevent heroin use in a patient who wants to use heroin; it can only facilitate a behavior change in people who have made a conscious decision to change. Thus, the paramount feature of a successful methadone program is what it does in ways *other than chemical* to help the patient rehabilitate himself (italics in original).

But if methadone neither compensated for a metabolic deficiency nor prevented continued heroin abuse, what was the advantage of maintaining addicts on methadone? Dr. Goldstein reasoned that "the sustained methadone dependence" served to break the "conditioned behavior" surounding heroin use, and to bring "the patient into the clinic daily, ensuring regular contact with the clinic staff, and introducing a degree of regularity into his disordered life." Thus no attempt was made to justify methadone as a "normalizing" or a preventive medicine; instead, it was defined principally as a powerful means of exerting a form of social control over street addicts. Not only did it attract addicts into participating in government-sponsored programs, and transfer the object of their dependency from an opiate procured illegally to an opiate obtained from licit sources, but it placed them on a highly effective kind of chemical parole. Their urine could be tested daily for illicit narcotics, and if they broke their parole—or the rules of the program—they could be denied the methadone they had become dependent on.

Methadone thus had changed in concept from a form of medical treatment, analogous with the insulin treatment of diabetes, to an incentive for rehabilitation programs. Signalling the change, Dr. Goldstein ended his presentation by cautioning:

> Nothing I have said should be interpreted as "debunking" methadone or derogating its importance. It is a fantastically effective tool for bringing addicts into a new and helpful kind of therapeutic environment. If they have sufficient motivation to enroll in a methadone program, that motivation can be nurtured by a good staff, can be transformed into a real desire for an alternative life style, more satisfying than that of a "junkie." No matter that the "metabolic disease" concept may be incorrect.

Methadone as public policy

In January 1969, when Richard Nixon assumed office, there were only 16 drug treatment programs receiving financial support from the federal government, and the main forms of treatment were detoxification and drug-free therapy. Almost all the agencies involved in the administration of these treatment programs, including the National Institute of Mental Health, the Office of Economic Opportunity, and the Department of Housing and Urban Development, were actively opposed to methadone maintenance. By 1973, however, the federal government was funding some 394 treatment programs offering methadone maintenance. In the intervening four years, there had obviously been a major shift in policy towards methadone.

To some extent, the expansion of treatment programs was a response to an expansion in the addict population during the 1960's, but the shift from detoxification to drug maintenance reflected a redefinition of the problem of addiction itself. Up until the mid-1960's, heroin addiction was generally thought to be a problem chiefly for the individual addict, and treatment therefore was aimed at freeing him from his dependence on the drug. By the early 1970's, however, heroin addiction had increasingly come to be regarded less as a problem for the individual addict than for society at large, since it was presumed that addicts were compelled to commit crimes to pay for their supply of heroin. The focus of policy thus changed accordingly from relieving the individual from the suffering and degradation of drug dependency to relieving the rest of society from the putative criminal behavior of addicts. As James Vorenberg and Irving Lukoff correctly noted, "the core of community concern is the relationship between addiction and crime."

Given this new view of the problem, the solution involved bringing the addict population under some form of social control. Since methadone maintenance, whatever its side effects, promised to transfer street addicts from a dependency on heroin, which they had to obtain at great cost from illegal suppliers, to a dependency on methadone, which could be dispensed legally under tight controls, it held great appeal to the young men in the Nixon Administration concerned with the problem of urban crime. Egil Krogh, then a deputy assistant to the President for domestic affairs, with special responsibilities for law enforcement, explained the Administration's interest in methadone in 1971 in the following terms:

> . . . [W]e found there was a cause and effect relationship fairly clear between heroin addiction and the need to commit crimes to support the habit. So we felt we needed to greatly expand the capability of the District of Columbia to treat those with the problem. . . . After a year we found that those [addicts] in high-dosage methadone had a marked decline in criminal recidivism. . . . I cannot piece out exactly what is attributable to narcotics treatment or police work, lights, a new court, but we feel all taken together have led to that result [decreased crime] and we would like to expand that type of treatment across the country.[36]

A Special Action Office for Drug Abuse Prevention was thereupon created, under Dr. Jerome Jaffe, to coordinate the expansion of "multimodality" treatment programs (which allow addicts to take advantage of either methadone maintenance or drug-free treatment).

Has methadone worked?

By 1973, the government had succeeded in expanding treatment programs to the point where virtually any qualified heroin user could receive methadone maintenance, if he wanted it. The waiting-lists for methadone had all but disappeared, and some 73,000 people were enrolled in maintenance programs across the United States. Yet as results were evaluated and compared with police data, it became clear that the widespread distribution of methadone was not going to solve the problems of crime, unemployment, or even drug addiction. To be sure, a large number of addicts were brought under some form of social control and, where urinalyses were effectively monitored, placed on a kind of chemical parole. But the main reduction in crime brought about by the use of licit methadone was in the realm of narcotics offenses (such as drug possession charges), which helped improve the appearance of overall police statistics, but did little to allay public concern over robbery, mugging, assault, and other street crime. Indeed, in 1973, despite the claim that the addict population had been freed from the compulsion to buy illicit heroin by the availability of methadone, there was a significant increase in the FBI crime index.

In addition, while heroin consumption may have decreased as methadone became more freely available—and certainly deaths attributed to heroin decreased—there is little evidence to suggest that overall drug abuse was reduced. The pattern found in most methadone programs was one of "poly-drug" abuse: When addicts were denied the euphoric reinforcement of heroin because methadone raised their tolerance to opiates, they quite commonly turned to amphetamines, cocaine, barbiturates, or other non-opiates. Moreover, the "leakage" of methadone from the maintenance programs into the illegal market created an entirely new drug abuse problem. In 1974, the Drug Enforcement Administration reported that deaths from illicit methadone have surpassed deaths from illicit heroin, and that methadone now constitutes a substantial share of the illegal traffic in drugs. At best, 7.5 million doses of methadone distributed annually by government-licensed clinics seem to have had the effect of shifting drug abuse from heroin to other equally damaging drugs.

Nor did methadone bring about the wholesale conversion of unemployed heroin addicts to productive members of society. While
results varied widely from program to program, few of the newer
programs even approached the high employment and retention rates
claimed by Dole and Nyswander. For those strongly motivated to
change their style of life, methadone no doubt assisted in their rehabilitation by lessening the compulsion towards heroin use. But for
the majority of methadone users, who continued to use other drugs
and to drop in and out of programs, methadone was merely one more
drug, freely obtained, which could be used to maintain their "habit."
Methadone failed to achieve the predicted results, not merely because the programs were inefficient or expanded too rapidly, but
because the basic assumption that it could somehow preclude drug
abuse, and force addicts to convert, proved to be untrue.

The unintended consequences

As policy, therefore, methadone maintenance rests on shaky foun-
dations. Originally, or at least when maintenance was first proposed
in the 1960's, it was widely assumed that a large proportion of heroin
addicts suffered from a permanent metabolic disorder which required that they be maintained on drugs for the duration of their
lives. Subsequently, however, this theory was all but abandoned by
most researchers in the field (or so diluted by qualifications that it
no longer justified drug maintenance). And if it is true that a large
proportion of heroin addicts would "mature out" of heroin use after
the age of 35 without the assistance of methadone, then the policy of
admitting almost all heroin users who desire methadone to maintenance programs may have the unintended consequence of prolonging addiction and increasing the population of addicts as a whole.
Nor could this problem be solved by more stringent entrance criteria,
since, as Dr. Jaffe points out, there is no way to determine in advance
if a candidate for a methadone program would be likely to abandon
heroin use on his own. Moreover, it is now widely believed, after the
Vietnam experience with addiction, that availability is a powerful,
if not the main, determinant of drug use. If drugs are not available, a
large proportion of the "users" will abstain from seeking them out.
The policy of making methadone readily available, then, may encourage, rather than discourage, drug use among a large group of
persons who otherwise would abstain.

The collapse of the "blockade" theory in the face of empirical findings also presents a dilemma for methadone policy. If high dosages

of methadone merely raise the tolerance for opiates of drug users, and drive them to other drugs for the euphoria methadone temporarily denies them, then the problem of heroin addiction is simply being expanded into a problem of poly-drug abuse, and it becomes difficult to justify the methadone policy as a "drug prevention" program. To be sure, methadone users can be placed under a tighter form of chemical parole through more sophisticated urinalysis techniques and more rigorous requisites for remaining in the program; however, such forms of behavior control raise the most difficult sort of ethical and legal questions: Can the state be justified in deliberately raising the tolerance of an addict for drugs by giving him higher dosages of an opiate than he would normally take, and then denying him the opiate when he fails to conform to the rules? At the very least, this would seem to be a form of punishment not proceeding from any "due process of law."

The alternative is to provide the addict only with a lower dose of opiates than he would otherwise take, thereby not increasing his tolerance. But low-dosage methadone programs do not seem to provide sufficient incentives to hold most hard-core addicts for any period of time. Most evaluations have found that low-dosage programs have had mainly transient populations who enter and leave the program within six months. Applying tighter controls against heroin and other forms of drug abuse in low-dosage programs would thus probably have the consequence of accelerating the turnover, and driving the hard-core addict away from the rehabilitation aspects of the program. In fact, as Dr. Avram Goldstein has pointed out, the only sort of addict who would remain in a program with low dosages and strong controls would be one who was strongly motivated to change his life style; and in this case, gradual withdrawal through reducing the dosage of methadone might be a more logical form of treatment than "maintenance."

Further, the massive methadone program—at the local as well as the federal level—tends to focus attention exclusively on heroin, which is only one aspect of the overall drug abuse problem. Methadone maintenance does not discourage the use of non-opiates like barbiturates, amphetamines, and cocaine, and may actually encourage poly-drug abuse. Therefore, agencies and personnel involved in the various methadone programs have a strong interest in emphasizing the menace of heroin—even when the rate of new addiction declines, as it has done in the past three years—and obscuring the dangers posed by other forms of drug abuse. The distribution of methadone by the government thus not only has failed to alleviate the problems of urban crime and drug addiction but may even have further complicated these problems by adding another illegal drug to the market (which, to some degree, compensated for the curtailed supplies of heroin from abroad), encouraging poly-drug abuse (by addicts who could no longer derive a euphoric experience from opiates), and prolonging addiction among some addicts who might otherwise have "matured out."

Social problems and chemical solutions

Perhaps the most difficult question in terms of public policy is why the government persisted in the methadone program on the basis of such questionable assumptions and equivocal results. In fact, the medical authorities and consultants who were most heavily involved in advising the White House on the methadone program were intelligent and thoughtful men who understood the quixotic nature of the theories about "blockades" and "metabolic disorders," and who realized fairly early that the mass distribution of methadone would not significantly reduce urban crime or eliminate drug abuse. They believed, however, that methadone would be a powerful lure for attracting and maintaining street addicts in rehabilitation programs. This was their motivation. The White House, however, had other things on its mind. It was interested mainly in crime. The experts therefore "sold" methadone maintenance to Egil Krogh, John Ehrlichman, and President Nixon as an "anti-crime" program, rather than as a "rehabilitation" program. The net result was that those with the technical competence to see the limits of methadone treatment chose not to deflate the unrealistic claim that methadone would substantially reduce crime.

The public, and especially the enlightened liberal community, was beguiled by the unchallenged rhetoric of the program. The notion that most crime was the product not of "criminals," but of "sick" individuals who could be cured by the distribution of an inexpensive medicine was most appealing. It fostered the hope among a large segment of the middle class that street crime could be eradicated by medical means. Unfortunately, criminal behavior—and addiction— proved to be more complex problems that did not lend themselves to simple chemical solutions.

FOOTNOTES

[1] Vincent P. Dole and Marie E. Nyswander, "A Medical Treatment for Diacetyl-morphine (Heroin) Addiction," *Journal of the American Medical Association,* Vol. 193, No. 8 (August 23, 1965), p. 80.

[2] *Ibid.,* p. 84.

[3] Vincent P. Dole and Marie E. Nyswander, "Rehabilitation of Heroin Addicts after Blockade with Methadone," *New York State Journal of Medicine,* Vol. 66 (1966), p. 2011-2017.

[4] *Ibid.,* p. 2016.

[5] *Ibid.*

[6] *Ibid.,* p. 2017.

[7] *Ibid.,* p. 2012.

[8] Vincent P. Dole and Marie E. Nyswander, "Successful Treatment of 750 Criminal Drug Addicts," *Journal of the American Medical Association,* Vol. 206, No. 12 (December 16, 1968), p. 2708.

[9] Frances Rowe Gearing, "Evaluation of Methadone Maintenance Treatment for Heroin Addiction: A Progress Report," Paper presented before the Epidemiology Section of the American Public Health Association (Philadelphia: November 13, 1969), p. 10.

[10] Marvin E. Perkins and Harriet I. Bloch, "Survey of Methadone Maintenance Treatment Programs," *American Journal of Psychiatry,* 126 (April 10, 1970), pp. 33-39.

[11] Gearing, *op. cit.,* figure 2.

[12] *Ibid.*

[13] James V. DeLong, "Treatment and Rehabilitation," in *Dealing with Drug Abuse,* foreword by McGeorge Bundy (New York, 1973), p. 176.

[14] Dole and Nyswander (1968), p. 2711.

[15] DeLong, *op. cit.,* p. 207.

[16] Dole and Nyswander (1968), p. 2711.

[17] Dole and Nyswander (1966), p. 2017.

[18] Herman Joseph and Vincent P. Dole, "Methadone Patients in Probation and Parole," *Federal Probation,* Vol. 34, No. 2 (June 1970), pp. 42-48; Dole and Nyswander (1968), pp. 2710, 2708.

[19] Gila J. Hayim, "Changes in the Criminal Behavior of Heroin Addicts: A One Year Follow-Up Study of Methadone Treatment" (Mimeographed, 1972), p. 57.

[20] The National Commission on Marijuana noted in reference to these claims: "Some studies use a man-year figure as a measurement of success although the conclusions drawn therefrom are especially likely to be distorted and misleading." See: *Drug Use in America: Problem in Perspective,* (Washington: U.S. Government Printing Office, 1973), p. 179.

[21] Gearing, *op. cit.,* figure 2.

[22] Hayim, *op. cit.,* p. 35.

[23] James Vorenberg and Irving F. Lukoff, "Addiction, Crime, and the Criminal Justice System," *Federal Probation* (December, 1973), p. 7.

[24] Irving Lukoff, "Issues in the Evaluation of Heroin Treatment," A Report to the Epidemiology of Drug Abuse Conference (Puerto Rico: February 12-14, 1973).

[25] In one such study, Lukoff found the correlation between low as opposed to high dosages and arrests to be an insignificant .009. Avram Goldstein in his report "Blind Controlled Dosage Comparisons with Methadone in 200 Patients" (3rd National Conference on Methadone Treatment: 1970) found: "Comparisons of 30, 50, 100 mg. daily dosages revealed surprisingly few differences." Jerome H. Jaffe in "Methadone Maintenance: Variation in Outcome Criteria as a Function of Dose" (3rd National Conference on Methadone Treatment: 1970) came to essentially the same conclusion.

[26] Jerome H. Jaffe, "The Maintenance Approach to the Management of Opioid Dependence" (unpublished, 1971).

[27] Joseph and Dole, *op. cit.,* p. 43.

[28] Quoted in T. George Harris, "As Far as Heroin is Concerned the Worst is Over," *Psychology Today* (August 1973), pp. 71, 75, 76.

[29] Interview in March 1973 with Richard Wilbur, Assistant Secretary of the Army for Public Health.

[30] Quoted in Harris, *op. cit.*, p. 76.

[31] *Ibid.*

[32] Charles Winick, "Maturing Out of Narcotic Addiction," *UN Bulletin of Narcotics,* Vol. XIV, No. 19 (1962).

[33] Carl D. Chambers and W.J. Russell Taylor, "Patterns of 'Cheating' Among Methadone Maintenance Patients," Paper presented at the Eastern Psychiatric Research Association Meeting (New York: November 7, 1970), pp. 328 ff.

[34] *Ibid.*, p. 331.

[35] *Ibid.*, p. 335.

[36] Press conference of John D. Ehrlichman, Egil Krogh, and Jerome H. Jaffe (Washington, D.C.: June 17, 1971). The degree to which the decline in crime in Washington was due to methadone is somewhat questionable since it began in 1969 when only 99 addicts in the entire area were receiving methadone.

How many games in town?
– the pros and cons
of
legalized gambling

JESS MARCUM & HENRY ROWEN

O NE of the little analyzed recent changes on the American scene is the rapid spread of legal gambling. As of this writing, 35 states have some form of legal gambling: 31 allow pari-mutuel betting at race tracks, eight have state lotteries, three permit off-track betting on horse races, three permit only charity bingo games, and one has casinos. Changes are coming rapidly. New Hampshire established its lottery in 1963, followed by New York in 1967, New Jersey in 1970, and Pennsylvania, Massachusetts, Connecticut, Michigan, and Maryland in 1971-73. New York passed a law in 1970 permitting off-track betting on horse races on local option, and in 1971 the New York City Off-Track Betting Corporation began operations. New Jersey began a daily lottery and Connecticut legalized off-track betting in 1972. In 1973, voters in Maine approved a lottery. In New York, the first stages of legislation to permit casinos have passed, and a referendum on casinos will be held this November in New Jersey. Moves to legalize gambling are under study in several other states, including Kentucky, Rhode Island, and Georgia.

This process has been driven largely by state legislators' desire for revenues. Not only have expenditures by state and local governments increased rapidly in the past two decades—more so than federal spending—but there has been resistance to employing the most important source of local revenue, the property tax. The prospect of getting tens or hundreds of millions of dollars per year from a commodity many people want to consume, without generating taxpayer opposition, has become hard to resist.

The revenue motive has been buttressed by the belief that legal gambling will drive out illegal gambling. Estimates of the amount of illegal gambling vary greatly, but gambling handles in the scores of billions of dollars annually and profits in the billions are frequently reported. Moreover, it is often held that illegal enterprises use gambling profits to enter the narcotics and other criminal trades, to buy into legitimate enterprises, and to corrupt law enforcement personnel. This concern led the Knapp Commission, appointed to investigate corruption in New York City's law enforcement system, to recommend the repeal of criminal laws against gambling.

Supporting these pragmatic arguments is a more philosophical one which holds that it is futile, indeed harmful, to try to ban an activity which is widely demanded and is available illicitly—often with the connivance of the police. Respect for the law is diminished. It is unreasonable and arbitrary to force people who want to gamble legally to go to the race track or to Nevada or the Caribbean—or to speculate in stocks, commodities, or stock options. Gambling is a victimless crime. It makes no more sense to try to prohibit gambling than to try to prohibit the consumption of alcohol. To be sure, some people gamble to excess just as some drink or smoke or eat to excess. But people who don't want to gamble don't have to, and those who do will find some way of doing it anyway; therefore they should have an opportunity to do so legally and conveniently.

Given the currency of this point of view, it is a pretty good bet that there will be a widespread adoption of legal gambling during the next decade. The consequences of such a development, however, are far from clear.

The key questions

The central issue is one of objectives. *The objective of maximizing tax revenues from gambling is by no means the same as the objective of eliminating illegal gambling in order to reduce corruption, or that of minimizing governmental interference with the exercise of personal preferences.* A given policy is unlikely to achieve all of these objectives. Moreover, even if these different goals are reconciled in a given policy, there is likely to be a conflict between it and another policy objective that most communities are likely to regard as important: keeping the total volume of gambling activity within reasonable bounds and seeing that it is conducted with a fair degree of public decorum.

The resolution of this central issue of objectives depends, as with most complex public policy issues, on a combination of facts, estimates, conjectures, and values. At this stage, although few reliable answers can be given, some important questions need to be asked and the available evidence used. One key question is: How much gambling would take place with widespread legalization? We estimate that the complete legalization of gambling throughout this country would lead to a large increase, probably about three times as much as the total amount of legal and illegal gambling that goes on today.[1]

Another key question is: How important are gambling revenues likely to be to state and local budgets? Here we conclude that the contribution from universal legalization would be modest, amounting at most to about five per cent of total state and local tax revenues.

Some other important questions on which some evidence is available and conjectures can be made are these:

• What would be the social consequences if a large increase in gambling occurs? For instance, how serious a problem might gambling addiction become?

• What would be the distribution of gambling losses across income groups? What would be the incidence of gambling taxes?

• Gambling-associated corruption in some communities (e.g., New York City) seems to be a serious problem. But is law enforcement corruption by gambling interests a serious problem across the nation? Is widespread infiltration of legal gambling enterprises by criminals likely to occur, and how might it be prevented? Are abuses similar to those that led virtually all forms of legalized gambling to be prohibited during the course of the 19th century likely to reemerge?

• How attractive does legal gambling have to be to drive out illegal operations? In particular, how much of a tax burden can the legal version bear and remain competitive?

• What should be the role of government? Should it be a prohibitor, regulator, operator, tax collector? Should public-benefit, non-profit corporations be established as operators? Should gambling be left largely to the market?

• What can be done to preserve public decorum? For example,

---

[1] A brief description of the methods used for estimating the present level of illegal gambling and the potential level given legalization is available upon request from the authors.

should gambling be intensely promoted and displayed as it is in Nevada or even as it is by the Off-Track Betting Corporation (OTB) in New York City?

• What should be the role of the federal government as the states increasingly compete with each other in offering gambling opportunities?

Varieties of gambling

In addressing these questions it is important to keep in mind variations in the characteristics of different games and in gambling behavior. There are important differences among lotteries, numbers, off-track betting, sports betting, and casinos, and also in the traditions and behavior of the citizenry of different communities. These need to be examined with some care if the consequences of legalization are to be understood.

Horse and dog racing. Betting on horse racing has been legal in many states for years. (Greyhound racing accounts for only a small fraction of all racing revenues and has much less growth potential than other types of gambling.) This acceptance is in part a class phenomenon; as the "sport of kings" it is distinguished from the more common forms of gambling. Moreover, since tracks are usually not easily accessible, the time and expense of going to them requires premeditation, which tends to discourage impulsive betting.

In 1971, revenues to the states from horse and dog racing were $550 million, and about an equal amount went to the tracks. This billion dollar take from the pari-mutuel pools comprised about 18 per cent of the $5.5 billion wagered.

How much might on-track betting be expanded? If racing were to be legalized in the 19 states which forbid it, night racing permitted universally, and additional racing dates granted (continuing a trend), we estimate that the volume and revenues of on-track betting would about double. Estimates of this kind are, of course, dependent on several uncertain variables. For one thing, the popularity of horse racing is not growing, and among young people it is actually declining. For another, the amount of on-track betting depends on opportunities for off-track betting. Betting on horses and on dogs interacts, and there are also interactions with other types of gambling. But if our estimate is correct, an additional $500 million in government revenues would probably be generated.

Definitions are important in understanding gambling, and such categories as "handle," "take," and "revenue" are often confused in the various types of gambling. In horse racing the categories are simple: The total amount wagered in the pari-mutuel pools is the "handle"; the total amount taken out of the pool before winners are paid off is the "take," which is equivalent to the gross profit; and "revenue" refers to the amounts that governments receive.

Finally, significant changes are taking place in horse race betting. Combination bets offering very-high-odds payoffs are becoming increasingly popular. The prototype is the daily double, which pays off on the winner of the first and second races as parts of a single combination wager. Payoffs average around $100 for a $2 ticket, in contrast with the average individual winner paying around $14. In recent years, many new forms of combination betting have appeared— Quinellas, Perfectas, Exactas, Twin Doubles, Five-Ten, Superfectas, and the like. In the Superfecta, Twin Double, and Five-Ten forms of wagering, the payoffs may become astronomical—$100,000 or more for a $2 wager.

These exotic bets are, in effect, lotteries and the reason for their popularity is clear: They offer a chance to win a fortune on a very small wager. The large payoffs also provide an incentive to engage in fraud. But the public's memory is usually short. Wagering and attendance fall off for a month or two after a fraud is exposed and then recover; however, the recent scandals at tracks in New York have led some tracks to abandon lottery-like bets.

Off-track betting. New York's legalization of off-track betting was a milestone in legalized gambling. In fiscal 1973, OTB's handle of $588 million produced gross profits of $99 million, of which $42 million in revenue was distributed to New York City and State. Early projections of government revenues from a mature New York OTB system went as high as $200 million a year, but recent estimates have been much lower. We estimate that off-track betting throughout the country would eventually produce about $1 billion in additional revenues. This estimate amounts to saying that the net revenue from off-track betting would equal that of on-track betting. Our figure for off-track betting could turn out to be too low, but if so, the on-track take is bound to be reduced. (It is not surprising, therefore, that the tracks in New York State have opposed the extension of off-track betting and have lobbied for a larger share of the revenues.) Another way of looking at this is that the total government revenues from full-scale legalization of both on-track and off-track betting would be about $2 billion, with less uncertainty in this total than in the split.

How does this potential compare with the current level of illegal bookmaking? We estimate net revenues (i.e., after paying off winners and after expenses of operation) to bookmakers at about $500 million, an amount about equal to current government revenues from the tracks. This is far below other estimates which usually assume $5 to $10 bet with bookmakers for every $1 bet at the tracks. (Our estimate, made several years ago, is supported by a recent survey of bettors in New York City made for the Fund for the City of New York.)

The extent to which legalized off-track betting would hurt book-makers is difficult to estimate. Bookmakers work largely on credit. Some large bettors prefer them because they can wager large sums without changing the odds, and because it is easier to avoid paying income taxes on net winnings. And many bettors prefer bookmakers because they take multiple bets such as parlays and "round robins." On the other hand, OTB has advantages. For one thing, bookmakers have been known to vanish mysteriously. And most give only 15-to-1 maximum odds to win, while OTB has no such limit. Bookmakers are reluctant to take bets on the exotic, high-odds forms of bets. Finally, OTB is, after all, legal. All in all, it is not unreasonable to guess that bookmakers would lose about half of their horse racing business in the event that off-track betting were to become legal and widely available.

Lotteries. The first American lotteries in recent times, in New Hampshire and New York, were not very successful. Then New Jersey showed the rest of the states how to do it right. The New Jersey experience (discounting sales to non-residents) can be extrapolated with fair confidence for the whole country. The result is a potential net revenue estimate for the entire country of approximately $1 billion a year.

Lotteries are coming into fashion for several reasons. Nowadays they are being run by state governments under strict supervision, and, so far, without scandal. They offer the possibility, however small, of becoming rich from only a small wager. The fact that about 50 per cent is taken out of the lottery pool before distribution to winners makes little difference to the players. If one buys a ticket, it doesn't matter much whether the prize is $500,000 or $600,000. If you win, you're rich. Further, the temptation to spend a great deal on lotteries is small.

There is another important consequence of the high odds for lottery players: For the vast majority of players, the sum wagered (or the handle) is totally lost. For example, in present pari-mutuel wagering on horses, out of $6 billion bet annually, some $5 billion is returned to the players and all of the players share this $5 billion more or less in proportion to the total amount of their wagers. There is some unevenness due to luck (and much less due to skill), but it averages out more and more as time goes by. In a lottery, no matter how much time goes by, luck never has a chance to average out, even in a lifetime. So although a few get rich by chance, most lose for good. Therefore, from the perspective of the average player the gross take for lotteries is the same as the handle.

There is relatively little illegal wagering on lotteries. It consists mostly of wagers on the Irish Sweepstakes and other foreign lotteries and probably produces illegal profits of no more than about $50 million a year.

Numbers. In the numbers game one may bet an amount from a few pennies to several dollars on any three digit number from 000 to 999. A number is randomly chosen each day (or more often) from some presumably random set of figures issued by the stock market, the treasury, race tracks, or elsewhere. (There are also other bets involving three or fewer digits.) The correct odds for a fair payoff are clearly 999-to-1. But the average numbers bank payoff is about 550-to-1, so that the gross take is 45 per cent. But by the time all expenses have been paid, the net return to the bank is probably about 10 per cent of the handle.

Numbers is an illegal lottery. But numbers has a special appeal because the bettor can pick his own number, the drawings are conducted daily instead of weekly or monthly, very small wagers can be made, and numbers "runners" are generally available wherever players are found.

Our estimate of the present illegal net revenue to the numbers bankers, which is a very approximate one, is about $250 million a year from a total handle of $2.5 billion. This volume is concentrated among blacks and ethnic groups in the older cities, especially in the East and Midwest.

Several states are now actively considering setting up lotteries which would be similar to the numbers game. (New Jersey has a daily lottery, but it does not permit bettors to pick their own numbers). Our estimate for the net revenue to governments that might be yielded by legalized numbers-type lotteries is $500 million. This potential is modest because numbers is not popular nationwide today, and probably would not become so even if offered legally.

Sports betting. Only Nevada now has legalized betting on sporting events, but proposals to legalize it elsewhere have been advanced. The owners, commissioners, and coaches of sports teams have strongly opposed legal wagering on the grounds that it would offer too many temptations for bribery. More important, it would hurt the image of sports. This opposition will persist, particularly against straight wagering on individual sporting events. (These objections should not be as strong to the lottery kind of sports pool betting popular in Great Britain, or to the football cards popular in the United States.)

In fact, there is a great deal of betting on sports today. Our estimate for the total net revenues from presently illegal sports betting is $500 million a year on a handle of $12 billion. Legalizing all types of sports betting might produce about $1 billion in revenue to states on a handle of about $33 billion. These net figures may seem low, but the gross take is as little as 2.5 per cent on baseball and as little as five per cent on other sports. These percentages are reduced even further when bookmakers are forced to change odds in order to try and equalize the money bet on both sides of a game. The gross percentage taken from all sports events is probably around six per cent of the money wagered. If we assume that half of this gross goes to expenses, three per cent is left. (Although this margin seems small, average sports bets are large relative to horse race bets; therefore the percentage required to cover expenses is much lower.) If sports betting were legalized, this is the share assumed to go to governments.

It is by no means certain, however, that such revenues could, in fact, be generated. Operating sports betting establishments is a hard line of work. Professional oddsmakers must set and move two-way prices, and this is a skilled and risky business. Wagering on sporting events could be run on a pari-mutuel pool basis rather than a fixed-odds basis, but it might be difficult to organize such pools effectively, and the public demand is very uncertain.

Casino gambling. The main casino games consist of dice or craps (which accounts for about one half of casino revenues), blackjack (about one fourth of casino revenues), baccarat, roulette, keno, and slot machines. (Keno is a type of lottery having "numbers"-like characteristics; if casinos become widely accessible, keno might cut into the illegal numbers handle.)

Our estimates of potential net revenues from complete legalization of casino games is $1.8 billion, from a total handle of $36 billion. This implies that the United States could ultimately support the equivalent of 10 "Nevadas." (Nevada, in 1971, had a total handle of about $3.6 billion.) In contrast, the present illegal annual net take from casino type gambling is, we estimate, a very much smaller $150 million. Such casino operations have not always been so modest. Illegal casino gambling flourished in the 1930's and 1940's in many states, but these operations have now largely disappeared. The operators in many cases moved to Nevada.

In horse racing, the pari-mutuel take or gross revenue is simply related to the total handle or amount bet. These relationships are more complicated in casino games, and most public discussion on this topic is highly confused. "Handle," more commonly called "drop," is defined in Nevada[2] for such casino games as craps, blackjack, and roulette as the total amount of cash and cash equivalents, such as markers or notes, in the box on each casino table at the end of each eight-hour shift, or more uncommonly at the end of each twenty-four-hour day.[3] The gross profit or "win" of a game is the amount of cash and equivalents in the box minus the deficit in chips from the chip rack. The "percentage hold" is the win divided by the drop. It is calculated for each table, for each type of game, and is summarized for every shift, for every day, and for the year to date. The percentage hold differs for each type of casino game and will, due to chance, fluctuate violently from day to day and even from month to month. At the end of a year, however, the figures settle down to fairly constant values. Craps will ordinarily hold about 18 per cent, blackjack 22 per cent, and roulette about 33 per cent of the drop. These numbers are known only from experience. They vary from casino to casino depending on the rules of the different games, different methods of handling credit play, and the different habits of the clientele.

The percentage hold is dependent on, but *not* equal to, the percentage favoring the house on an individual bet. In roulette, to take the simplest example, all individual bets (excepting one obscure and little used bet) have a common fixed house percentage of 5.26 per cent.[4] The other casino games such as dice and blackjack have vary-

---

[2] This description applies with only slight differences to Puerto Rico and to casinos in other countries.
[3] Most of the cash in the box has been exchanged for gaming chips from the table chip rack which are used to make bets. Some cash it bet directly, and if the bet is lost, the cash goes into the box. If the bet is won, it is paid in chips. The box is never opened at the table.
[4] If one kept track of each individual roulette wager made and called the total of all such wagers the handle, in the long run the house would hold about 5.26 per cent of the handle so defined. Of course, no records are kept of the total amount of individual wagers made in the casinos, except in rare instances where

ing house percentages applicable to the different bets available to the player, and one can give only an average percentage against the players.[5]

In Nevada, the state and local government combined tax on casino gambling is about seven per cent of gross profits. This is much less than Nevada could obtain in taxes; they are kept low, perhaps, because Nevada tries to maximize tourism. We assume that a 75-25 division of gross casino profits would be possible, with the casino operators keeping 75 per cent and the remaining 25 per cent going to governments.

This leads to the question: Who should operate casinos? In New York State, it has been proposed in initial legislation that casinos be operated by the state or by a public-benefit corporation instead of by private operators. There are arguments both ways. In favor of state-operated casinos, it can be said that a greater *percentage* of the profits would ultimately go to the states (but probably smaller *total* revenues), infiltration of criminals into the operation would be much more difficult, corruption in the granting of franchises would be avoided, and policing of operations would be easier. Private franchising, on the other hand, has the advantage of generating more demand and hence revenues, and it avoids having the moral authority of the state eroded by direct association with casino operations.

The experience of Puerto Rico in contrast to that of other Caribbean casinos is instructive on at least the issue of consumer demand. Puerto Rican gambling, closely controlled and supervised, evidently seems to be sterile and non-competitive in contrast with the higher-limit, easy-going operations found, for instance, in the Bahamas. Despite accusations that Bahamian casinos have underworld connections and that cheating sometimes occurs, the customers have not

---

particular tables have been "clocked" for some reason. However, each casino keeps elaborate totals of the drop in the game boxes, so that handle defined in this way is a quantity continuously and accurately recorded. In all discussion of "handle" and "hold" and "take" which we have seen, no one ever bothers to make it clear that there are two possible ways of defining and computing these numbers, so that it is never made clear why percentages of "handle" held are sometimes quoted in the 15 to 30 per cent range and other times in the one to five per cent range.

[5] On the crap table, the average wager has about a two per cent advantage to the house; in blackjack, this figure is probably closer to three per cent, whereas in baccarat it is about 1.25 per cent. Finally, the per cent of the *drop* held for each individual game is more or less proportional to the percentage in favor of the house on *individual* wagers. In roulette the figures are 33 per cent for the hold versus five per cent on an individual bet, in blackjack 22 per cent versus about three per cent, and in craps 18 per cent versus about two per cent. There is no hold or drop figure for baccarat because most dealings are in cash from a bankroll on the table.

been deterred. On the contrary, it appears that the gambling public is attracted to operations spiced by rumors of underworld involvement.

The experience of the Howard Hughes ventures in Nevada is also instructive. A few years back Hughes entered Nevada, purchased six large casinos, and quickly became by far the largest operator in the state. This empire had much of the bureaucratic flavor of a state-run operation in contrast to the smaller, more individualistic operations of the other hotel-casinos. Business in the Hughes casinos fell off, and it has been widely reported that the Hughes organization in Nevada has made no money.

Credit policies will also surely make a difference. Private casinos give large amounts of risky credit for good business reasons. The ability to take the optimum credit risk with each player is a valued characteristic of a casino manager and his staff. It is hard to believe that state-operated casinos (even through the medium of public-benefit corporations) could efficiently run a risky credit operation. Another problem concerns the liberal use of free food, drinks, rooms, and travel—the present *modus operandi* of the Nevada casinos. And there is also the lavish entertainment which is an integral part of private casino operation. Somehow, one cannot envision this sort of Las Vegas-like operation being run by bureaucrats.

Whatever the comparative advantage of private casino operations, the problems of controlling them should not be underestimated. The British experience with casinos is instructive here. Chemin-de-fer was the only legal casino game permitted in England until the 1960 Betting and Gaming Act legalized more extensive casino operations. The number of casinos increased rapidly and by 1968 reached a total of more than 100 in London alone, of which at least 10 were quite large. Unfortunately, there was no clear authority responsible for casinos. As a result, many were owned and controlled by foreigners, violence occurred as control of many small casinos was contested, and protection payments were extracted. When things had clearly gotten out of hand, the government finally passed the Gaming Act of 1968, appointed a Gaming Board, and adopted strict licensing regulations. Almost all the smaller casinos which had caused most of the trouble were forced to close; the larger ones that were allowed to remain open were supervised and forced to remove all foreigners from direct control, tourist gambling "junkets" were forbidden, and all casinos were made to operate as private clubs. Foreigners wishing to join a gambling club must now wait 48 hours before membership is approved, clubs may be open only from 2:00

p.m. until 4:00 a.m., and casinos with restaurants are now required to route restaurant patrons away from gaming tables.[6] As a consequence of the strict licensing procedures, the number of casinos is much reduced, but the abuses have largely disappeared.

The lesson of the British experience is that too little regulation can cause problems. On the other hand, if an American state decides to have casinos in order to make money and draw tourists, then too much regulation will be counterproductive. States now contemplating having casinos would certainly do well to study carefully both the British and Puerto Rican experiences, as well as that of Nevada, in formulating their own policies.

Bingo. Some states allow bingo for avowed charitable purposes and the handles are already very large. As with other types of gambling, a shift in attitudes has occurred. Many large bingo centers which flourished along with casino gambling in the 1930's and 1940's were closed down by local authorities in the 1950's. For example, in the Ocean Park-Venice and Long Beach areas of California some 15 to 20 bingo parlors (locally called Bridge-O) flourished as late as 1950. Bingo today is permitted in a few of the large Nevada casinos and these operations have usually been quite successful. But now, proposals for removing restrictions are being advanced in a number of states.

Our estimate for the net potential revenue for full legalization of bingo is $500 million a year. Our estimate of the net current revenue from widespread, often technically illegal, but tolerated, bingo games is $100 million.

Card Playing. The main card games which rightfully come under the category of organized gambling are panguinge (or "pan," for short) and the many varieties of poker. Other gambling card games such as gin rummy and pinochle are usually played man to man and do not involve a house take.

In Nevada, about 10 of the casinos have card rooms where poker and pan are played. The revenue is modest but the operators believe that many of the patrons of the card rooms will sooner or later play at nearby casino tables. Outside of Nevada, the only large card rooms operating legally are in California, which has local option for draw poker. The main center is Gardena, in Southern California,

---

[6] Other restrictions are no advertising, no tipping of croupiers, no liquor served in gambling areas, no gambling in any casino by casino employees, and regulation of odds on games.

which has five large draw poker establishments. As a result, the property tax rate is very low compared to that of surrounding municipalities.

Our estimate for the present net revenue from illegal organized cards is $50 million; net revenue with legalization of cards, based largely on the Gardena experience, is estimated to be $200 million.

Slot machines. Three (or multiple) reel slot machines, or "one-armed bandits," are tolerated in many localities, although legal in few. In Nevada, each casino has hundreds of such machines available from denominations as low as one cent per play to a high of $5, and it is not unusual for a large Las Vegas casino to gross $7,000 or more a day from its machines. The slots may be designed to return on the average any desired percentage of the amount played to the customer. In the large casinos, a common figure is about an 85 per cent return to the players. It is not unusual in supermarkets, drug stores, and similar locations for slot machines to have a "hold" of 50 per cent or even more.

Our estimate for the present net revenue from illegal slot machine operations is $70 million a year. If they were legalized and made widely available, the estimated annual revenue to the states is $500 million. There are also other coin-operated games, legal and illegal, but the amounts of money involved in them are comparatively small.

Full legalization: the potential revenues

Present reported revenues from legal gambling, our estimates of the net revenues from current illegal operations, and the potential from nationwide legalization are summarized in Tables 1, 2, and 3. Currently the nationwide gambling handle is about $30 billion a year, one-third legal and two-thirds illegal. The states get a little under $1 billion in revenues while the illegal operations net less than $2 billion. With wide-open, nationwide legal gambling, our estimate is that the total handle would be about $100 billion and, assuming a high tax rate, that the total revenues to the states would be about $7 billion.

There are, of course, several qualifications and uncertainties about these numbers. The assumption that all the major types of games will be legalized in every state is clearly an overestimate, since it is doubtful that even 10 years from now there will be complete legalization in half of the states. Many states, especially in the Midwest,

TABLE 1. *Present Reported Legal Gambling Revenues for Major Games*

	HANDLE	GROSS TAKE	GOVERNMENT REVENUE
	(IN BILLIONS OF 1973 DOLLARS)		
Racing (on-track)	5.50	1.00	.50
Off-Track Betting	.55	.10	.06
Lotteries	.50	.30	.20
Casinos	3.60	.70	.04
Total	10.15	2.10	.80

TABLE 2. *Present Estimated Illegal Gambling Revenues*

	HANDLE	GROSS TAKE	OPERATORS NET REVENUES
	(IN BILLIONS OF 1973 DOLLARS)		
Off-Track Betting	5.50	1.00	.50
Lotteries	.20	.10	.05
Numbers	2.50	1.00	.25
Casinos	2.00	.40	.15
Sports Betting	12.00	.70	.50
Bingo[1]	.30	.15	.10
Cards[2]	—	.07	.05
Slot Machines[2]	.40	.10	.07
Total	22.90	3.52	1.67

[1] Excluding games operated by churches or charities.
[2] Other than in casinos.

TABLE 3. *Future Potential Legal Gambling Revenues*[1]

	HANDLE	GROSS TAKE	GOVERNMENT REVENUES
	(IN BILLIONS OF 1973 DOLLARS)		
Racing (on-track)	11.00	2.00	1.0
Off-Track Betting	11.00	2.00	1.0
Lotteries	2.50	1.20	1.0
Numbers	4.00	1.00	.5
Casinos	36.00	7.20	1.8
Sports Betting	33.00	2.00	1.0
Bingo[2]	2.00	1.00	.5
Cards[3]	—	.80	.2
Slot Machines[3]	4.00	1.00	.5
Total	103.50	18.2	7.5

[1] There might also be a sizable amount of illegal gambling in the future.
[2] Excluding games operated by churches or charities.
[3] Other than in casinos.

may be slow to legalize any sort of gambling. (These "prohibition-ist" states, however, will not have a large proportion of the nation's population.) Moreover, some kinds of gambling will not become uniformly available even where permitted by state laws, but will be concentrated in particular centers. This will be especially true of casinos, which are likely to be established initially in resort areas.

It will probably be a long time before gambling casinos appear in Manhattan.[7]

In addition, there is a great deal of uncertainty as to how the various types of gambling will interact with one another. On the one hand, competition among the various forms of gambling may increase the revenues to some types at the expense of others; this could make some of our individual estimates and the total too large. On the other hand, widespread legalizing might lead to reinforcement. Many people who had never gambled before might become addicted players. If this were to happen, then our estimates could turn out to be too low. Therefore, we put an uncertainty factor of about two on these estimates. If the negative factors prevail, our estimates may be high by a factor of two; if the positive factors prevail, then they could be low by a factor of two. This uncertainty factor of two is only a slightly educated guess. It might be, say, one and a half or three, but almost surely not 10.

In any case, we emphasize that these projections assume that gambling has been widely legalized and that the industry has matured. Within the next decade, perhaps half of the expected potential might be realized.

The projected $18 billion gross take shown in Table 3 would be the sum lost by gamblers to operators. Out of this total would come the costs of running the gambling enterprises, the return on investment, and the amounts retained by or transferred to governments. To put these figures in perspective, the losses to players if gambling on this scale had occurred in 1973 would have come to about two per cent of total personal income. (Our estimates are that losses actually were about 0.6 per cent.) This is about twice the share of personal income spent on gambling in Great Britain. But if Britain is a "nation of gamblers," as it has been called, how can our projection of gambling at twice the British level be justified? First, lotteries, as such, are illegal in England and they contribute much of our estimate. Casino gambling in England, now greatly restricted, is far below the level we project for the United States. Moreover, sports betting on individual games is very small in England compared even to our present illegal levels, let alone to our projected legal levels. In short, we are assuming a greater variety of games with a wider appeal than exists in England. Second, the British are poorer than we are, which means that we have more discretionary

---

[7] As this article goes to press, a group of mid-town Manhattan businessmen have proposed legalizing casino-restaurants in the Times Square section with the stated objective of rehabilitating the area.

income available for entertainment. In effect, we are assuming that gambling expenditures increase more than proportionately as per capita national income increases.

Here again we face the uncertainty in our estimates. If England represents a saturated gambling condition, and if the higher income elasticity argument doesn't hold water, then our estimates for the United States could well be too large. But if all forms of gambling are legalized, and if our high standard of living permits proportionally larger gambling expenditures, and if this country becomes truly a "nation of gamblers," then our ultimate projections could be too low.

Illegal gambling: How much is there?

The estimates for current revenues from illegal gambling shown in Table 2 are a handle of about $20 billion and a gross take of $3.5 billion. The gross take is the total amount lost by players. Out of it come payoffs to law enforcement personnel (we estimate that these payoffs total roughly $500 million a year). The gross take also covers the salaries and other costs of running a large number of illegal organizations. Operators net take, estimated at about $1.7 billion, is the sum retained as profits by illegal operators after expenses.

Our estimates of illegal gambling contrast sharply with other published estimates, which have almost all been considerably higher, ranging up to 20 times as much. There appear to be two distinct causes for these inflated estimates. One is the motive of arousing public attention to the dangers of illegal gambling: the higher the estimate, the more menacing the threat. The second is confusion among the terms "handle," "gross take," and "net take." For example, John Scarne (in *Scarne's Complete Guide to Gambling*) estimates an annual betting handle of $500 billion. He claims, however, that only half of this is bet through the medium of organized gambling, where there is such a category as "house take"; the other half is private gambling. Scarne also uses the definition of "handle" in casino gambling that counts every bet made rather than the much more useful definition that equates handle to drop. The difference exaggerates the estimated handle by a factor of about seven.

Another mistake is to confuse handle with either gross or net revenue. An instance of this occurred in the *Advocates* television program on gambling aired in January 1972. The moderator, Mr. Dukakis, began by saying that illegal gambling in the United States amounted to at least $20 billion, which seemed to refer to the handle. The next panel member to speak, Mr. Jack Cole, then said that the underworld "rakes off" an estimated $50 billion a year from the action, which seemed to refer to gross take.

Confusion may be understandable on a television show, but many writings exhibit similar misunderstandings. Rufus King, in a 1967 study prepared for the President's Commission on Law Enforcement, concluded that the gross handle of illegal gambling is not less than $20 billion a year, an estimate similar to ours. He then stated that "of this, the annual 'take' of the gambling promoters—i.e., the profits for organized crime—is $6 to $7 billion per year. And out of the latter, some $2 billion per year finds its way directly and indirectly into the hands of corrupt public officials and law enforcers."

There are several difficulties here. First, the annual "take" of $6 to $7 billion would be one third of the handle. But in sports betting, which is a large part of the total, the take is only about six per cent, and in casino gambling the take is about 20 per cent of the (properly defined) handle. Second, King goes on to confuse the gross take with the net take by saying that the annual take is the same as the profits for organized crime.

Exaggerated and confused estimates have also been set forth by more authoritative sources. The President's Commission on Law Enforcement in 1967 repeated King's estimate of a profit of $6 to $7 billion per year. President Nixon's 1969 message to the Congress on organized crime exhibited the familiar confusion: "Estimates of the take from illegal gambling alone in the United States run anywhere from 20-50 billion dollars, a figure larger than the entire federal administrative budget for the fiscal year 1951." Once again, it appears that "handle" has been converted into "take."

Gambling revenues and state budgets

Does the existence of a substantially smaller scale of illegal gambling than has widely been assumed make any difference? For one thing, it indicates that although illegal gambling may be a significant problem in certain communities, its seriousness as a nationwide problem may have been exaggerated. For another, it suggests that if the diagnoses of so many alleged experts are as faulty as they appear to be, their remedies might also be questioned, whether they advocate more rigorous law enforcement, or opt for wholesale legalization.

If the profits from illegal gambling are inflated, so too are expected government revenues from its legalization. Today Nevada gets about 40 per cent of its state-level revenue from gambling taxes, New York State about three per cent, and New Jersey about five per cent. In the not too distant past, several states got much larger proportions of their revenues from gambling. For example, in 1946 New Hampshire and Rhode Island each obtained 16 per cent of their revenues from the tracks. But that was back when the states had fewer responsibilities and very much smaller budgets than they do today. And there was less competition. Perhaps one fourth of the New Jersey lottery sales and a majority of New Hampshire's sales have been to non-residents, and with the spread of legal gambling their non-resident trade is shrinking.

In order to get a sense of what gambling revenues might mean for all of the states together, assume that the amount of gambling we estimate would occur in a fully legalized nationwide system were taking place today. Our projected gambling revenues of $7.5 billion in 1973 dollars come to 2.0 per cent of total taxes collected by all levels of government, and 5.5 per cent of total state and local revenues. This amounts to about 25 per cent of the yield from property taxes, and is about equal to the combined total of state gasoline and cigarette taxes, or to the present level of federal revenue sharing.

For some states, of course, the share of gambling taxes would be much higher than this average, and a higher share would mean dependence. But dependence on gambling revenues would create a conflict with other state objectives, including that of regulation to avoid abuses. Where revenues conflict with regulation, the incentive to subordinate the regulatory function is strong and may be overwhelming. It is foolish for a state government to believe that it can rigorously control gambling enterprises to protect the public welfare if doing so will result in a clear and negative impact on the public purse. The fact that the administration of lotteries in several states is lodged in state finance departments suggests how this conflict between regulation and revenue is likely to be resolved.

In the view of the Bank of New South Wales, this conflict has been evident in Australia: "The states have become more involved in direct operations of lotteries and dependent on the maintenance of legal betting. They have therefore acquired a vested interest in stimulating gambling as a means of raising revenues." The same phenomenon has been noted with respect to the Italian state lottery.

Clearly, $7 billion is not a trivial sum. Though it is not nearly enough to solve the revenue problems facing the states, it may well be enough to get some of them hooked on gambling.

Gambling and organized crime

Not only are the profits from illegal gambling almost certainly less than the huge sums usually cited, there is also doubt about the relationship between illegal gambling and "organized crime"—and, indeed, about just what is meant by "organized crime." Most of the discussions on this subject suggest the following conclusions:

1) All of the profits from illegal gambling go to "organized crime."

2) Organized crime is synonymous with the "syndicate" or the "Mob" or the "Mafia" or "La Cosa Nostra," which operates on a nationwide scale.

3) This "organized crime" which controls illegal gambling is the same organization that controls narcotics, extortion, prostitution, some labor unions, loan sharking, and other nefarious operations.

Although there is no question about the existence of criminal organizations and of links of some kind among some of them, the evidence in support of propositions as sweeping as these is far from convincing. The publicly available evidence is consistent with a pattern of local control of illegal gambling (i.e., illegal gambling in Los Angeles is, by and large, run and controlled by local Los Angeles people, whereas illegal gambling in New York is controlled and run largely by New Yorkers). This pattern, in fact, seems to prevail. The ties among these local organizations seem to be weak at best and often non-existent. Moreover, although there is certainly some interconnection between illegal gambling and the other types of crime mentioned above, a high degree of overlap has not been established. It is a more plausible conjecture that some operators engage only in gambling while others also engage in other criminal activities. We estimate that gambling proceeds are divided about evenly between these groups. And of the group that runs both gambling and other illegal activities, only some are likely to have ties to "organized crime." Again, perhaps the proportions are about equal.

An approximate check on the degree of involvement of "organized crime" in gambling can be made by calculating the per capita incomes implied by various estimates. The FBI has estimated that "La Cosa Nostra" or the "Mafia" has a membership of about 6,000. If all gambling profits went to its members, the per capita amounts

involved, using both the more or less "official" profit estimates of
$6 billion a year and ours of $1.7 billion, yield $1 million and
$300,000 a year per member respectively from gambling profits
alone. Although millionaires have undoubtedly been made from the
profits of crime, it is obvious that the average income of members
of the Mafia is not this large. Certainly, our conjecture on the pattern of gambling control yields a more plausible, although probably
still too high, estimate of gambling income to members of the
"Mafia."

The acceptance of a lower estimate of illegal gambling profits and
corruption payments should also affect arguments for legislation
based on the elimination of this source of corruption. The Knapp
Commission report has been cited above. Another report, issued in
1972 by the Committee for Economic Development (CED), urged
that all laws against casual gambling be repealed and that all organized gambling be taken over by the government. The report
argued that "such action would erode the corruptive power of organized crime, now heavily fortified by illicit gambling profits. And
it would provide a sizable source of public revenue."

The wholesale legalizing of gambling in order to lessen police
corruption is a drastic remedy. The situation in New York City may
justify the Knapp Commission's position, but we doubt that either
it or the CED group was in a position to forecast the consequences
of legalization. A more careful and selective approach to legalizing
gambling in New York, and a fortiori elsewhere in the country,
seems prudent.

The case for trying to eliminate illegal gambling through legalization rests on several propositions that, at the least, require examination. One argument often advanced is that profits from gambling
flow into other criminal activities such as loan sharking or narcotics
distribution. This proposition seems to rest on the premise that
these other illicit activities need permanent subsidies or that they
incur large "start-up" costs. To be sure, some illegal operations are,
in effect, conglomerates that no doubt derive strength from having
interlinked activities, but the notion that gambling provides essential support to other criminal activities that would seem to be
capable of generating profits on their own seems far-fetched as a
general proposition. Indeed, the possibility must be considered that
the cutting off of illegal gambling funds will cause some elements
of "organized crime" to intensify their activities in narcotics and
other illicit trades or to search for other kinds of illegal activities to
enter. If illegal organizations were profit maximizers, they would

already have developed these other activities. But a model which attributes a degree of organizational slack to illicit firms suggests that the erosion of gambling profits would lead to a search for other sources. It is not obvious which model is the more appropriate one, but it might be excessively optimistic to assume that reductions in illegal gambling would result in *no* increase or even a decrease in other kinds of crime.

Finally, it is true that if the community is willing to go far enough in legalizing gambling, imposing low taxes on it, and enforcing the laws, the market share of illegal gambling operators will certainly fall. But it should be noted that a policy of imposing very low taxes on legal gambling in order to compete more effectively with illegal operations is not consistent with a policy of maximizing revenues. Moreover, based on our figures, the illegal market share could be reduced from two thirds of the present total ($20 billion out of a $30-billion national handle) to a smaller share of a much larger total, and still be absolutely quite large.

Who gambles?

One view of gambling is that it is a useless activity, a luxury, and ought to be subject to taxation. This was the view of the British Select Committee on Betting Duty in 1924:

> Your committee are unanimous in the view that betting is a useless thing except insofar as it gives pleasurable excitement for some and for others an escape from the monotony of their daily world. It is in the main unproductive except to the bookmakers. In others, it is not inaptly described as a "mugs game," as practiced by the great majority of backers. It is a foolish occupation or habit. It is a pure luxury and a fitting subject for taxation unless there are strong reasons for allowing luxury to escape.

On this view, gambling taxes can be avoided by not gambling. Nevertheless, if the poor are more likely to gamble than the rich, the operational effect of taxing gambling would be to transfer income from the poor to those better off. More generally, if this country is going to experience a major growth in gambling, we need to know much more than we do about who gambles, how much they lose, and the probable incidence of gambling addiction. And we also should know more about what happens to the gambling propensity of a community over time as incomes increase. For a given availability of gambling opportunities, should we expect to see proportionally more, less, or the same amount of gambling over the next

20 years? Or say by 1984? George Orwell's forecast in his famous novel was this:

> Heavy physical work, the care of home and children, films, football, beer, and above all, gambling filled up the horizon of their minds. The lottery, with its enormous weekly prizes, was the one public event to which the proles paid serious attention and the principal thing for which some of them lived. It was their delight, their anodyne, their intellectual stimulation.

But what is known? As with much about gambling, very little, although there seem to be better data in Britain than in the United States. A Social Survey in the United Kingdom in 1950 and several surveys since then have shown that the incidence of gambling is highest in low-income groups. For example, the frequency of betting on horses and on football pools is much greater in the working class than in the upper and middle classes. The principal exception to this pattern seems to be casino gambling, because the casinos have been designed to appeal to the affluent.

Some evidence on differences in the kinds of bets made by different socio-economic groups has been provided by the British publication *Sporting Life,* which showed that a shop that served the lower-class areas and that handled smaller bets had, on the average, both higher costs and higher profits. For each pound bet, the poor bettors got a worse return than did the upper-income bettors. The big bets tend to be at short odds and on horses more likely to win, but most bets in working-class areas are on long shots or combinations, on which the operator has a larger takeout. These are, in fact, the only rational bets for the poor to make, for only these long-odds bets offer them any chance of winning a really significant amount of money.

Within the United States, early surveys taken for the New York City Off-Track Betting Corporation showed that its customers were similar to the general population but with a bias toward above-average income and education. Its most frequent bettors (those placing 100 or more bets a month with OTB), however, were below average in income and education (24 per cent had incomes below $7000). If we take account of amounts bet, it appears that OTB's handle is biased somewhat towards the low end of the income distribution. A similar inference can be drawn from a survey of New York State lottery ticket purchasers made in 1969. Evidently, the willingness to wager a small amount was actually less at high incomes than at lower ones. The Quayle survey in New York showed gambling on numbers to be concentrated in middle-income and low-income black and Puerto Rican groups, although whites were also substantially represented. The survey also showed that heavy sports betting with bookies is disproportionately concentrated in the middle-income group.

For the United States as a whole we know little about the incidence of gambling as a function of people's incomes. We would expect to find that the incidence of gambling varies with different types of games, and this is suggested by the evidence. But the data on distribution we have seen are too sketchy to be of much use for the purpose of determining policy.

Addiction and corruption

We can, however, say within the confidence limits stated above that gamblers currently lose something over $5 billion a year and that legalization might see such losses tripled. But how should one interpret a projection of a possible $100-billion gambling handle? As we have seen, the handle is an index of the total number of gambling transactions (i.e., the amount of gambling), and thus can be interpreted as a measure of the preoccupation of people with gambling and the amount of time they spend doing it. On this view, it will be an important aspect of many people's lives. This preoccupation is likely to be manifested in two specific and troubling ways: gambling addiction and an altered community atmosphere.

Although little is known about the incidence of gambling addiction, it can be a serious problem. Concern about compulsive gambling was expressed by the Gaming Board in Britain in its 1969 Report:

> The major objection however to the use of entertainment and dancing as a means of attracting people to take part in gaming must be that it increases the number of people who acquire a taste for this activity. Some proportion of them will eventually be compulsive gamblers. It is not at present possible to form a view as to what that proportion is likely to be—the information on which such a view must be based is not available. Nor is it possible to predict what proportion of compulsive gamblers may eventually achieve a cure. It is frequently argued that the innocent enjoyment of the majority should not be interfered with for the sake of a small minority whose weakness leads them into difficulties. For want of information, this argument must be broadly accepted, but with important reservations. It may well be less expensive in the long run (both in money and in terms of human suffering) to limit somewhat the opportunities for people to be led into gaming in the first place, than to attempt to cure those who subsequently develop compulsive cravings. It would seem particularly important that oppor-

tunities to acquire a taste for gaming should not be made too readily available to young people.

The line between meeting a legitimate demand for gaming and going too far can be a fine one. Landau, the former head of the Israeli lottery, believed that weekly drawings would sell better than fortnightly ones and so advocated them, but he felt that drawings every two days were an indication of a sick society.

The importance of learning more about the incidence of gambling addiction and the conditions in which it develops is suggested by analogy with drug addiction. For many decades, drug addiction was thought to be a minor social problem affecting Chinese immigrants, jazz musicians, and a few other special groups, but now it has emerged as a prominent national concern. Gambling addiction is evidently not a major problem today, but if we reflect on how little we know about the psychology of addiction, it might make us consider the possibility that it could develop into a serious social ailment.

The effect of gambling activities on the general atmosphere of the community will also be of wide concern. Many who do not disapprove of gambling in general will oppose it in their own community. It is especially troublesome when the state uses its power to force gambling establishments on communities that do not want them. For example, objections to having OTB outlets have occurred in some neighborhoods in New York. The usual way this concern has been dealt with is by segregating gambling activities in resort towns and in separate jurisdictions (Gardena serving the Los Angeles area, Covington in Kentucky serving Cincinnati—years ago but no longer—and, most importantly, Nevada serving the United States as a whole).

Zoning of gambling has a good deal of merit. It has been applied strictly by European countries, which have usually restricted casinos to watering places, kept them out of major cities, and banned local residents from entry. Although restrictions of this severity would not be acceptable in the United States today, this approach has much to commend it. Localities willing to accept gambling can get the financial benefits while the residents of places unwilling to live intimately with it can travel moderate distances to do their gambling. People who do not find themselves in the desired type of community will move to the other. However, the desire of legislators for revenue, or businessmen for trade, or libertarians for removing constraints may prevent a sensible pattern along these lines from emerging.

How rational is gambling?

Adam Smith viewed gamblers as conceited men who believe that their fortune is greater than that of their neighbors and who overrate their chances of gain and underrate their chances of loss. But if one considers the near universality of gambling from earliest recorded history, one wonders about this view. Moreover, an examination of gambling behavior in different countries today shows some interesting regularities. For example, in a number of countries for which data on legal gambling are available, net expenditures on gambling seem to fall within the range of 0.4 per cent to 1.0 per cent of national income.

Various attempts have been made to account for gambling behavior. Some scholars have developed the "pleasurable excitement" and "escape from monotony" themes of the 1924 British Commission. Others stress the fact that many people believe life is dominated by chance and they just might get lucky. A third group focuses upon the skill and computational activities involved. Still others emphasize the importance of social group interactions that often occur in the gambling environment. Psychiatrists have suggested that gambling behavior increases sublimation of oedipal aggression against one's father, that it is a substitute for masturbation, that it is a defense against feminine identification which takes the form of excessive masculinity, and that bettors have an unconscious wish to lose. It seems plausible that several of these motivations may play a role, but there is much to be said for economizing on explanations.

Perhaps the simplest is that people gamble for money. This explanation may seem paradoxical, because on the average they lose. For example, a 50-cent lottery ticket has an actuarial value of around 25 cents. Milton Friedman and L. J. Savage have shown, however, that this kind of purchase can be explained by assuming that the gambler has a particular utility preference for money: Over a range of income levels, he has an increasing marginal utility for money—in contrast to the usual assumption that the marginal utility of money decreases monotonically as wealth increases. It isn't necessary to postulate a preference for thrills or risks. All a person needs is a desire for a large sum of money. This prospect is precisely what a lottery offers.

If lottery-like games can be explained with some economy of means, what about games that offer lesser odds (in the 100-to-1 to 1000-to-1 region), like numbers or combination bets such as Exactas? For people who play these games, saving would be a more reliable way of amassing some money. But suppose we assume a life beset with crises, a life that makes saving difficult or impossible, and also assume a high personal time rate of discount and a limited ability to borrow money (and then only at a high rate of interest). For such people, it may not be irrational to play unfair games, even though the mathematical expectation is negative. Such games might seem to offer the only hope of accumulating a lump sum.

It is only when one gets to short-odds games, played repetitively, where money is put right back into the game, that we must resort to "pleasurable excitement" or to the various other kinds of non-economic explanations.

Motivations for gambling are important to understand because they provide insights useful for public policy choices. For example, almost everybody who bets on a lottery loses. This seems to be why individual outlays on lotteries are small and lottery playing is non-addictive. Consequently, the long-odds "lottery" type of market probably can be satisfied in a number of ways. Competition among a well-run lottery, numbers, and combination bets of various kinds may be keen. Increases in the take from one of these games are likely to be at the expense of the others. For the shorter-odds types of games—especially those where repeated, rapid play is possible, as in casinos—the commodity being sold is a more complicated "package." The psychological involvement is more addiction-causing. Moreover, these types of games are probably less close substitutes for one another and hence less strongly competitive. This is good from the point of view of the revenue maximizer because the market can be partitioned and developed, but the social consequences of widespread availability of this class of games may be serious.

The federal role

The federal government has generally been hostile to gambling, legal or illegal. It has imposed a 10 per cent tax on most forms of gambling, exempting only casino games and money wagered in pari-mutuel pools and state lotteries where drawings are based on horse race results. It prohibits the transmission of lottery tickets across state lines and forbids banks to sell them. The FCC forbids the broadcasting of lottery drawing results. Gambling winnings are taxed, in contrast to the practice in many countries. Bookmakers in Nevada are prohibited from accepting out-of-state bets by telephone and are burdened with the 10 per cent tax.

If legal gambling expands, it seems unlikely that the federal role can long remain what it is today. Increased competition among states is likely to lead to a demand for a stronger federal role. On this question, the history of competition among the states in Australia is instructive. In 1902, the central government refused to accept mail for Tasmania's lottery because other states felt that money was being drained from them. Addresses of convenience and agents were therefore used to sustain sales. In 1931, New South Wales introduced a lottery, in part to keep money from going to Tasmania and Queensland. In 1954, Victoria persuaded Tattersall's lottery to move there from Tasmania because it was attracting too much money away from Victoria. Tasmania responded by licensing another operator who provided bigger prizes than Tattersall's. The main effect of all this competition was to increase the stakes, reduce the interval between ticket sales and drawings, and produce more frequent drawings—a process we now observe at work in the United States.

The federal government in the United States will also be under pressure from legal gambling interests to remove obstacles such as the taxation of gambling winnings and the 10 per cent betting tax. Exempting winnings would certainly help shift action away from illegal operations. It also would help expand the total amount of gambling.

Weighing the alternatives

State legislators have several factors to weigh in choices on gambling. Arguments in favor of legalization are increased tax revenues, reduced corruption, increased tourism, and removal of restrictions on personal choice. On the other hand, general legalization will increase substantially the amount of gambling, and this will have uncertain but probably significant consequences on addiction and community atmosphere. Gambling taxes will not do much to ease the burden of taxes in most states; and in the few states where these taxes might reach a substantial level, they will create a relationship of dependency. Moreover, legislators should be aware of the conflict between the function of government as regulator and its possible role as operator; there is much to be said for limiting government's role to that of regulator. States that permit widespread gambling will also want to consider seriously the possibilities of limiting the "spillover" effects by adopting strict zoning provisions.

On the fundamental issue of legalization, the states are faced with three broad options:

1. *No change.* This would mean foregoing comparatively small tax revenues and living with existing illegal gambling and corruption, which in many states is not a serious problem. This policy would avoid the social costs associated with increased gambling. And if neighboring states offer gambling services, the abstaining state's citizens will not be terribly deprived. No doubt some states will prefer this alternative for at least the next decade.

2. *Selective legalization.* This would mean legalizing only the most easily controlled forms of gambling. States that choose this alternative would accept on-track betting, lotteries, and perhaps numbers (in states that have large illegal numbers business) and, possibly, off-track pari-mutuel betting on horses. Another possibility is sports betting on a pool or pari-mutuel basis of the British type. Casinos, sports betting on individual games, card parlors, and slot machines would be excluded. A difficult problem these states will face is deciding where to draw the line.

3. *General legalization.* Some states may legalize virtually all types of gambling. They will then have to live with the various consequences of that decision.

Our findings are not sufficiently certain to predict what will happen with confidence; still less do they enable us to say what a state should do. But our analysis does suggest the existence of illusions and misconceptions about the consequences of legalized gambling, and the importance of looking closely at its possible impact. No one knows what the long-term effects of legalizing gambling would be. Yet we can find out a good deal by examining our experience to date with illegal and legal gambling. The variation in gambling patterns across states and over time provides a wealth of data, and further analysis of British data would also be very useful. Some research has begun and even these limited results are helpful. But much more needs to be done.

Does Punishment Deter Crime?

GORDON TULLOCK

TRADITIONALLY there have been three arguments for the punishment of criminals. The first of these is that punishment is morally required or, another way of putting the same thing, that it is necessary for the community to feel morally satisfied. I will not discuss this further. The two remaining explanations are that punishment deters crime and that it may rehabilitate the criminal. The rehabilitation argument was little used before about 1800, presumably because the punishments in vogue up to that time had little prospect of producing any positive effect upon the moral character of the criminal.[1] *

But with the turn to imprisonment as the principal form of punishment—a movement which occurred in the latter part of the 18th and early part of the 19th century—the idea that the prison might "rehabilitate" the prisoner became more common. The word "penitentiary" was coined with the intent of describing a place where the prisoner has the time and the opportunity to repent of his sins and resolve to follow a more socially approved course of action after his release. The idea that prisons would rehabilitate the criminal and that this was their primary purpose gradually replaced the concept of deterrence as the principal publicly announced justification for the punishment system. I should like to defer discussing my views as to why this occurred until the latter part of this article, but here I should like to point out that, whatever the motive or the reason for this change, it certainly was not the result of careful scientific investigation.

So far as I have been able to discover, there were no efforts to test the deterrent effect of punishment scientifically until about 1950. At that time, several studies were made investigating the question whether the death penalty deterred murder more effectively than life imprisonment. These studies showed that it did not, but they were extremely primitive statistically. This is not to criticize the scholars who made them. Computers were not then readily available, the modern statistical techniques based on the computer had not yet been fully developed, and, last but by no means least, the scholars who undertook the work were not very good statisticians. Under the circumstances, we cannot blame them for the inadequacies of their work, but neither should we give much weight to their findings.

* All footnotes may be found at the end of this article.

Moreover, even if it were the case that the death penalty did not deter murder, it would not automatically follow that deterrence does not work in general. The argument is frequently made that life imprisonment is actually a more severe punishment than the death penalty and it might turn out to be true—at least in the eyes of potential murderers. If this were the case, then one would anticipate that life imprisonment would have a greater deterrent effect than would execution. But in any event, the findings obtained in these early studies were largely the result of their very primitive statistical techniques.

Statistically testing deterrence is not easy because the prospect of punishment obviously is not the *only* thing that affects the frequency with which crimes are committed. The crime rate varies with the degree of urbanization, the demographic composition of the population, the distribution of wealth, and many other circumstances. Some statistical technique is necessary to take care of these factors—and such techniques are now available. Using multiple regression (or, in a few cases, a complicated variant on the Chi-Square test), it is possible to put figures on each of these variables into the same equation and to see how much they influence the dependent variable which, in this case, is the rate of a specific crime. Although there are difficulties, this procedure will give a set of numbers called coefficients that are measures of the effect of *each* of the purported causative factors on the rate of commission of the given crime. If punishment deters crime, it will show up in these figures as a coefficient that is both significant and negative. A number of other things in the equation may also show up as affecting the crime rate, but the purpose of this article is to discuss only whether *punishment* does or does not deter crime.

One of the basic problems with any kind of statistical research in the field of criminology is the appallingly poor quality of the data. Any study will have a great deal of what the statistician calls "random noise" in it. Most of the studies mentioned below use the FBI's *Uniform Crime Report* statistics, and almost all of the authors have made comments about how bad these statistics are. I am happy to say that the Law Enforcement Assistance Administration has begun a project aimed at a sharp improvement in crime statistics, and hence we can anticipate that such research will be a great deal easier in the future. All of the studies I will report are based on the earlier and poorer statistics, but in about a year or so there should be a new generation of studies drawing upon the much better data that will be available at that time.

THE recent studies in deterrence come partly from economists and partly from sociologists. As an economist myself, I may be pardoned for starting with the economic studies, but I should say that, due to the long delay that intervenes between research and publication, it is not at all obvious which discipline actually had priority.

Most economists who give serious thought to the problem of crime immediately come to the conclusion that punishment will indeed deter crime. The reason is perfectly simple: Demand curves slope downward. If you increase the cost of something, less will be consumed. Thus, if you increase the cost of committing a crime, there will be fewer crimes. The elasticity of the demand curve, of course, might be low, in which case the effect might be small; but there should be at least *some* effect.

Economists, of course, would not deny that there are other factors that affect the total number of crimes. Unemployment, for example, quite regularly raises the amount of crime and, at least under modern conditions, changes in the age composition of the population seem to be closely tied to changes in the crime rate. The punishment variable, however, has the unique characteristic of being fairly easy to change by government action. Thus, if it does have an effect, we should take advantage of that fact.

The 19th-century utilitarians had drawn this conclusion, and when economists in the 1950's and early 1960's began turning their attention to the problem of deterrence, this rather simple application of economic theory was one of the first things that occurred to them.[2] The first econometric test of this theoretical deduction from economics was performed by one of Gary Becker's graduate students, Arleen Smigel Leibowitz, in her Master's thesis.[3] The basic design of this research project was reasonably sophisticated, although, as can be seen below, it has been improved upon since then. Leibowitz used as her basic data the crime rate and the punishment for a number of different crimes in each state in the United States. She took into account both the severity of punishment (i.e., the average prison sentence) and the probability that punishment will actually be imposed (i.e., the percentage of crimes whose perpetrators are caught and sent to prison). A number of essentially sociological factors that might affect the crime rate were also included in her multiple regressions. Leibowitz's findings revealed an unambiguous deterrence effect on each of the crimes studied—that is, when other factors were held constant, the states which had a higher level of punishment showed fewer crimes. Such crimes as rape and murder were deterred by punishment just as well as (indeed, perhaps better than) burglary and and robbery.

Another of Becker's students, Isaac Ehrlich, in his doctoral dissertation went over much the same ground as Leibowitz but with a much more sophisticated and careful statistical methodology. The results, which are available in full text in his dissertation and in a somewhat abridged form in an article,[4] once again indicate that punishment does deter crime.

Further work along the same general lines was carried out by Llad Phillips, Harold L. Votey, Jr., and John Howell. In general, these scholars used the same basic data and analytical methods as Leibowitz and Ehrlich, and confirmed their findings. More recently, this group of scholars has used the same data and similar methods in an effort to produce more detailed and specific results.[5] These studies, which are of great interest in themselves, are relevant to our present purpose only in that, as a sort of by-product, they contain further confirmation of the basic finding that punishment does deter crime. Further, Phillips has run a time-series test using national data in his multiple regression to supplement the cross-sectional tests on state data.[6] It also produced similar results. Last along this particular line, Morgan Reynolds in his doctoral dissertation has treated the same basic research design en route to some new results in another area.[7]

In addition to these studies using essentially the same data on crime and punishment in the 50 states, there are two important studies using different data. Michael Block compared the crime rates for Los Angeles police districts with the likelihood in each of these districts that offenders would be caught and sent to prison, and found a clear deterrence effect.[8] And R.A. Carr-Hill and N.H. Stern carried out a study using data drawn from England and Wales and, once again, determined that punishment does deter crime.[9]

Joseph Magaddino and Gregory Krohm, using California county data, have begun work which, from the results shown by their first regressions, apparently will lead to the same conclusion.[10] David Sjoquist and Phillips, Votey, and Donald Maxwell investigated somewhat different problems, but their statistical outcomes provide further support for the deterrence theory.[11]

Finally, some students under my direction attempted to make a cost-benefit analysis of certain property crimes, primarily burglary, from the standpoint of the criminal—that is, they looked into the question of whether crime does pay. The data were particularly bad in this area, as the reader can well imagine, but they supported the conclusion that most people who took up the profession of burglary had made a sensible career choice. They did not make very much from burglary, but they were not very high-quality laborers and would have done as badly (or worse) if they had elected honest employment.[12] This is not of direct relevance to the deterrence hypothesis, but it does seem to indicate that at least some criminals make fairly rational decisions with respect to their careers, and hence that raising the price of crime would presumably reduce the frequency with which it is committed.

Recently this point of view has been questioned by a short study by Michael Sesnowitz.[13] (The article was commented upon by Krohm and a reply was made by Sesnowitz.[14]) Following an approach rather similar to that used by my students, Sesnowitz found that burglary did not pay in Pennsylvania. Basically, the difference between Sesnowitz's results and those which I would have expected comes from the fact that there are no data on the amount of time served by burglars in Pennsylvania who are sentenced to jail rather than prison. Sesnowitz assumed that the average jail sentence was the same as the average prison sentence for burglary (43 months). But since it is illegal in Pennsylvania for anyone to spend more than 23 months in jail (as opposed to prison), it is most unlikely that this is so; and if adjustments for this discrepancy are made, the results wind up rather similar to those obtained by my students. Incidentally, Pennsylvania apparently does have an exceptionally high punishment level for burglars—and, correspondingly, an exceptionally low rate of burglaries, just as the deterrence hypothesis would predict.

So much for the economists; let us now turn to the sociologists. All the economists I have cited began their studies under the impression that punishment *would* deter crime. All the sociologists I am about to cite began under the impression that it *would not* and, indeed, took up their statistical tools with the intent of confirming what was then the conventional wisdom in their field—that crime cannot be deterred by punishment. When they found out they were wrong, they quite honestly published their results, although they found it rather difficult to get their work accepted in the more conventional sociological journals.

The first of these sociologists was Jack Gibbs, who published a study in the *Social Science Quarterly* which indicated that punishment did indeed deter crime.[15] His statistical methods were basically rather different from those used by the economists—indeed, speaking as an economist, I would say they were more primitive; but the fact that the same conclusion comes from two different statistical techniques is further confirmation of its validity. The publication of this paper set off a spate of other papers by Louis Gray and David Martin, Frank Bean and Robert Cushing, and Charles Tittle.[16] All of these scholars took up their cudgels with the intention of demonstrating that Gibbs was wrong, and all ended up agreeing with him. In the process, they greatly expanded and improved upon his work. Moreover, they continued using statistical tools that were somewhat different from those that had been employed by the economists; hence, their work can be taken as an independent confirmation of the economists' approach.

The sociologists were very much interested in a problem that had also concerned the economists, but not so vitally. This is the question whether the severity of the sentence or the likelihood that it will be imposed is more important in deterring crime. In my opinion, this is not a very important question. Suppose a potential criminal has a choice between two punishment systems: One gives each person who commits burglary a one-in-100 chance of serving one year in prison;[17] in the other there is a one-in-1,000 chance of serving 10 years. It is not obvious to me that burglars would be very differently affected by these two punishment systems, although in one case there is a heavy sentence with a low probability of conviction, and in the other a lighter sentence with a higher probability of conviction.

I would suggest that the appropriate technique is simply to divide the average sentence by the frequency with which it is imposed, and to use that as the deterrent measure. Most of the sociologists and a good many of the economists mentioned above have attempted to determine which of these two variables is more important. Leaving aside my theoretical objections, I do not think the statistics are accurate enough for the results obtained from these tests to be of much value. Be that as it may, more often than not the researchers have found that the frequency with which the punishment is applied is of greater importance than its severity.

THE first studies in this field, the ones I criticized at the beginning of my survey of the empirical literature, dealt with the death penalty. Recently Ehrlich has returned to this problem and, by using a much more sophisticated method, has demonstrated a very sizeable deterrence payoff to the death penalty for murder.[18] His figures indicate that each execution prevents between 8 and 20 murders. Unfortunately, the data available for this study were not what one would hope for, so not as much reliance can be put upon his results as one normally would give to work by such a sophisticated econometrician. Earlier, and using a quite different set of statistics and a different method, I arranged to have a graduate student do a preliminary study of the same issue; his results showed that each execution prevented two murders. Here again, however, the data were bad and the methods were suitable only for a preliminary exploration.[19]

It should be emphasized that the question of whether the death penalty deters murder is a different one from the question of whether we wish to have the death penalty. One widespread minor crime is failing to return to the parking meter and put in a coin when the time expires. I take it that we could reduce the frequency with which this crime is committed by boiling all offenders in oil. I take it, also, that no one would favor this method of deterrence. *Thus, the fact that we can deter a crime by a particular punishment is not a sufficient argument for use of that punishment.*

In discussing the concept of deterrence, I find that a great many people seem to feel that, although it would no doubt work with respect to burglary and other property crimes, it is unlikely to have much effect on crimes of impulse, such as rape and many murders. They reason that people who are about to kill their wives in a rage are totally incapable of making any calculations at all. But this is far from obvious. The prisoners in Nazi concentration camps must frequently have been in a state of well-justified rage against some of their guards; yet this almost never led to their using violence against the guards, because punishment—which, if they were lucky, would be instant death, but was more likely to be death by torture—was so obvious and so certain. Even in highly emotional situations, we retain some ability to reason, albeit presumably not so well as normally.

It would take much greater provocation to lead a man to kill his wife if he knew that, as in England in the 1930's, committing murder meant a two-out-of-three chance of meeting the public executioner within about two months than if—as is currently true in South Africa —there were only a one-in-100 chance of being executed after about a year's delay.[20]

Another example can be drawn from the American South. Before about 1950, there was a great deal of violence among blacks, particularly on Saturday nights. The local authorities took the view that this was an inherent matter of black character, and hence were reluctant to punish it severely. It has been pointed out that the reluctance of the police to punish such "black" traits was probably the principal reason for their existence. A black who slashed another black's face with a razor on Saturday night would probably merely be reproved by the police and, at most, would get a short term in jail. A white who did the same thing to another white would probably get several years in prison. The difference between the statistical frequency with which blacks and whites performed this kind of act is thus explicable in terms of the deterrence effect of punishment as it was then administered.

It should be noted that thus far I have said nothing whatsoever about how well-informed criminals or potential criminals are as to the punishments for each crime in each state. For punishment to have a deterrent effect, potential criminals must have at least some information about its likely severity and frequency. Presumably, the effect of variations in punishment would be greater if criminals were well-informed than if they were not. In practice, of course, potential criminals are not very well-informed about these things, but they do have some information.

Reports of crimes and punishments are a major part of most newspapers. It is true that most intellectuals tend to skip over this part of the newspaper, but the average person is more likely to read it than some things that appeal to intellectuals. And an individual who is on the verge of commiting a crime or has already taken up a career of crime is apt to be much more interested in crime stories than is the average man. He should have, therefore, a rough idea of the severity of punishments and of the probability that they will be imposed. This information should affect the likelihood that he will choose to commit a given crime.

Nevertheless, the information that he will have is likely to be quite rough. Undoubtedly, if we could somehow arrange for people to have accurate information on these matters, we would get much better coefficients on our multiple regression equations for the deterrence effect of punishment. But since governments have a motive to lie—i.e., to pretend that punishment is more likely and more severe than it actually is—it is unlikely that we can do much about improving this information. Still, the empirical evidence is clear. Even granting the fact that most potential criminals have only a rough idea as to the frequency and severity of punishment, multiple regression studies show that increasing the frequency or severity of the punishment does reduce the likelihood that a given crime will be committed.

FINALLY, I should like to turn to the issue of why "rehabilitation" became the dominant rationale of our punishment system in the latter part of the 19th century and has remained so up to the present, in spite of the absence of any scientific support. The reasons, in my opinion, have to do with the fallacy, so common in the social sciences, that "all good things go together." If we have the choice between preventing crime by training the criminal to be good—i.e., rehabilitating him—or deterring crime by imposing unpleasantness on criminals, the former is the one we would *like* to choose.

The Reverend Sydney Smith, a follower of the deterrence theory, said a prison should be "a place of punishment, from which men recoil with horror—a place of real suffering painful to the memory, terrible to the imagination . . . a place of sorrow and wailing, which should be entered with horror and quitted with earnest resolution never to return to such misery . . ." [21] This is an exaggeration. Our prisons do not have to be that bad; the deprivation of liberty in itself may be a sufficiently effective punishment. But in any case, deterrence necessarily involves the deliberate infliction of harm.

If, on the other hand, we can think of the prison as a kind of educational institution that rehabilitates criminals, we do not have to consciously think of ourselves as injuring people. It is clearly more appealing to think of solving the criminal problem by means that are themselves not particularly unpleasant than to think of solving it by methods that *are* unpleasant. But in this case we do not have the choice between a pleasant and an unpleasant method of dealing with crime. We have an unpleasant method—deterrence—that works, and a pleasant method—rehabilitation—that (at least so far) never has worked. Under the circumstances, we have to opt either for the deterrence method or for a higher crime rate.

FOOTNOTES

[1] Of course, they might prevent him from committing the crime by making it physically impossible. Cutting off both hands of a forger and hanging them about his neck probably had no effect on his desire to commit forgery, but certainly made it very hard to do.

[2] See Gary Becker, "Crime and Punishment: An Economic Approach," *Journal of Political Economy*, 76 (March/April, 1968), pp. 169-217. See, also, Gordon Tullock, "The Welfare Costs of Tariffs, Monopolies, and Theft," *Western Economic Journal*, 5 (June, 1967), pp. 224-32; and "An Economic Approach to Crime," *Social Science Quarterly*, 50 (June, 1969), pp. 59-71.

[3] Arleen Smigel Leibowitz, "Does Crime Pay: An Economic Analysis" (unpublished Master's thesis, Columbia University, 1965).

[4] Isaac Ehrlich, "Participation in Illegitimate Activities: An Economic Analysis" (unpublished Ph.D. dissertation, Columbia University, 1970); and "Participation in Illegitimate Activities: A Theoretical and Empirical Investigation," *Journal of Political Economy*, 81 (May/June, 1973), pp. 521-65.

[5] Harold L. Votey, Jr. and Llad Phillips, *Economic Crimes: Their Generation, Deterrence, and Control* (Springfield, Va.: U.S. Clearinghouse for Federal Scientific and Technical Information, 1969); Harold L. Votey and Llad Phillips, "The Law Enforcement Production Function," *Journal of Legal Studies*, 1 (June, 1972); Llad Phillips and Harold L. Votey, Jr., "An Economic Analysis of the Deterrent Effect of Law Enforcement on Criminal Activity," *Journal of Criminal Law, Criminology, and Police Science*, 63 (September, 1972); and Llad Phillips and Harold L. Votey, Jr., "The Control of Criminal Activity: An Economic Analysis," in *Handbook of Criminology*, ed. by Daniel Glaser (Chicago: Rand McNally & Co., forthcoming).

[6] Llad Phillips, "Crime Control: The Case for Deterrence," in *The Economics of Crime and Punishment*, ed. by Simon Rottenberg (Washington, D. C.: American Enterprise Institute for Public Policy Research, 1973), pp. 65-84.

[7] Morgan Reynolds, "Crimes for Profit: The Economics of Theft" (unpublished Ph.D. dissertation, University of Wisconsin, 1971).

[8] Michael Block, "An Econometric Approach to Theft" (Stanford University, mimeographed paper).

[9] R. A. Carr-Hill and N. H. Stern, *An Econometric Model of the Supply and Control of Recorded Offenses in England and Wales*, rev. (University of Sussex: School of Social Science, 1972).

[10] Joseph P. Magaddino and Gregory C. Krohm (untitled paper, in progress).

[11] See David L. Sjoquist, "Property Crime and Economic Behavior: Some Empirical Results," *American Economic Review*, 83, no. 3 (1973); and Llad Phillips, Harold L. Votey, Jr., and Donald Maxwell, "Crime, Youth, and the Labor Market," *Journal of Political Economy*, 80 (May/June, 1972).

[12] William E. Cobb, "Theft and the Two Hypotheses," in *The Economics of Crime and Punishment*, ed. by Simon Rottenberg (Washington, D. C.: The American Enterprise Institute for Public Policy Research, 1973), pp. 19-30; Gregory C. Krohm, "The Pecuniary Incentives of Property Crime," *idem*, pp. 31-34; and J. P. Gunning, Jr., "How Profitable is Burglary," *idem*, pp. 35-38.

[13] See Michael Sesnowitz, "The Returns to Burglary," *Western Economic Journal*, 10 (December, 1972), pp. 177-81.

[14] Gregory C. Krohm, "An Alternative View of the Returns to Burglary," *Western Economic Journal*, 11 (September, 1973), pp. 364-7; and Michael Sesnowitz, "The Returns to Burglary: An Alternative to the Alternative," *idem*, pp. 368-70.

[15] Jack Gibbs, "Crime, Punishment, and Deterrence," *Southwestern Social Science Quarterly*, 48 (March, 1968), pp. 515-30.

[16] Louis N. Gray and J. David Martin, "Punishment and Deterrence: Another Analysis of Gibbs' Data," *Social Science Quarterly*, 50 (September, 1969), pp. 389-95; Frank D. Bean and Robert G. Cushing, "Criminal Homicide, Punishment, and Deterrence: Methodological and Substantive Reconsiderations," *Social Science Quarterly*, 52 (September, 1971), pp. 277-89; and Charles R. Tittle, "Crime Rates and Legal Sanctions," *Social Problems*, 16 (Spring, 1969), pp. 409-23.

[17] This is actually somewhat higher than the risk that burglars now face in most parts of the United States.

[18] Isaac Ehrlich, "The Deterrent Effect of Capital Punishment: A Question of Life and Death." This is to be published in the *American Economic Review*.

[19] Since I cannot possibly claim to have read everything that has ever been written on the subject, I have been conducting part of my research in this area by asking people who hear my speeches or read my papers to tell me if they know of any other articles or books in which the effectiveness of deterrence has been tested in a reasonably scientific manner. I have never received a positive response to this question, but I repeat it here.

[20] These figures are for blacks killing blacks, not for blacks killing whites, or, for that matter, whites killing whites.

[21] Sydney Smith, *On the Management of Prisons* (London: Warde Locke and Company, 1822), pp. 226, 232.

Crime
and punishment
in
England

JAMES Q. WILSON

However much we Americans may deplore the apparent political and economic decay of England, there persists among nearly all of us the admiring view that at least with respect to criminal justice, the English know how to do things properly. The images about British justice with which we have been supplied by countless reporters and storytellers remain unsullied and intact—the quiet, competent, incorruptible bobby; the stern but fair judge; the quick and certain punishment for wrongdoers; the respect and deference shown by all ranks of the English population toward unarmed constables; the safety and security of the meanest streets of London. To be sure, we are aware of some incidents of terrorist violence and an occasional football riot, but these are isolated and modest exceptions to the normal state of affairs.

This view of English crime and justice follows naturally upon a more general perception of British society widely taught and believed in the United States. There is thought to be in Britain a broad consensus in moral and legal matters—no competing value systems either generate crime or stimulate disrespect for the law. To these common habits of mind is joined a pragmatic disposition to devise rational and useful schemes for insuring both private rights and public safety—careful, formal trials for anybody accused of a crime, and prompt and severe sentences for anybody convicted of one. What we perceive, in short, is a legal system codified by Blackstone and supported by a sentencing policy devised by Bentham, all operating in a society described by Bagehot.

It would make for a fine literary effect if I could show at this point that the very opposite of these suppositions is, in fact, the case. Unfortunately, however, the reality of British justice, while quite different than is popularly imagined, is by no means the exact reverse of its image. The current state of criminal justice in England and Wales is enormously complex—in part because it is almost as diverse and lacking in central direction as its American counterpart; in part because it is the object of a strenuous debate over its purposes and practices; and in part because it is struggling, inadequately, to cope with a level of crime undreamt of as recently as 20 years ago. What can be said, I believe, is that if the economic crisis of the country were not uppermost in the minds of everyone, the problem of crime might well be; by the same token, if the government were in a position to increase expenditures on anything (which it very nearly is not), it might arguably give highest priority to the expansion and improvement of the police and the prisons.

It is clear that the current economic and political crisis powerfully affects the prospects for any bold action to deal with crime. What is not clear is whether that crisis—or rather the change in society and popular attitudes that have contributed to that crisis—has itself been a cause of the steep increase in crime that has occurred in recent years. It is clear that the political economy of England has come very near to collapse; whether the civic virtue of its people is in an equally perilous state—and, if so, whether from the same causes—is not at all clear.

What can be said is this: England and Wales are in the grip of their most steeply rising crime rate of this century. This crime wave has stretched the police service and the capacity of the prison system almost to the breaking point. Accompanying (and perhaps contributing to) the increase in crime have been changes in the criminal justice system that have substantially lessened the probability that any given offender will be penalized or separated from the rest of society—and this is especially true of young offenders. While certain cases are still dealt with swiftly, this is generally true only for less important ones or (not necessarily the same thing) ones in which the likely penalty is trivial. The congestion and delay in the disposition of serious cases has increased dramatically. Finally, there are signs of what I would call, at the obvious risk of some trans-Atlantic ill will, the "Americanization" of English criminal justice— by which I mean that well-intentioned officials and advisers in Her Majesty's government seem to have learned little from the mistakes made by their counterparts in the United States. There is scarcely a single ill-advised recommendation of the President's Commission on Law Enforcement and Administration of Justice that the British Home Office and its various advisory councils do not seem determined to repeat.

Crime and its "causes"

It is widely believed that in the United States the crime rate is vastly—incomparably—larger than it is in England. Indeed, even if the comparison is restricted to the largest cities, the differences are supposedly enormous—London is claimed to have only a small fraction of the crime reported in New York. In fact, comparing all "serious" offenses ("indictable offenses" in England and "Index Crimes" in the United States), the United States has more, but not vastly more, than England. In 1973, there were 4,116 "Index" crimes per hundred thousand population reported to the police in the United States, and 2,760 "indictable offenses" per hundred thousand reported in England and Wales. The London Metropolitan Police reported 355,248 indictable offenses in 1973; the New York City Police Department reported 475,855 Index crimes the same year. The populations of the two cities are approximately the same.

"Index offenses" and "indictable offenses" are not exactly the same thing, and in consequence some may feel that any gross comparison of English and American crime figures is misleading. To a degree, that is true. But consider one or two specific crimes that are more or less commonly defined and commonly counted. There were 1,211 burglaries for every hundred thousand persons in the United States in 1973; there were 800 burglaries for every hundred thousand persons in England and Wales that year. A difference, to be sure, but not one so vast as is often supposed. And if one were to adjust the English and American figures for the differences in the availability of things worth stealing—color television sets, 10-speed bicycles, fancy camera gear—the burglary rate in England might well appear even higher than is reported.

Another objection to the English/American comparison is that we are dealing only with *reported* offenses. We know, of course, that many offenses go unreported. It is possible that citizens report to the police a higher proportion of all burglaries in England than in the United States. Until the results of a British survey of criminal victimization are published, we will not know. But in the meantime, we can examine the rates for one crime—auto theft—which we know from surveys to be quite accurately reported in this country, and which we need not believe is any less completely reported in England. By my calculations, in England and Wales there were 2,056 motor vehicles stolen out of every one hundred thousand owned by households in 1973, a theft rate *twice as great* as in the United States, where there were just over a thousand stolen automobiles for every hundred thousand registered.

Nor are English thefts petty. F. H. McClintock and N. Howard Avison estimate that the average value of the property stolen per burglary or larceny in 1965 was in excess of $100 (now it is no doubt more) and they note that the greatest increases in theft have occurred in the category of high-loss crimes.

There *are* major differences in English and American crime rates, but primarily with respect to violent crimes. In 1973, 1680 murders were reported to the New York police but only 110 were reported to the London Metropolitan police. The total of 72,750 robberies reported in New York was nearly 27 times greater than the 2,680 robberies reported in London. Londoners may be only a little less dishonest than New Yorkers but they are vastly less violent.

England, including London, has experienced a great increase in the rate of reported serious (i.e., "indictable") offenses, but the increase in certain violent offenses, notably robbery, has been even greater. In 1955, there were only 823 robberies in all of England and Wales; in 1974, there were 8,666. This was a tenfold increase in number and, since the population did not grow much during this period, nearly a tenfold increase in rate. The rise has been even greater in London: There were 237 robberies reported there in 1955 but 3,151 in 1974, a thirteenfold increase. As a result, a larger percentage of all thefts are now accompanied by violence than was the case 10 or 20 years ago. In 1955, Colin Greenwood reports, less than three tenths of one per cent of all London thefts were robberies; by 1969, it was nearly one per cent, and it continues to grow. (In comparison, about 17 per cent of all New York thefts are robberies.)

The very great restrictions placed by English law on the private possession of firearms has apparently not impeded the increase in robbery. Blunt and sharp instruments—pick handles and knives, primarily—continue to be the favored weapon in armed robberies, accounting for over half. The number of robberies in which firearms—notably, shotguns—were used or carried has also increased greatly. Colin Greenwood concludes that there has been a steady increase in the use of violence in the commission of theft, that the number of robberies in which weapons were used has increased at least as fast as the number of robberies, and that there has been a sharp rise in the proportion of armed robberies in which the available weapon was a firearm. Despite legal restrictions, the steady shift from unarmed to armed robbery has proceeded apace—where there is a will, there is a way.

Race and violence

Though the trends are ominous, London has a long way to go before violence there approximates violence in New York (or most other large American cities). What accounts for this great difference could occupy a speculative mind for years. I am aware of no scientific or systematic evidence that would shed light on it. One possibility will occur immediately to an American reader—the differences in the composition of the population, or to be blunt, race.

Certainly if you were to ask a taxi driver, hotel clerk, or news vendor in London, he would explain the increase in violent crime, especially robbery, by the presence of West Indians. The American term for robbery of the person on a street following a sudden attack —"mugging"—has caught the fancy of the English, and one finds frequent reference to it in the press, even though it lacks any precise legal definition. There is no doubt that muggings have increased in London—from 674 in 1968 to 1,544 in 1972, according to the police. The total is still, by American standards, ridiculously small—the prospect of four or five muggings a day in a city of eight million persons is not likely to inspire fear in the hearts of a Manhattanite. It is widely believed that these muggings are the work of black youths, but it is impossible to verify this. Though the Metropolitan Police (i.e., Scotland Yard) records the race of those whom it arrests, it will not divulge the data, nor will the Home Office, to which the police commissioner reports. A confidential study on race and crime was in fact made by the Statistical Unit of Scotland Yard, but the results are closely guarded.

Map displays of robberies and other violent crimes, however, show that these crimes are common in the heavily West Indian sections of London, such as Lambeth and Brixton, and on or near London Underground (i.e., subway) lines that serve those and similar areas. The authorities refuse to publish data on these matters, fearing that such facts would be exploited by anti-immigrant politicians and would unduly inflame popular prejudices. (Presumably the government would release the data if they would tend to soothe popular fears.)

Whatever may be the relationship between race and violent crime, immigrants cannot, by any stretch of the imagination, account for more than a small fraction of the total increase in crime in England. The rate at which indictable offenses are committed began rising in about 1930, quadrupling in the two decades before 1950. There was a pause just after World War II, with a few years of declining crime rates, and then an even more rapid surge began in 1955 that has continued, with a brief respite in 1972-1973, to the present. Crime has increased during the last two decades at a rate of about 10 per cent per year (about the same as the rate of increase in the United States). Though immigration to England was also increasing during this period (the number of persons living in Great Britain who were born overseas doubled between 1951 and 1971), the fraction of the total population born abroad has been quite small—3.2 per cent in 1951, 5.5 per cent in 1971. (The British census does not report the number of persons born in Britain of foreign or mixed parentage.)

Furthermore, most immigrants either are not "colored" (they are from Canada, Australia, New Zealand, Ireland), or are Asians (Indians and Pakistanis), whom every observer believes have lower than average crime rates. The proportion of persons living in England born in the West Indies is very small indeed—less than two per cent for Britain as a whole, only slightly more than two per cent for London. Finally, McClintock and Avison, studying criminal repeaters, found that well over 80 per cent of the known recidivists were born in England or Wales.

Causes or conjectures?

What, then, can account for the great increase in English crime rates? There is no agreed-upon answer to that question, nor is there likely to be one. It is instructive for Americans to contemplate the problem, however, because the increase in English crime, in many ways so similar to the increase in the United States, cannot be explained by the various "causes" regularly advanced in this country. Race, as we have seen, may explain some of the increase in violent crime, but it cannot explain much of the increase in crime generally. Nor can the increased youthfulness of the population account for much of the change. The number of boys under the age of 17 increased between 1961 and 1971 by eight per cent in Britain and nine per cent in the United States—a contribution to the rising crime rate, no doubt, but scarcely the decisive one. In England as in the United States, it is not simply or even primarily the growth in the *numbers* of young persons but rather the increased rate of crime *among* young persons that has caused crime rates to rise. Put in technical terms, the age-specific crime rate has increased, most notably among the younger age groups. For example, in 1951 only 1,164 out of every 100,000 males between the ages of 17 and 21 were convicted of an indictable offense in England and Wales. By 1973, that had quintupled: Now 5,522 out of every 100,000 males in that age group were found guilty. (The conviction rate for persons over thirty increased only slightly.)

Trying to explain the increased criminality of the young in England is as frustrating as trying to explain it in the United States. Narcotics addiction, which may explain some part of American crime rates, cannot explain more than a tiny fraction in England, where there are very few addicts (though the few that exist are quite likely to have criminal records, despite the availability of heroin from government clinics). Nor can the rising crime rate in England be accounted for by rising unemployment, increased income inequality, or deepening poverty. In 1961, the unemployment rate in Great Britain was 1.4 per cent; in 1973, it was 2.7 per cent. During the years in which crime was rising the fastest, unemployment was virtually nonexistent; the two recent years (1971 and 1972) in which unemployment exceeded three per cent were followed by two years in which, for the only time in the last two decades, the crime rate actually went down.

So also with income inequality. The government reports there has been a steady decline since at least 1961, and probably earlier, in the proportion of the national wealth owned by the richest tenth of the population and a corresponding increase in the proportion owned by the least wealthy tenth. Being aware of these facts, no one in England tries to explain crime rate changes by the pauperization of the workers, though most recognize that crime is more common among *certain kinds* of lower-income families.

What kinds? The association between crime and aspects of family life, repeatedly established in America, has also been shown to operate in England, beginning in 1925 with the pioneering study by Sir Cyril Burt of young delinquents in London, and continuing with Professor Sprott's 1954 study of delinquent and nondelinquent areas in a working-class mining town. The familial contribution to English crime does not, however, depend on whether the family is "broken"—i.e., whether one parent is absent owing to divorce or desertion—or on whether the mother is working. Absent or working parents are no more likely to have delinquent children than intact, at-home families; it is the *behavior* of the parents that is crucial. Discord, the absence of affection and consistent discipline, and improper moral instruction are the causal factors; on this, the studies of Lee Robins, Barbara Wootton, Simon Yudkin, Harriet Wilson, and John Mays all seem to agree.

That it is the behavior rather than the number of parents that accounts for delinquency helps explain why youthful crime can increase in England though there has been no increase in the proportion of single-parent families (they accounted for less than seven per cent of all households in both 1961 and 1971). What we would like to measure, but obviously cannot, is the change that has occurred in the quality of family life in the last two decades. Though it may pain the sophisticated to encounter such apparently Victorian sentiments, it seems inescapable that we have witnessed a change in the moral quality of family life that has had, along with other factors, a profound effect on the general level of public safety and security.

What these other factors may be is largely a matter of conjecture. What is striking—and, given the tendencies of American thought, salutary—is the absence in England of the kinds of conjectures heard in the United States. Neither the authorities nor the scholars in Britain "explain" rising crime by reference to poverty, drug abuse, relative deprivation, social or political frustration, rising unemployment, or the absence of legitimate opportunities. Such factors simply cannot account for the crime increase in England; one suspects they cannot account for it in the United States, either, but that our parochial perspective has prevented us from seeing that.

Crime is rising in virtually every society for which reliable data are available. Though it is possible different causes are at work in different countries, it is also possible—and, given the similarity in the trends, more than likely—that some general factors are operating on a world-wide scale. Three immediately come to mind: the growth of urbanization and affluence; the spread, especially among the young, of the cult of personal liberation and unfettered self-expression; and the change in attitudes of the young toward authority, schooling, and the family. There is no way of testing the effect of the subjective forces, but there is some evidence of the importance of the objective ones. For example, in England as in America, the rise in thefts from automobiles is, as Leslie Wilkins has shown, closely related to the rise in the number of registered motor vehicles. The more opportunities for theft, the more thefts will be committed, other things being equal.

The police and crime

One of the things that may not be equal is the risk associated with crime, and one of the factors that may influence that is the number and efficiency of the police. In theory, the English police are locally controlled organizations that might, were the theory fact, have as great difficulty in adjusting their jurisdiction, resources, and training to changing criminal conditions as have their American counterparts. In reality, there is a sizeable degree of national control, financing, and standardization of the police service. Half the cost of each local force is paid for out of national funds disbursed by the Home Office. Regulations governing almost every feature of police service are promulgated by the Home Secretary, and Her Majesty's Inspector of the Constabulary carries out detailed reviews to insure that these regulations are obeyed by every local force. There is a single Police College, at Bramshill, through which virtually all of the up-and-coming senior officers have passed, or will pass, on their way to command positions in the various local forces. Each prospective constable is expected to have served in at least one other jurisdiction before he is appointed to head a local force. One dramatic measure of the degree of national control is the fact that within the last decade, the number of local police forces has been reduced from 125 to 43. A comparable reduction—by two thirds!—in the number of American police departments is simply unthinkable.

These consolidations, regulations, and training schemes are aimed at improving police efficiency. They are not, however, accompanied by equally significant increases in money or manpower. Metropolitan London, with a population of about eight million, has only 21,000 police officers (New York City has a third again as many); London has about the same number of police today as it did 40 years ago, when crime was only a fourth as common.

The failure of the police establishment to increase in size during a period of increasing crime and greater public disorder has been accompanied by a sharp drop in the proportion of reported offenses cleared by an arrest or confession. Between 1938 and 1954, a period when crime rates were more or less stable, the "detection rate" (i.e., the proportion of all reported crimes that the police believe they have "cleared up") was between 40 and 50 per cent. As the crime rate began going up in 1955, the detection rate began going down. From 1955 to 1965, according to McClintock and Avison, it dropped by 10 per cent. This rate has continued to drop down to the present, and is lowest in the biggest cities.

There are grave difficulties in relying too heavily on "detection rates" as a measure of police efficiency, or indeed as a measure of anything. The number does not discriminate between serious and trivial offenses, between crimes solved by arresting a hitherto unknown suspect and crimes admitted to by a person already in custody, and between crimes (such as burglary) that typically require police action for their solution and crimes (such as drug abuse) that are known of only because an arrest has already been made. Nevertheless, there seems little doubt that the chances that any given offender will be caught for a crime today are substantially less than his chances of being caught 10 or 20 years ago, and that his chances of being caught are lowest in the largest cities with the highest crime rates. Roughly, a robber had one chance in two of being caught in 1955, but only one chance in three in 1975. This, however, is a higher risk of apprehension than what he would face in a large American city—there, he would have only one chance in four of being caught.

One reason for the greater risk facing the English robber may be found in the nature of his offense. Robbery is still a relatively infrequent crime and, so far as one can tell, disproportionately practiced by professional or semi-professional criminals. One might think that the professional could, by his skill, more easily evade detection than the amateur, but in fact whatever advantage he acquires by virtue of craftiness is offset by his tendency to repeat the crime (thereby increasing his risk of apprehension in any given year) and to work with confederates (thus putting him at the mercy of potential informants).

A dramatic example occurred recently of the way in which the police can capitalize on these aspects of professional crime. In 1972, there were 72 bank robberies in London (there were 183 in New York that year). By 1974, Scotland Yard had cut that number to

17—a drop of better than 75 per cent. As it turned out, most of the bank robberies were committed by one of two major gangs, one member of which turned Queen's evidence in return for a promise of leniency in his own case. He implicated his associates, who were arrested and given long prison terms. In the United States, by contrast, a large number of banks are robbed by lone wolves, acting almost on impulse, who may evade capture for long periods of time. Ordinary street muggings, by contrast, are, in London as well as in New York, the impulsive acts of young offenders and are thus difficult to check by police strategies alone.

Police powers

The ability of the English police to reduce crime may also be assisted by the kinds of legal powers they possess, powers in some important respects more ample than those of the American police. For example, a constable may stop and search any person he reasonably suspects of carrying arms, dangerous drugs, or stolen goods. An American officer in most jurisdictions would be limited to frisking suspicious persons for weapons (i.e., "patting them down"); to search beyond this, and to seize drugs or stolen goods, could only be done legally if the search were pursuant to a warrant or incident to a lawful arrest (which in turn requires that the crime be committed in the officer's presence or that the officer have probable cause—and not mere suspicion—that a felony had been committed by the person about to be arrested).

Furthermore, an English officer may enter a building without a warrant and search the premises in which he reasonably suspects that a person who has committed a crime is hiding. An American officer would be well-advised to obtain a warrant before entering a building, even if he has probable cause to believe that there is a suspect inside.

Finally, in England an arrested person has the right to speak to an attorney (a "solicitor"), "provided that no hindrance is reasonably likely to be caused to the processes of investigation, or the administration of justice by his doing so." In other words, the police may exclude a solicitor from the questioning of an arrested person. In America, such an exclusion is permissible only if agreed to by the accused.

Perhaps of greatest importance to the operation of the English police system is that evidence gathered in violation of the rules will not automatically be excluded from the trial—in theory, no one goes free merely because the constable has blundered. The constable, on the other hand, is liable for serious civil, administrative, and criminal penalties if he acts improperly. Nor is this only a theoretical possibility. In 1974, 84 London officers were prosecuted and 51 were found guilty of various offenses; in another 116 cases, disciplinary action was taken. Over 90 officers resigned from the force before the completion of a criminal or disciplinary inquiry.

The American courts have used a different system to control the police: Exclude from a trial improperly gathered evidence in order, so the theory goes, to reduce the incentive for using improper means. No one can measure the extent to which the exclusionary rule as enforced in the United States results in lower rates of arrest and conviction, and thus higher rates of crime. In routine cases—the burglar caught in the act, the robber identified by an eye witness, the assaulter accused by his victim—the rule probably makes little difference. In more complex cases, where searches and interrogations are required, it may make some difference. In cases involving no complaining witness, such as drug violations, the rule may be of decisive importance.

Crime has not been the only problem to face the British police. Since 1972, there have been over 1,300 public demonstrations in greater London, 54 of which involved disorder resulting in the arrest of over 600 persons. Nearly 300 police officers were injured, as were a large but unknown number of participants and spectators. One demonstration, at Red Lion Square in June 1974, was especially difficult and ugly. A right-wing group, the National Front, sent about 900 persons on a march; about a thousand left-wing opponents staged a countermarch; nearly a thousand police officers were on hand; and 51 persons were arrested, 54 were injured, and there was one fatality.

Here, as with ordinary crime, the British police enjoy somewhat greater powers than their American counterparts. A demonstrator in London may be arrested for using threatening, abusive, or insulting words, or for carrying a sign displaying such words, or for using indecent language. American officers could not ordinarily make lawful arrests on such charges. They may, of course, arrest people for such behavior, but the charge must be for a real or claimed breach of a valid statute, such as resisting arrest or disorderly conduct.

The London police are upset by the violence which increasingly confronts them and with the behavior of the courts in punishing it. About 3,000 London bobbies were assaulted in 1974, an increase of 12 per cent over 1973. Sir Robert Mark, Commissioner of the Metropolitan Police, is openly critical of the penalties given—or not given—to unlawful and violent demonstrators. Of the 758 charges brought against demonstrators during the past three years, 575 resulted in convictions, but only 18 resulted in prison sentences—and of these, 12 were for only one month. Only 10 of the 105 convictions for assaulting a police officer produced imprisonment. "The ability to mainatin a satisfactory standard of public order in its widest sense is impaired . . . by pusillanimous laws and pusillanimous courts," Mark declared in August 1975.

Despite the rise in violent crime, the advent of terrorism in London, the continued wave of disorderly demonstrations, the frequent injury to police officers, and the increased use of firearms by criminals, there appears to be no sentiment for arming the police. "Nothing could be sillier or more irresponsible," Mark recently said to the officers at the Bramshill Police College, "than to suggest in public that in the foreseeable future the police are likely to be armed as a routine measure. There has never been less likelihood or justification for such a proposal. . . . This is a proposal with which the overwhelming majority of policemen would probably refuse to comply."

Reforms and revisions

Just as the London police are increasingly finding themselves, contrary to custom and legend, in an adversary role with the citizenry, so also are they discovering that, contrary to custom and legend, not all their ranks are models of integrity and rectitude. In February 1972, just two months before Mark became the new commissioner, two Scotland Yard detectives were sentenced at the Old Bailey criminal courts to long prison terms for corruption. On taking office, Mark was appalled by what he saw and even more by what he suspected. "I don't know what they [the detectives] do to the enemy," he said, "but by God they frighten me." Mark, like most reform-minded police commissioners elsewhere, soon discovered that the detective service is a separate, virtually autonomous unit of the force with its own leaders and rules. Peter Brodie, for six years head of the Criminal Investigation Department (CID), was widely thought to have the inside track for the post of commissioner. When Mark, a man who had never served in the ranks of the Metropolitan Police (he had been chief constable in Leicester), was appointed instead, Brodie resigned. Mark promptly drew the battle lines with the CID, threatening to put its entire membership back in uniform, giving command over detectives to uniform officers at local police stations, creating a new unit (A10) to investigate complaints against officers, and requiring that meetings between detectives and informers be reported to superior officers.

The head of the Flying Squad was suspended from duty on charges of having gone on a Cyprus holiday with James Humphreys, the alleged "Emperor of Pornography" in London; the officer then resigned from the force. Humphreys himself boasted that he had 40 Scotland Yard men in his pocket. Of the 40, 22 have resigned, 12 are under investigation, and 6 were cleared. In all, Mark and the A10 unit investigated over a thousand cases against officers, with more to come. As of June 1975, 22 officers had been convicted on bribery or corruption charges, 20 awaited trial, and 12 had been acquitted, though nine of the 12 plus another 45 officers not formally charged had been suspended from duty or otherwise disciplined. Over 300 officers had resigned in the face of investigations.

None of this should have been surprising. It would be astonishing were it otherwise. Detectives in every force depend on informers to solve crimes. To acquire informers requires cultivating criminals. To make an arrest often requires inducing an informer to cooperate, and it is inevitable that in some cases improper means—planting evidence, using force—will be used to secure that cooperation. The London police, like their colleagues in New York, must enforce laws dealing with a number of so-called "victimless crimes." The supposedly enlightened British policy of tolerating prostitution but banning solicitation, of allowing gambling but only on licensed premises, and of permitting government clinics to prescribe heroin for addicts has not by any means eliminated the opportunities for police corruption or abuse of power in dealing with prostitutes, gamblers, pornographers, or drug users. Indeed, to a casual visitor, the abundance of obscene publications suggests that their illegality is not a matter of utmost concern to the police, just as the bewildering and often meaningless laws governing the licensing of and membership in gambling and night clubs seem almost an invitation for abuse and manipulation.

Commissioner Mark is fully aware of these problems and determined to deal with them squarely. He is just as determined, however, to confront what he takes to be the deficiencies in the rest of the criminal justice system. He is unsparing in his criticism of lawyers and judges—the former for obstructing the search for the truth, the latter for allowing the guilty to be lightly punished. For years, in a way unthinkable for most politically cautious (because politically vulnerable) American police chiefs (Edward Davis of Los Angeles is a conspicuous exception), Mark has pressed for revisions in the laws of criminal procedure. He was among those who, in 1967, objected to the ability of a lone juror to prevent the conviction of a guilty man. The response was a law (presented by a Labour Party minister!) that allowed for convictions by a less-than-unanimous jury, in general by 10 out of the 12 jurors (the actual formula is much more complex). By the same law, the Criminal Justice Act of 1967, the defense was required to disclose before the trial any alibi the accused planned to offer so that the police might investigate it (the entirety of the prosecution's case must be disclosed in advance).

Now Commissioner Mark and others are pressing for additional changes. He would like to waive the need for a police caution—that timeless and familiar phrase by which the arrested party is warned that what he says can be used in evidence against him; in the United States, it is known as the "Miranda warning." As Mark puts it, "The credibility of the accused should be related to his spontaneity rather than to that period of reflection and professional consultation between his original interrogation and trial, a period which has produced . . . some of the most ingenious and highly paid fiction of our time." He would also like to weaken the right not to testify in one's own trial, not perhaps by compelling testimony, but at least by allowing the prosecution to put the accused in the witness box, ask him questions, and call to the jury's attention any refusal to answer.

Mark is convinced that the system of justice is unduly biased in favor of the guilty. He would like to see a higher proportion of those who face trial be convicted, arguing that 40 per cent of those who plead innocent are acquitted, a proportion he believes unrealistically high. In all of this, he has encountered fierce opposition. His critics, among them Lord Wigoder, an officer of the Criminal Bar Association, and Michael Zander, an author and member of the London School of Economics, argue that juries are not often wrong—much less, as Mark put it, "occasionally stupid, prejudicial, and barely literate."

The vigorous argument between Mark and Zander over the acquittal rate of juries has stimulated some interesting research on jury behavior. In my view the data thus far do not show the English juries are unreasonably inclined to acquit serious offenders.

Of greater interest to an American, however, is the remarkable importance the jury retains in the British criminal justice system. In 1973, according to Zander, 40 per cent of the persons charged in the English Crown Courts pleaded not guilty, and thus were tried before a jury. In the same year, fewer than nine per cent of the persons proceeded against on felony charges in the California Superior Courts saw a jury—the rest were handled by the judge acting alone, usually on the basis of a guilty plea. Plea bargaining in America has drastically reduced the frequency of trials, whether with or without a jury.

Sentencing and corrections

The English response to rising crime rates during the 1960's appears, in the aggregate, to have been quite different from that in the United States. In America, the combined state and federal prison population declined from about 213,000 persons in 1960 to about 196,000 in 1970—a drop of approximately nine per cent. In England and Wales, however, the average daily population of prisons increased from 20,857 in 1961 to 25,634 in 1970—a rise of about 23 per cent.

These changes in the size of the prison population might lead one to suppose that British judges, unlike their American counterparts, responded to rising crime rates by getting tougher. That would be quite misleading. The English prison population may have gone up because judges became more severe, because there were more criminals being brought before judges who had a constant or even declining propensity to imprison, or because the kinds of crime being committed were becoming more serious.

Two things can be said: First, the chances of going to prison for having committed a serious crime are much greater in England than in America (which may help explain why English crime rates are lower than American ones). Second, the chances of going to prison for having committed a serious offense are declining in England (which may help explain why English crime rates are rising).

Take robbery, a major crime with a more or less common definition in the two countries. Because there are no national data in the United States on court dispositions, I will compare English experience with that of California, a state with relatively good statistics. In England in 1971, 26 per cent of the reported robberies resulted in some form of confinement—prison, detention center, or Bortsal (reformatory). In California in 1970, only four per cent of the robberies resulted in persons being put in custody in a jail, prison, or juvenile camp. Stated another way, England, which had only one sixth the number of reported robberies, actually sent more persons to prison or its equivalent than did the state of California.

This does not mean that English judges are six times as severe as California judges. There are, roughly speaking, two kinds of courts: the major trial courts (in California, the Superior Courts; in England, the Crown Courts) and the lesser courts that dispose of cases summarily or handle juveniles (in California, municipal and juvenile courts; in England, magistrates' and juvenile courts). If one looks only at the Superior or Crown Courts, it is not clear that English and American judges are very different. For example, among robbers appearing before Superior or Crown Court Judges, about the same proportion (well over 80 per cent) were convicted, and of these about the same proportion (perhaps three fourths) received some form of custodial sentence. (Unfortunately, we cannot compare the length of the sentences, since that is not reported in California, though it is in England.)

Far more important than the behavior of trial court judges in explaining the differing degrees of risk for robbers in the two countries is what happens to those robbers who never appear in the major trial courts at all, because they are not caught by the police, or are released by the prosecutor without charges, or are handled by the lesser courts, or are treated as juveniles. Compared to California, in England a robbery is more likely to be solved by an arrest, a person arrested is more likely to be prosecuted, and a person prosecuted in a local court or as a juvenile is more likely to be confined. Any exact comparison of British and American dispositions is imposible, however—the American data are nonexistent. But it would appear that a major reason why the risk of crime is higher in England is that young offenders, who of course account for a large fraction of all crime, are treated more severely there than in the United States.

Though the risks facing a criminal in England are high, they have been getting smaller. In 1966, 2,146 persons were brought into court charged with robbery. The great majority—85 per cent—were handled in Crown Courts (then called Courts of Assizes and Quarter Sessions). Of these, over 90 per cent were convicted; of those convicted, 60 per cent were sent to prison and another 25 per cent were placed in Borstals, or detention centers. Only 11 per cent were given some noncustodial sentence. For those going to prison, the typical sentence was two to three years. Nearly a third were sen-

tenced for over three years. So far, the image of English justice
seems confirmed: certain penalties, firmly applied.

The handful of robbers, all juveniles, dealt with in Magistrates'
Courts were treated quite differently. Though nearly 90 per cent
were found guilty, only 38 per cent of these were given some custodial sentence (a detention center or school for a few months) and
none was sent to prison.

By 1974, the pattern had changed substantially. In that year
3,651 persons were brought into court charged with robbery. But
owing in part to the fact that young persons now made up a much
larger proportion of those committing robberies, a greater fraction
—nearly a third—of these cases were handled in juvenile court. Of
those tried in Crown Court (all adults), about the same proportion
as in 1966 were convicted, but a somewhat lower percentage of
these were sent to prison—51 per cent in 1974 compared to 60 per
cent in 1966. The prison terms remained about the same. But in
Magistrates' Court, the proportion found guilty was lower (79 per
cent in 1974 compared to 89 per cent in 1966), and of those convicted, a smaller proportion were given custodial sentences (20 per
cent in 1974 compared to 38 per cent in 1966). And whereas this
more lenient treatment affected only about 300 accused robbers in
1966, it affected over a thousand in 1974.

In short, the probability that an accused robber would be given
a custodial sentence in England and Wales fell from 62 chances out
of 100 in 1966 to 47 chances out of 100 in 1974. The proportion of
reported robberies, rather than of prosecuted robbers, that result in
a custodial sentence is, of course, even smaller and has also been
declining—from 30 chances in 100 in 1966, to 20 in 100 in 1974.

It is unlikely that these changes in sentencing patterns are the
result of any centrally made decision. The English judiciary, like the
American, is constitutionally independent of executive authority
and, again like the American, is not organized or disposed to implement uniform sentencing policies. Since the early 1960's, there
have been annual conferences of judges at which sentencing was
discussed and, since 1966, a newly appointed magistrate must take
a training course that includes sentencing exercises. The Home Office also has published a handbook on sentencing. For all that, however, there remain substantial disparities in sentencing, and for essentially the same reason they exist in the United States—courses,
conferences, and handbooks are all very well, but when public officials are given substantial discretionary power, they will not surrender it, they will use it. Sentencing conferences have not been

effective in this country and there is little reason to suppose they are more effective abroad.

This would certainly explain why there appears to be as much disparity among the sentences of various judges in England as there is in other countries. One study, for example showed that the proportion of young persons given probation was 12 per cent in one town and 79 per cent in a neighboring one. Another study found equally wide disparities among Magistrates' Courts dealing with juveniles in London; still another found wide differences in the proportion of adults sent to prison in the Magistrates' Courts throughout England and Wales.

Rehabilitation, deterrence, and justice

Nonetheless, the broad changes in English sentencing patterns, however unevenly they are proceeding, seem consistent with, if not dictated by, the policies of English governments extending back well into the last century. The rehabilitative ideal has been the object of the same veneration in England as in America. Originally that ideal was to be sought within the penitentiary. The Gladstone Report of 1895 urged that prisons be designed to develop the "moral instincts" of their inmates and thus to "turn them out better men and women, physically and mentally, than when they came in." But soon rehabilitation was thought to require non-prison alternatives. Borstals for "youth training" were created. But most important, the "major objective of English penal policy" in the years after the Gladstone Report came to be, as Richard F. Sparks has written, "to keep as many offenders as possible out of prison."

A major step in the direction of increased reliance on noncustodial policies was the Criminal Justice Act of 1967, authorizing a court to suspend a sentence of imprisonment that does not exceed two years and, even more importantly, *requiring* that sentences not in excess of six months be suspended unless the offense was a violent one or certain other conditions were met. A Parole Board was also created, authorized to release from prison persons who had served one third of their sentences (or 12 months, whichever was greater). In 1972, another Criminal Justice Act was passed that modified the 1967 law—suspended sentences were no longer mandatory, but still strongly urged. It also instructed judges not to sentence anyone to prison who has not already been in prison unless they were satisfied that no other method of dealing with him was "appropriate."

Noncustodial treatment programs became very popular among British penal reformers of all political persuasions. Sir Arthur Peterson, then the permanent secretary (i.e., senior civil servant) at the Home Office, was reported as expressing doubts in 1973 about the value of prison even for protecting society from offenders and as hoping that falling crime rates (they did decline, briefly, in 1973 before shooting up again) would reduce opposition to the further development of noncustodial programs. The California Treatment Program (CTP), which had been praised (prematurely, as it turns out) by President Johnson's Crime Commission, was also widely hailed in England. In 1970, William F. Deedes, then a Conservative member of parliament and now the editor of the *Daily Telegraph,* endorsed the CTP approach—intensive probation and treatment programs for offenders returned to the community rather than sent to prison—unaware that as he spoke a reanalysis of the CTP data in the United States showed that claims for its crime-reduction potential had been exaggerated.

A policy of decarceration was supported by Robert Carr, Conservative Home Secretary, and continued by Roy Jenkins, his Labour successor. In late 1975, the Home Office Planning Unit described to an interviewer its major task as being to find a way of reducing the size of the prison population, partly to save money and end overcrowding but also, it frankly admitted, because of the ideological view that prison is an inappropriate way of dealing with offenders.

Despite the hope that prison populations could be reduced, they have in fact grown. This is not the result of the sentencing practices of judges but of the rise in the number of crimes being committed: On this, the careful studies of Richard F. Sparks are quite conclusive. Indeed, if the harsher prewar sentencing practices were still in effect, the prison population today would be vastly larger than it is. In 1968, for example, about three fifths of all those in prison were discharged after only four months. Furthermore, as in the United States, those sent to prison tend to have many previous convictions, though often not many previous prison sentences. Of the more than 2000 adult men sent to prison in 1967 for having committed a violent crime (other than murder), over 87 per cent had one prior conviction and over 55 per cent had five or more prior convictions. Despite these long records, over a third had never been in prison before and over half had only been in once.

England would seem ripe for the kind of debate that has recently developed in the United States over the crime-reduction potential of prisons, either by virtue of their deterrent effect on would-be offenders or their incapacitative effect on actual ones. As yet, little informed debate on this issue has emerged, in part because official circles in England are less willing than those in the United States to concede the inefficacy of rehabilitation. In America, persons of both parties and at all levels of government—President Gerald Ford, Senator Edward M. Kennedy, Governor Edmund Brown of California, Attorney General Edward H. Levi—are aware of and have taken fully into account the findings of Robert Martinson and others that rehabilitation programs, noncustodial as well as custodial, have been ineffective. No such recognition has yet been expressed by comparable British officials, even though British scholars—notably Roger Hood, Leslie Wilkins, and Sir Rupert Cross—have come to almost precisely the same conclusions as their American counterparts.

Where British scholarship has lagged has not been in studies of recidivism but in those on deterrence. Statistical analyses in the United States have consistently, though not conclusively, supported the view that the higher the probability of arrest and imprisonment in a given jurisdiction, the lower the crime rate, other things (such as the characteristics of the population) being equal. I am aware of only one British study of this sort—a 1973 paper by R. A. Carr-Hill and N. H. Stern. Applying the customary econometric techniques to data for the police districts of England and Wales, they found that, other things being equal, the greater the probability of arrest, the lower the rate of indictable offenses. There was also a significant, though weaker, relationship between imprisonment and crime—the higher the proportion of convicted persons receiving custodial sentences, the lower the offense rate. These results are similar to those obtained with American data, yet there has been little effort in England either to test further the approach or to weigh seriously its policy implications. The Home Office, which boasts, in addition to a Planning Unit, a Research Unit and a Statistical Unit, does not seem inclined to pursue this line of inquiry.

Instead of attempting, soberly and carefully, to analyze the criminal justice system to discover and measure such effects as it might have on crime rates under alternative sentencing policies, English opinion seems instead on the verge of a major ideological brawl between "liberal" and "conservative" opinion. The chairman of the Howard League, Louis Blom-Cooper, and others are pressing vigorously for abolition of prison for all but the most dangerous criminal offenders and for greater reliance on "a continuing programme of adjustment" for most offenders based on "the control and supervision of offenders within the community" on terms to be set not by judges, but by administrative authorities who would decide which, if any, of their charges "needed" confinement. The treatment perspective, the indeterminate sentence, and the use of (never clearly specified) "community" resources is a view very much alive and well in England; the report of the Advisory Council on the Penal System regarding young offenders goes far in this direction, though not quite as far as Mr. Blom-Cooper, a member of the Council who dissented from the report, would like.

At the opposite end of the spectrum is Sgt. Leslie Male, chairman of the Police Federation, who is calling, on behalf of his organization, for more police, more prisons, and more jail sentences —instead of fines—to counter the "frightening" increase in crime.

At issue is not simply the question of public safety versus prison amenities or deterrence versus rehabilitation, but issues of justice. Roger Hood, at Oxford, for example, favors offenders spending less time in prison, but he argues that the terms of their time inside and their supervision outside should be set by judges on the basis of determinate sentences and legal criteria, not by administrators on the basis of indeterminate sentences and therapeutic objectives. It is a view that has come to be widely held in the United States but official circles in England tend to dismiss it by referring to Hood, wearily, as "that due process fellow."

Crime and British politics

Thus far the primacy of economic issues and (by American standards) the infrequency of serious violent crime has permitted the debate over the criminal justice system in England to proceed sedately, in measured tones, among a small group of attentive observers. The complaints of Sir Robert Mark and the far tougher statements of the Police Federation may be harbingers of what is to come if crime continues to rise at its present rate, and if each governmental commission examining the matter continues to respond by devising new ways of putting offenders back on the street as quickly as possible.

British politics handles crime differently from American politics, and not simply because the British have less violent crime. Party control of nominations for seats in the House of Commons and the absence of much in the way of an independent local government reduce significantly the opportunity or incentive for a person to launch or expand a political career by developing a following around a certain issue. There are a number of American politicians who have used "crime in the streets" as an issue, often with success; such behavior is far less likely in England. Political advancement comes more from party conformity than from popular appeals. On the other hand, American elected officials have had great difficulty in changing the American criminal justice system—the very decentralization, party weakness, and governmental fragmentation that make issue appeals so rewarding make legislative or administrative action on the basis of those appeals so difficult. The major federal piece of crime legislation—the Safe Streets Act of 1968—changed little in the criminal justice system except the amount of federal money spent on it. There have been a number of changes at the state level, but they have been piecemeal and often inconsistent.

British public officials, though not attracted by the political appeal of crime, can, as members of the majority party, participate in making substantial changes when they are so inclined. The entire criminal courts system was reorganized by the Courts Act of 1971, sentencing rules were altered substantially by the Criminal Justice Act of 1967 and again by the Criminal Justice Act of 1972, and capital punishment was abolished by the Murder Act of 1965. It would be unthinkable—and perhaps unconstitutional—for such sweeping national changes to be voted by the American Congress, yet the arenas in which changes might occur, the states, are poorly staffed or researched, and thus knowledge of current policy is lacking—to say nothing of good ideas about future practice.

However much greater the British political capacity to act may be, that capacity has not yet extended to devoting significantly greater resources to criminal justice—the police are understaffed, and the number and variety of correctional institutions and programs are inadequate. Even the British tradition of a speedy trial has suffered under the crush of business in the major Crown Courts. In 1973, a person being proceeded against in the Old Bailey (the Central Criminal Court in London) had to wait in excess of six months for a trial if he were out on bail and nearly four months if he were in custody. Most importantly, the inclination to test carefully the consequences for crime of alternative sentencing policies does not yet seem great.

English virtue, at least as measured by the violent crime rate, is not collapsing under the weight of political turmoil and economic crisis. Crime began going up in the 1950's, long before Britain's problems became as grave as they are today. But the present problems are straining its ability to respond to crime and perhaps impeding its ability to think about them.

Learning about crime— the Japanese experience

DAVID H. BAYLEY

LIKE the United States, Japan is modern, affluent, urbanized, and industrial. Politically and economically, Japan is part of the "developed" world. But there is one area where Japan is remarkably and perplexingly different— the incidence of criminality.

The number of crimes committed annually in Japan in recent years is actually lower than 25 years ago. In 1948, the peak postwar year for crime, there were 1,599,968 non-traffic offenses committed under the Japanese penal code; in 1974, there were 1,211,055. The crime rate—the incidence of crime per unit of population— is declining; in 1974, there were 112 crimes committed for every 10,000 persons. (This includes all penal code offenses, no matter how trivial, except for traffic violations.) Contrast this with the United States, where yearly increases in crime make dramatic headlines, and are considered as inevitable as death and taxes. In 1974, including only the seven categories of serious crime (murder, forcible rape, robbery, aggravated assault, burglary, larceny-theft, and auto theft) that the FBI uses to compute its crime index, there were 480 crimes for every 10,000 persons. In other words, there are over four times as many serious crimes per person in the United States as crimes of any sort per person in Japan.

An individual is 10 times more likely to be murdered in the United States than in Japan; 13 times more likely to be raped; and six times more likely to be the victim of theft. The most mind-boggling statistic concerns robbery, an offense that has a lot to do with the anxiety Americans feel about "crime in the streets." The likelihood of being robbed in the United States is *208 times* greater than in Japan. Last year there were 436,000 robberies in the United States, compared with 2,100 in Japan. The difference between these figures is not due to statistical quirks. Robbery—theft accompanied by violence or the threat of violence—is defined identically in the laws of both countries. However, because possession of handguns is prohibited in Japan without official permission—which is given only to the police, the armed forces, and the members of international shooting teams—it is much less easy to intimidate, threaten, or coerce. While it is true that people kill, not guns, as gun advocates in the United States assert, the absence of guns nonetheless makes certain kinds of crime more difficult to commit.

Comparison of crime rates in major urban areas in both countries shows the same remarkable differences. There are three times more serious crime per person in New York City than there are crimes of all sorts per person in Tokyo. (So that New York City does not seem a particularly bad American example, it should be noted that, according to FBI statistics, there are at least 45 cities in the United States with higher crime rates.) New York City has 10 times more murders per person than Tokyo, 11 times more rapes, and 235 times more robberies. Almost as many homicides are committed each year in New York City as in all Japan—1,600 versus 1,900—although New York City has only one tenth the population.

Narcotics offenses are a trivial problem in Japan, compared with the United States. Last year just under 10,000 persons were charged with drug-related offenses in Japan. Most of these were in connection with amphetamines (87 per cent). In the United States, over half a million people were arrested for narcotics violations. The proportion of arrests involving hard drugs was twice as high in the United States as in Japan (14 per cent versus six per cent). In Tokyo, only 35 persons were charged with offenses involving hard drugs in 1974. Another thousand were arrested for the use or sale of amphetamines, and 119 in connection with marijuana. This record would be considered astonishing in any large American city.

Japan's low level of drug offenses represents a double success—not just the achievement of a low incidence but the overcoming of what was once a large problem. During the mid-1950's and early 1960's, six times as many people were being charged with amphetamine offenses in Japan, and five times more with hard-drug offenses. The Japanese experience suggests that drug contagion may be beaten, a prospect almost unimaginable to most Americans.

Is the difference in criminality between Japan and the United States, shown by official figures, the result of misreporting? No. To be sure, more crimes are committed in both countries than are known to the police, but the rates of underreporting of crime, according to independent surveys in both countries, are the same or higher for the United States, depending on the type of crime. True crime in Japan is estimated to be about 80 per cent higher than what is reported, while true crime in the United States is 100 per cent higher. Official figures thus represent a real difference in criminality between the two countries.

The difference in public safety between Japan and the United States can be experienced and felt; it makes a difference in the way people live. Japanese streets and public places are habitable, even at night. Streets do not become deserted when the sun goes down, and very few areas of Japanese cities are considered "out of bounds," given over to juvenile gangs, prostitutes, and criminals. Americans who live in Japan gradually unlearn old anxieties: They are no longer apprehensive at the sound of a following footstep, the sight of lounging teenagers, or a personal request for directions. Japan is a poignant reminder of the innocence Americans have lost without wholly appreciating it.

American theories of crime

Why should there be this dramatic difference in criminality and public safety between these two wealthy, modern nations? Or what does the United States have that Japan doesn't? One place to look for explanations is among the theories that Americans produce to account for their own rising crime rate.

Crime is frequently attributed by Americans to social modernity. Rising crime rates are thought to be an inevitable consequence of modern industrial life. But there is not much to choose on this score between Japan and the United States. The economic structures of both countries are very similar: From a quarter to a third of the GNP of each country is produced by manufacturing, only three to six per cent by agriculture and fishing. Japanese agriculture is more labor-intensive than American, so more people work on farms than in the United States—17 per cent versus four per cent. This difference in occupational structure is too small to account for the disparity in national crime rates, and the difference between Japan and the United States is as great in urban crime rates as it is in rural crime rates. Japanese as well as Americans are among the most highly educated people in the world. Virtually all Japanese complete nine years of schooling, and the vast majority—over 80 per cent—finish high school. A larger proportion of Americans go to college, but since crime rates decline with education, this factor should have the effect of lowering the American crime rate relative to the Japanese. Both populations are thoroughly exposed to mass media. Official estimates are that 95 per cent of all households in both countries have television sets; radios are even more common. The daily circulation of newspapers per capita is greater in Japan than in the United States.

Japanese are not quite as rich, however, as Americans. Though Japan is within the top 20 nations in the world in per capita income, ranking with Great Britain and Finland, per capita income is about 60 per cent of American levels—roughly $3000 versus $5000. This difference, though substantial, cannot account for the higher criminality in the United States. Few people would contend that affluence alone makes people criminal.

Americans often blame crime on urbanization, and especially population congestion. Newspapers have recently fed this line of speculation by reporting experiments showing that overcrowding among rats produces social deviance. Japanese experience refutes this explanation, unless one assumes that Americans and Japanese react very differently to crowding. The Japanese population is 10 times more densely concentrated than the American—about 110 persons per square mile, as opposed to nine per square mile. Though the proportion of people living in urban areas is the same in both countries—70 per cent—urban densities are significantly higher in Japan. There are about 4,000 persons per square mile in the New York metropolitan area, compared with 14,000 per square mile in Tokyo. One fourth of the entire Japanese population—25 million people—live within 37 miles of downtown Tokyo. The United States would have a population density similar to Japan's if 50 per cent of all Americans lived in a space the size of the state of California.

Americans believe that the criminal justice system—police, prosecution, courts—bears a large responsibility for curbing the incidence of crime. When crime rates rise, the criminal justice system is thought to be failing. In recent years, inefficient policing and lenient sentencing have frequently been blamed. There would be less crime, it is argued, if there were more policemen, better trained and better equipped, so that more criminals were caught, and if sentences upon conviction were stricter, so that offenders spent more time behind bars. But if Japanese practices are a guide, Americans expectations are misplaced. There are fewer policemen relative to the population in Japan than in the United States—one officer for every 563 persons versus one officer for every 410 persons. In New York City, before the recent cutbacks, there was one officer for every 186 persons; in Tokyo there is one officer for every 287 persons. On the other hand, because the territory of Japan is much smaller than the United States, Japanese policemen are more concentrated geographically—one officer for every 0.76 square miles in Japan as opposed to one for every 7.1 square miles in the United States. In Tokyo there are 182 policemen per square mile, in New York City only 51. If, therefore, changes in police coverage can affect the crime rate, the crucial ratio would seem to be between policemen and area, not between policemen and population. This argument is rarely made, however; recommendations for increased personnel are usually justified in terms of population growth. Proportionately, the Japanese spend more of their national wealth on policing than Americans do—0.80 per cent of GNP in Japan, 0.56 per cent in the United States. Relative to Japan, then, the United States could afford to increase police personnel in order to lower the policeman/territory ratio. One might speculate that this might, following the Japanese model, reduce crime somewhat.

Contrary to what might be expected, court sentences are not more severe in Japan than in the United States. In recent years about 96.5 per cent of Japanese convicted of crimes were sentenced to payment of a fine, and only 3.5 per cent were sentenced to imprisonment. Moreover, a majority of those sentenced to prison were given a suspended sentence. Though experts agree that these sentences are much more lenient than in the United States, the point is not easy to substantiate statistically. Because of the multiplicity of criminal-justice jurisdictions in the United States, data are not available on average sentences for similar offenses across the country. They are available for Japan, because there is a uniform penal code and a unified court system. One expedient is to compare sentencing in United States federal district courts, for which there is summary information, with all courts of first instance in Japan, on the assumption that court practices concerning federal crimes are reflective of judicial norms in state and local courts. In 1971, the average prison sentence given by United States federal district courts was three and one-half years. In the same year in Japan, 94 per cent of persons sentenced to prison terms without labor served one year or less. Fifty per cent of persons sentenced to prison terms with labor served one year or less and 40 per cent more served three years or less. In Japan, therefore, 90 per cent of all persons sentenced to jail terms served not more than three years. Comparing penal sentences for the few crimes common to United States and Japanese criminal codes, the average sentence for counterfeiting is 40 months in the United States, 15 months in Japan; for forging public documents, 31 months in the United States, 11 months in Japan. Stricter sentences are also not the explanation for the dramatically lower rate of narcotics offenses in Japan. Sentences for offenses involving hard drugs in Japan average two years, as opposed to between five and six years in United States. Japanese law does provide for compulsory hospitalization, and the practice is to take addicts off drugs immediately, to go "cold turkey." The death penalty does exist in Japan, and is most commonly given for murder attendant upon robbery. During the period 1968 through 1972, 68 persons were executed—about 13 per year.

In the late 1960's, burning cities and the findings of a national commission prompted Americans to discover violent national traditions generally unacknowledged in history books. Finding that violence was "as American as apple pie," as Rap Brown said, Americans began to blame the past for contemporary criminality. Unfortunately for this line of argument, traditions of violence are by no means unique to the United States. Japan has them as well. Student demonstrations, for example, more sustained and more violent than the antiwar movement in the United States, have been a fixture of Japanese politics for a generation. Assassination of political figures has a much larger place in Japanese history than in American history. And the tradition continues, forcing the Japanese police to maintain close watch over radical groups of both the left and the right. The wounding of Ambassador Reischauer in the early 1960's by a knife-wielding assailant was not nearly as surprising in Japan as it would have been in the United States. Within memory Japan embarked on a brutal and far-flung imperial adventure. Its soldiers, too, have had their My Lai. The samurai warrior, armed with two curved swords, is a prominent figure in contemporary popular culture. Japanese television is as inundated with bloody samurai dramas as American television has been with shoot-outs at the OK corral. If America has a cult of the gun, Japan has a cult of the sword. Japanese history is no less blood-soaked or cruel than American history. It would be difficult to argue that contemporary Japanese culture bears fewer traces of its own past than American culture does of its own past.

Informal social controls

So where do we turn if modernity, congestion, the criminal justice system, or violent traditions do not explain the difference in crime rates? An alternative approach is to free ourselves from American views about the causes of crime and examine what Japanese society does to control deviance that Americans do not customarily consider. Rather than measuring Japanese criminality against American theories, let us consider it against the perspective of Japanese practice.

The key to social discipline in Japan lies in the greater vitality of informal controls over individuals. Japan relies less than the United States on formal institutions of government—such as police, prosecutors, and courts—to curb criminality. Order is maintained through active informal supervision of personal behavior by family, workmates, and neighbors. This informal system has three interlocking features that contrast sharply with American social practices: the vitality of informal groups, the legitimacy of authority, and the assumption by informal groups of responsibility for maintaining social order.

Despite industrialization and urbanization, Japan has preserved the cohesion of small-scale social groups more successfully than the United States. Personal identity for Japanese, who prize mobility and individual autonomy less than Americans do, is dependent on membership in particular groups. Social position is defined more idiosyncratically than in the United States. A Japanese is not just an engineer, but an engineer with Mitsubishi, educated at Tokyo University; not simply a civil servant, but a civil servant in the Accounting Section of the Ministry of Finance with 15 years seniority; not simply a brother, but a brother in the Matsuoka family of the Setagaya ward of Tokyo, formerly of Kurashiki in the Okayama Prefecture; not simply a police officer, but an Inspector in the Crime Prevention Section of the Shibuya Police Station. While in the United States people are also known by their associates, in Japan they are almost unrecognizable without these affiliations. This explains why personal introductions and name cards specifying social location are so crucial in Japan. They ensure that the newcomer is affiliated with, and hence responsible to, people who are known and trusted. The American cocktail party makes Japanese acutely uncomfortable because it forces them to interact with anonymous, essentially interchangeable people.

Because of their dependence on particular groups, Japanese are extremely sensitive to the regard of these associates. They shrink from any action that might jeopardize their acceptability, for the greatest calamity that could befall them would be exclusion. Then they would be outcasts, eternal strangers without the emotional fulfillment of belonging. As a result, Japanese have, in the apt phrase of one commentator, a "heightened sense of the fatefulness of their antisocial impulses." Americans, by contrast, value social mobility; they want to be able to pull up stakes, to sever dependency, to be autonomous. It is instructive that the classic American tale of rejection and loss of roots, that of Philip Nolan, the "man without a country," involves statelessness—the loss of national affiliation. The consequences of severing other associations seem to arouse fewer fears for Americans. And, since the Vietnam war, it may be that even national association is less prized than before.

This is not to suggest that Americans do not value the regard of their fellow human beings at work, home, play, worship, and so forth. The difference between Japanese and Americans is not the difference between being "inner-directed" and "other-directed." What is different is the scale and anonymity of the reference groups. Japanese live within stable networks of named people; Americans live in a more impersonal human environment, where people are substitutable. Social constraints in Japan are thus less diffuse than in the United States; they are overlaid with the emotions of personal attachment.

The capacity for exerting the kind of social control found in Japan has been eroded in the United States. For example, a larger proportion of families remain intact in Japan than in the United States. In the United States about four marriages in 10 end in divorce; in Japan, although divorce can be obtained by mutual consent, only one marriage in 10 fails. There are fewer families headed by women in Japan—five per cent versus 12 per cent. The average number of persons living in households is about the same in both countries, approximately 3.2, but the number of persons living alone is greater in the United States. Americans are probably the most mobile people in the world, and this has a direct effect on the cohesiveness of families and neighborhoods. About one fifth of all Americans change their residence each year, about half of these moving to another state. By contrast, only about eight per cent of Japanese change residence each year. The average American moves 14 times during his lifetime; the average Japanese, five times. Moreover, Americans move farther, often for thousands of miles. Japanese move within a space somewhat smaller than California, which enhances the opportunity for renewed face-to-face contact with relatives, schoolmates, and friends. Until recently, most Japanese workers, both salaried and hourly, kept the same employer all their lives. Though this situation has changed significantly in the past two decades, labor turnover rates in manufacturing are still half the American rates.

Neighborhoods are also more cohesive in Japan. For example, most have institutions of informal government, known as *chokai*, that collect dues, elect officers, undertake projects, and disseminate information. The *chokai* are not creations of law but rather traditional institutions, centuries old. Similar organizations have been lost in most places in the United States and must now be reinvented, often as a direct response to soaring crime and a need for greater security.

There is, then, a structural difference between Japanese and American society that is critically important to the incidence of crime. Japanese are surrounded by tight networks of known individuals to whom they are connected by blood or shared experience, and whose regard is essential for emotional security. This produces a capacity for informal constraint of behavior that is very much stronger in Japan than in the United States.

The legitimacy of authority

The Japanese also more readily accept the legitimacy of such informal authority. The characteristic posture of a Japanese before authority is subservience and compliance; the characteristic posture of an American is self-assertion and suspicion, often resentment. Japanese police officers working around American military bases are shocked at the truculence of servicemen caught breaking the law. While Japanese offenders admit their guilt and throw themselves on the mercy of the officer, Americans deny wrongdoing, challenge the officer's right to intervene, and demand to see a lawyer. Guilty pleas in court are more common in Japan than in the United States—95 per cent versus 80 per cent of all prosecutions. Moreover, many of the American guilty pleas are technical—

the result of plea-bargaining—and do not indicate repentance or admission of error. Plea-bargaining is illegal in Japan. The compliant nature of Japanese offenders is shown by an amazing fact: 90 per cent of all Japanese criminal cases are prosecuted without the necessity of jailing an offender to guarantee his court appearance. At no time from detection through trial is the offender detained.

In the United States, arrest marks the beginning of the criminal justice process; in Japan, the end. Police efficiency is measured in the United States by the proportion of cases "cleared by arrest." Such a figure is meaningless in Japan.

Confronted by authority, Americans struggle and conform; Japanese submit and repent. Admissions of guilt and a display of contrition are conditions for reacceptance of an offender into Japanese society. They indicate that the individual recognizes and acknowledges his transgression against the standards of the community; resocialization has begun. Though contrition is also rewarded in the United States, it is not required for reacceptance. All that is necessary is for the offender to meet the requirements of punishment—to pay his debt, to serve his time.

The efficiency of these two criminal justice systems is sharply affected by the customary responses of the people to authority. Suspects are found by the Japanese police in connection with 57 per cent of all known offenses, while the comparable figure in the United States is a bare 20 per cent. Of these suspects, 68 per cent are prosecuted in Japan, compared with 80 per cent in the United States—a generous estimate based on the rate of prosecution for the FBI's seven categories of serious crime. At these rates, the Japanese prosecute in connection with 38 per cent of known criminal offenses; Americans, 16 per cent. Since admissions of guilt occur in 95 per cent of prosecutions in Japan, and 80 per cent in the United States, conviction is assured with respect to 35 per cent of known offenses in Japan, against 13 per cent in the United States. By the yardstick of convictions, the Japanese criminal justice system is almost three times more efficient than the American.

To the extent that the Japanese criminal justice system deters crime, it does so not because it is severe, but because it is certain. The chances of escaping exposure and censure are much less in Japan than in the United States. The cornerstone of the American philosophy of crime control is deterrence: People will not commit crimes if punishment is prompt and strict. Official action is supposed to reinforce the development of conscience, the internalization of

moral restraint. Japanese experience suggests that the relationship
between formal action of a criminal justice system and the incidence of crime is more complex. Rather than official action prompt-
ing compliance with social norms, compliant attitudes toward authority enhance the efficiency of official action. The Japanese police
look good because the offender will admit guilt in order to obtain
social acceptance. Because authority is informally present throughout society and people accept its legitimacy, criminal justice officials in Japan have a comparatively easier time detecting and
prosecuting offenders than their counterparts in the United States.
There is a disturbing implication in this for the United States:
Once the volume of crime becomes very large, and the system
becomes overloaded—as one can argue has already happened in
the United States—then both the efficiency of law-enforcement
and its deterrent effect decline. Because official efficiency and the
volume of crime are reciprocally related, a spiral of increasing
crime and decreasing efficiency would be difficult to reverse. Formal systems of control work best when they are needed least. Unfortunately, the converse is also true.

Law and morality

The last feature in the Japanese system of crime control that
needs stressing is the permeability of the boundary between formal and informal authority. Police, prosecutors, and courts possess
not merely legal authority, as in the United States, but moral
authority as well. Japanese police officers sermonize considerably more often than American officers: They lecture people of
all ages and stations on the obligations of being a "proper Japanese," on manners, on courtesies appropriate to elders, on the danger of bad companions, and on the obligations of friendship. Americans tend to separate moral and legal authority, assigning them
to different persons—legal authority to policemen, moral authority
to priests, teachers, and relatives. They resent the assumption by
either set of the other's role. A moral figure that helps the police
is a "fink"; a legal figure that sermonizes is told to make a formal
charge or else "bug off."

Formal and informal roles, legal and moral ones, interpenetrate
in Japan because government is not considered a created entity—it
is not the result of an explicit act of fabrication by an existing
community, the product of making a constitution. Government is
not added on to community; it is intrinsic to community, as par-

entage is to family. Its role is larger than law, and consequently more difficult to circumscribe. Government officials, such as policemen, have a legitimacy, a moral stature, that they do not have in the United States. They are agents of the community's moral consensus as well as its statutory prescriptions.

The homogeneity of the Japanese population has undoubtedly been important in allowing community and government, morality and law, informal and formal authority, to become combined. Because subcultural groups are few and their numbers very small, there is almost universal agreement on what it means to be Japanese, as well as the value of being so. The largest minority group, two per cent of the population today, are the *burakumin,* historically outcasts who performed menial and unclean tasks, such as butchering and leather-working. They are not physically distinct, and to most Japanese are an "invisible race." The next largest minority groups are the Koreans, one half of one per cent of the population, and the Chinese, scarcely more than one quarter of one per cent. Altogether, less than three per cent of the population have minority status, and the majority of these are solidly Japanese in appearance and culture. While the melting pot of American society is still bubbling and giving off smoke and fumes, Japanese society has produced an ingot of uniform quality.

As Japanese policemen are accepted as moral actors, Japanese citizens are expected to assist policemen actively. The responsibility for maintaining law and order does not belong exclusively to police, prosecutors, and judges. The roles of private citizen and public official mutually interpenetrate. For example, almost every neighborhood in Japan has a crime prevention association composed of citizen volunteers and led by their own officials. These associations, working closely with local police stations, distribute material on household security, warn residents about new forms of crime, post reminders in public places about the importance of telephoning the police promptly if any suspicious events occur, maintain half a million "contact points" in private homes where crime-prevention information may be obtained, and sell special locks and fasteners for doors and windows. In many neighborhoods the associations organize street patrols, some with distinctive uniforms, that give special attention to monitoring the behavior of juveniles during the evening hours in popular entertainment areas. Officers in each police station are designated to work with the associations; they are also given office space and secretarial assistance. Planning and operation of the associations are strictly matters of local initiative, though the associations are organized into prefectural and national federations. Each level receives some financial contribution from a parallel level of government—*chokai*, ward, city, prefecture, or nation.

Americans, on the other hand, are unsure of their relations with the police when they are not charged with an offense. Though recognizing that they have a duty to cooperate with the police, they interpret this narrowly, and have devised no mechanisms for giving assistance to the police in an organized, reliable, routine way. Though vigorously defending the right of self-defense, Americans believe that policing should be left to formal authorities. They are suspicious of individuals who go out of their way to lend assistance. Group assistance especially has bad reputation, having become associated in American history with vigilantism. In American tradition, citizen assistance does not supplement police activities, it supplants them. It springs from a breakdown of formal control and is therefore apt to be unregulated and lawless. In recent years, attempts have been made to organize block and neighborhood crime-prevention associations, largely in core areas of major cities. Very often they are regarded by law-enforcement personnel as meddling nuisances or outright threats to law and order.

In summary, the fundamental reason why Japan has a crime rate that is significantly lower than the United States is because its people are encapsulated by familiar small-scale groups that articulate norms of right behavior—norms that are similar from group to group—and apply informal pressure to conform. Economic growth, industrialization, and technological modernization have not produced social atomization in Japan. Though Japan has experienced the same great economic changes as the United States during the past century, its society remains vitally cellular. The economic and social basis for grouping has changed, but the subordination of individuals to groups with responsibility for them remains. Japan is unique among industrial societies in its ability to create and maintain tribe-like groups of small scale. This is fundamental to maintaining low levels of criminality.

The small size of Japan also makes some contribution to its relative peaceableness, but it is unclear how much. While the policemen are concentrated, so too are the people, creating congestion that would be intolerable to many Americans. The size of Japan also reduces the fragmenting effects of mobility. It is tempting to say that limited space has forced the Japanese to learn to live together, that tribalization stems from overcrowding. But there is surely nothing necessary about a response of this sort to crowding. If the citizens of other nations—the United States, for example— were similarly congested, they would simply turn on one another, raising the incidence of violence and mayhem. Customs and values, not geography or density, are the important determinants of Japanese orderliness.

The future of the American system

Two final observations about crime and law enforcement in the United States are prompted by this examination of the Japanese experience. First, the levels of criminal behavior that Americans find so disturbing may be the inevitable consequence of aspects of national life that Americans prize—individualism, mobility, privacy, autonomy, suspicion of authority, and separation between public and private roles, between government and community. The United States may have relatively high levels of criminality because it is inhabited by Americans.

Second, given American traditions, it is questionable whether law enforcement agencies can be much more effective in curbing criminality than they are now. The record so far would indicate that government, unless supported by more vigorous informal social sanctions, cannot contain crime without running the risk of transforming the scope and character of its operations in ways that would threaten other values basic to the American way of life. Moreover, reliance on formal agencies of the criminal justice system may be more than merely ineffective—it may undermine their public support. It is more than a coincidence that rising concern with crime in the United States is accompanied by fierce criticism of the criminal justice system. Though different people have their particular scapegoats, most would agree that the "system" is not working well. Of course it is not: It is being asked to do what it cannot do—namely, take the place of decaying processes of informal social control. Americans are in the tragic and paradoxical position of depending more and more on law-enforcement institutions whose authority they increasingly question and reject.

The Rehabilitation of Punishment

MARC F. PLATTNER

A remarkable turnabout has recently occurred in the perennial debate about how America should deal with its convicted criminals. For over a century, American penology had subscribed to the rehabilitative ideal and its practical concomitant, the indeterminate sentence, which tailors the length of a convict's prison term to his prospects for and progress toward the "cure" of his criminal tendencies. From 1870 through the 1960's, this position represented the "enlightened" view, and reformers strove, with considerable success, to have it embodied in public policy. Then, suddenly, the tide of advanced opinion on this matter began to turn. There emerged a wave of skepticism, and even hostility, toward the theory and practice of prisons that were based upon the rehabilitative ideal, and a wave of concern about the unfairness that characterizes a system of indeterminate sentencing. This assault upon the received doctrine has rapidly been gaining support from all parts of the political spectrum, culminating this year in a host of books, articles, and reports advocating the abandonment of the indeterminate sentence and of rehabilitation as the justification for imprisonment. Politicians as diverse in their views as President Ford and Senator Kennedy have endorsed a return to determinate sentencing, and several state legislatures seem to be moving in this direction.

The dynamics of this abrupt 180-degree turn in elite opinion are fascinating, and reveal a good deal about the situation of American social thought in the mid-1970's. The old consensus in favor of rehabilitation had been based on the liberal embrace of what Daniel P. Moynihan has called (in a slightly different context) the "therapeutic ethic." That is, political liberalism came to accept the understanding of man and society associated with the dominant trends in the behavioral sciences and psychiatry. This included a view of crime as a form of "deviant" behavior, whose causes lay in individual or social pathology. Hence criminals could not properly be regarded as bearing moral responsibility for their actions, or as deserving of punishment. Instead, they were themselves the victims of some kind of social or psychological "disorder," and were thus in need of treatment by experts in the behavioral sciences.

Since the amount of treatment required obviously varied depending upon the characteristics of the individual offender, judges were granted wide discretion in deciding the length of the sentence (e.g., one to 20 years). And since the criminal's potential for responding to rehabilitative techniques could not be accurately predicted in advance, parole boards were given wide discretion in deciding whether and when to release a convict before he had served the maximum term imposed by the court. (According to the strict rehabilitative theory, of course, there should be no legislatively or judicially imposed maxima or minima at all; sentences should be totally indeterminate, with behavioral experts enjoying complete freedom to determine when an offender had been sufficiently "cured" of his criminal tendencies to return safely to society.) Although the involuntary confinement of the convict for purposes of treatment curiously resembled a form of punishment, proponents of the rehabilitative theory denied that any punitive intention was involved, citing as an analogy the involuntary confinement of the mentally ill. Punishment and the punitive attitude, they argued, were an expression of a barbaric desire for vengeance, which had no place in an enlightened modern society.

Although the intellectual reaction against the rehabilitative theory did not gather real force until the 1970's, its sources can be found in the general social and intellectual ferment of the 1960's. One development that obviously must be cited in this context is the generally heightened interest in the problem of crime and the emergence of "law and order" as an issue of intense public controversy. The reason for this was simple: the extraordinarily steep rise in crime rates during the 1960's. Yet, while the crime explosion produced considerable political pressure for a policy of "getting tough" with criminals, it was not sufficient in itself to transform liberal opinion. Ramsey Clark, a staunch defender of rehabilitation, remained the preeminent liberal spokesman on this issue. The subsequent turn against rehabilitation cannot be explained primarily as a conservative reaction to rising crime rates. It was made possible only by a discrediting of rehabilitation from the left, part of a larger attack on the postwar liberal consensus that viewed America as a fundamentally just society.

In regarding law-breaking as a result of the "sickness" of the criminal, and as amenable to "treatment" by experts in the behavioral sciences, the rehabilitative theory implicitly assumes that the laws that are broken are just ones. Once this assumption is seriously questioned—as it was by the New Left—the rationale of the rehabilitative theory falls apart, and its application in practice takes on a new and sinister cast. Convicts no longer appear as disturbed individuals receiving much needed and compassionate care for their disabilities, but as more-or-less heroic rebels being forcibly remolded to accept the ways of an unjust society. Similarly, the behavioral scientists who treat them no longer appear as enlightened and impartial experts guided by some transpolitical notion of health, but as the henchmen of the ruling class and its self-interested view of what constitutes socially acceptable conduct.

A number of developments during the late 1960's lent plausibility to this critique. One was the *internal* attack condemning social scientists and psychiatrists as well-paid agents of the political status quo, which was led by radical, mostly younger members of these professions. Another was the imprisonment of antiwar protesters and black militants, who were sympathetically regarded, and indeed often admired, by the liberal community, and hence could not easily be branded as candidates for therapeutic help. In addition, the generally heightened sensitivity to issues of race and class led liberals to look with disfavor upon institutions where preponderantly poor and black inmates were being treated by white, middle-class professionals. Given the prevailing intellectual climate, it was but a short step to regard prisoners as simply one more unjustly oppressed group in American society.

T HE radical critique of the rehabilitation-oriented prison was given its first systematic popular expression in Jessica Mitford's *Kind and Usual Punishment,* published in 1973. Miss Mitford's basic premise was that the criminal law is not the embodiment of neutral principles of justice, but a "codification of the self-interest" of the dominant elements in American society. The prison is a weapon of class oppression, and what is billed as "rehabilitation," far from being a humanitarian effort to help disturbed individuals, is simply a subtle and insidious way of grinding down enemies of the existing order: "For the prison administrator, whether he be warden, sociologist, or psychologist, 'individualized treatment' is primarily a device for breaking the convict's will to resist and hounding him into compliance with institution demands, and is thus a means of exerting maximum control over the convict population. The cure will be deemed effective to the degree that the poor/young/brown/black captive appears to have capitulated to his middle-class/white/middle-aged captor, and to have adopted the virtues of subservience to authority, industry, cleanliness, docility."

Despite the savageness of Miss Mitford's attack on liberal reformers (and on their hero, Ramsey Clark), her book was well received by liberal audiences. Though this may be attributed in part to the general vulnerability of liberals to attacks from their left, it was also due no doubt to Miss Mitford's powerful depiction of the practical abuses spawned by the rehabilitative theory. The most frightening of these abuses involved the use of "behavior-modification" techniques on unwilling prisoners. According to Miss Mitford's account, "advanced" prison systems were already employing various kinds of drug therapy and were contemplating the use of neurosurgery. But even where such chilling instruments were not em-

ployed, Miss Mitford showed how the unfettered reign of behavioral scientists readily led to tyrannical and unjust control over the
fate of prisoners. At the Patuxent Institution in Maryland, a "total
treatment facility" for "defective delinquents," all inmates were
committed for absolutely indeterminate sentences, to be released
only when the staff determined that they had been "cured." The
result was that those prisoners who refused to cooperate or whose
progress did not satisfy the social workers and therapists—a group
comprising 46 per cent of the inmates paroled from 1955 to September 1965—were confined beyond the maximum sentence imposed for the crime they had committed.

A constant refrain throughout Miss Mitford's book is the hatred
felt by prisoners for the indeterminate-sentencing system, which
they feel forces them to play a "treatment game" they do not
believe in, subjects their lives to the arbitrary whims of correctional authorities, and produces unjustifiable disparities in the
amount of time served for similar crimes. One did not have to share
Miss Mitford's own implicit condoning or even approval of criminal
behavior to sympathize with the prisoners' complaints against compulsory therapy and the indeterminate sentence. Indeed, an elo-
quent and prescient indictment of this mode of dealing with criminals was made by the British theologian C. S. Lewis in a brilliant
essay, "The Humanitarian Theory of Punishment," which was published in 1948:

> On [the] remedial view of punishment the offender should, of course,
> be detained until he was cured. And of course the official straighteners
> are the only people who can say when that is. The first result of the
> Humanitarian theory is, therefore, to substitute for a definite sentence
> (reflecting to some extent the community's moral judgment on the
> degree of ill-desert involved) an indefinite sentence terminable only
> by the word of those experts—and they are not experts in moral
> theology nor even in the Law of Nature—who inflict it. Which of us,
> if he stood in the dock, would · ɔt prefer to be tried by the old system?
>
> It may be said that by the continued use of the word punishment
> and the use of the verb "inflict" I am misrepresenting Humanitarians.
> They are not punishing, not inflicting, only healing. But do not let us
> be deceived by a name. To be taken without consent from my home
> and friends; to lose my liberty; to undergo all those assaults on my
> personality which modern psychotherapy knows how to deliver; to be
> remade after some pattern of "normality" hatched in a Viennese
> laboratory to which I never professed allegiance; to know that this
> process will never end until either my captors have succeeded or I
> grown wise enough to cheat them with apparent success—who cares
> whether this is called punishment or not?

It is doubtful, though, whether this critique of the rehabilitative
theory would have influenced the recent American debate if it had
not been offered in the radical guise in which Miss Mitford presented it.

T HERE was also a strand within American liberal thought, how- ever, that was able to supply a basis for opposition to the ther- apeutic ideology—namely, the concern for civil liberties and the rights of individuals. Insofar as the rehabilitative theory asserted that the criminal was "sick" and hence not morally responsible for his crime, it also implied that the convict—like the confined mental patient—was not competent to exercise his rights. And insofar as the rehabilitators were acting on the basis of expert knowledge and a concern for the welfare of the individuals they were treating, the interference of the courts would be unnecessary or even harmful to the prisoners themselves. Although most civil libertarians were probably personally sympathetic to the apparently compassionate character of the rehabilitative theory, it was inevitable that their concern with individual rights and due process would eventually cause them to turn against it. And, indeed, this is what has hap- pened. In defending the rights of prisoners who claimed they were being penalized because of their political views or denied parole on insufficient grounds, civil-liberties lawyers were led to challenge in court the authority of the rehabilitative experts. And as they saw how the system operated, and learned how intensely their clients—the prisoners themselves—opposed it, many civil libertarians came to reject root and branch the rehabilitative theory and its corollary, the indeterminate sentence.

One source of objections to the indeterminate-sentencing system was its obvious unfairness in subjecting offenders convicted of similar crimes to wildly disparate periods of imprisonment. At least one study revealed that different judges varied considerably in the sentences they would impose for identical criminals convicted of identical offenses. Moreover, the wide discretion granted to judges and parole boards made it possible for their personal biases to in- fluence their decisions about confining or releasing convicts. Lib- eral critics were particularly sensitive to the possibility that such discretion could lead to longer terms for the poor and the black.

Another aspect of the indeterminate sentence attacked by some legal scholars was its use as a form of preventive detention. An important part of the justification for holding some prisoners for long terms under indeterminate sentences was the belief that they would present a danger to the community if they were released. But a number of studies showed how uncertain and inaccurate predictions of dangerousness tended to be, which meant that many prisoners were being confined because of a mistaken belief that they would return to crime.

In this context, mention should be made of the "decarceration" movement, which has played a significant role in recent discussion about prisons. Much of the original impetus toward decarceration came from within the rehabilitative professions themselves. In the treatment of the mentally ill, psychiatrists promoted a movement away from reliance on large state hospitals and toward outpatient care whenever possible. A similar development took place in re-

gard to correctional institutions in the 1960's, and prison populations fell, while the use of probation and parole increased. Although
this trend was supposed to achieve greater success in rehabilitating offenders, doubts quickly arose as to whether "community-based
corrections" were in fact producing this result. Nonetheless, proponents of decarceration, like historian David Rothman, continued
to defend it on other grounds: It was less expensive, more humane,
and less restrictive of individual freedom than institutionalization.
In fact, as the evidence mounted that rehabilitation of offenders in
any setting was not succeeding, the case for decarceration, from a
civil-libertarian standpoint, grew all the stronger. If the rehabilitators
could not accomplish what they promised, how could depriving
their patients of liberty be justified at all? In this situation, the
conflict between civil-liberties lawyers and behavioral scientists
became more intense, and even the right of psychiatrists to confine
mental patients involuntarily was increasingly challenged.

THE coup de grace to the rehabilitative theory was administered by the social scientists themselves. As the number and
kinds of treatment programs proliferated, and as more controlled
and rigorous studies were made of their results, the findings revealed that they were not succeeding in reducing recidivism. A
massive survey of rehabilitation programs undertaken by Robert
Martinson and his colleagues—first reported on in an article by
Martinson in the Spring 1974 issue of *The Public Interest*—concluded that there was "no clear pattern to indicate the efficacy of
any particular method of treatment." Given the moral and political
questioning of the rehabilitative theory that was already taking
place, the effect of the Martinson study was devastating. The tide
of opinion turned decisively against rehabilitation as a justification
for the imprisonment of criminals.

The conclusion that Jessica Mitford had drawn from the discrediting of the rehabilitative theory was that prisons should simply
be abolished. This "abolitionist" position was based on a rejection
of the three other justifications commonly offered for imprisonment: 1) incapacitation of convicted criminals; 2) deterrence of
other potential lawbreakers; and 3) retribution. Miss Mitford glibly
denied the effectiveness of prisons in curtailing crime through performance of the first two functions, and simply brushed aside the
case for retribution. Nor did she suggest a new form of criminal
sanction to replace imprisonment. Since Miss Mitford is neither a
utopian nor a fool, she presumably did not really believe that the
United States or any other political community could maintain itself
without any criminal sanctions whatsoever. Her call for the abolition of prisons made sense only as a tactic forming part of a larger
strategy for revolutionary political and social change.

The abolitionist program was destined for failure since very few,
even on the left, were upon reflection prepared to accept Miss
Mitford's suggestion that imprisonment should not be employed

for even the most serious crimes. Thus the ultimate effect of the successful critique of the rehabilitative theory was to spark scholarly interest in other functions performed by prisons. Rising crime rates had already begun to focus attention on the incapacitative and deterrent effects of imprisonment. While liberal opponents of the indeterminate sentence tended to be particularly disturbed by the overly long periods of confinement it sometimes allowed, others attacked the indeterminate-sentencing system for releasing many serious offenders without any period of confinement at all. These critics argued that the frequent failure to incarcerate even repeat offenders who committed serious crimes substantially weakened the legitimate incapacitative function of the prison sanction, and that the general uncertainty as to whether a prison sentence would be imposed severely reduced its deterrent capabilities. Moreover, sophisticated statistical studies by economists and sociologists indicated that, contrary to the conventional wisdom among penological champions of the rehabilitative theory, deterrence did indeed "work"—i.e., greater certainty and severity of the sanction did produce a lower rate of crime. Finally, there was even a new willingness to take seriously the old-fashioned concept of retribution—which, in the aftermath of Watergate and the Pardon, no longer seemed quite so barbaric or unreasonable, even to many liberals.

THE wide-open nature of the current discussion of criminal sanctions has led to a reexamination of first principles and to a generally more philosophic level of discourse. This development is reflected in two recently published books on the subject: *Doing Justice* (Hill and Wang, $9.95), the report of the predominantly liberal Committee for the Study of Incarceration written by Andrew von Hirsch; and *Punishing Criminals* (Basic Books, $10.95), written by the conservative social scientist Ernest van den Haag.

The argument of *Doing Justice* is heavily influenced by civil-libertarian concerns and a "basic mistrust of the power of the state." It therefore rejects the rehabilitative theory and the indeterminate sentence on many of the grounds discussed above. Yet it acknowledges, albeit somewhat grudgingly, "at least a partial acceptance of this society's laws: one that permits us to consider violators as, by and large, deserving of punishment." The return to common sense of liberal thinking about crime is nowhere better illustrated than by the following passage from the Introduction to *Doing Justice*, written by Committee members Willard Gaylin and David Rothman:

> One of the sad consequences of the appropriation of the term "law and order" by the extreme right wing as a euphemism for racist feelings that were unfashionable to articulate was that the intellectual community, repelled by the implicit racism, turned away from the legitimate rights that such words imply. The authentic need to investigate the essential importance of both law and order was slighted. Instead, the intellectual community focused all too exclusively on the

neglected rights of the criminal offender, forgetting that, while this was a compassionate and necessary pursuit, the welfare of the community was the primary concern of a system of criminal justice.

The Committee's recognition that the criminal justice system must serve the welfare of the community is reflected in its acceptance of deterrence as a reason for imposing criminal sanctions. But given their intense concern for the individual and his rights, von Hirsch and his colleagues are understandably reluctant to allow deterrence or any other crime-control considerations to serve as the primary rationale for punishing particular individuals. Invoking the names of Immanuel Kant and John Rawls, they argue that the claims of justice must take precedence over purely utilitarian considerations. Hence they focus upon the old-fashioned concept of *desert* (a "somewhat less emotionally loaded" synonym for retribution) as the chief justification for punishment. Criminals should be punished because the acts they have committed *deserve* it. And the severity of their punishment should be proportional to the "seriousness" of their crime.[1]

There is, however, another theme that is sounded repeatedly throughout *Doing Justice*—an insistence that the sanction of imprisonment be sparingly used. In the Introduction, Gaylin and Rothman put it this way:

> . . . central to our conception, essential to its balance, is a commitment to the most stringent limits on incarceration.
>
> It would be better to ignore the recommendations of the Committee entirely than to accept any part of them without that focus on decarceration about which all its other arguments pivot. . . . To abandon the rehabilitative model without a simultaneous gradation downward in prison sentences would be an unthinkable cruelty and a dangerous act.

In accordance with this view, the Report recommends that even for the most serious violent offenses—"perhaps" with the exception of murder—no prison sentences should exceed five years, even for repeat offenders. Similarly, it suggests that for crimes like burglary and auto theft, incarceration should not be employed at all (instead, the punishment, apparently even for repeat offenders, would be no more than "stiff schedules of intermittent confinement involving substantial deprivations of offenders' leisure time").

Despite what the statement by Gaylin and Rothman quoted above seems to imply, the Report's reliance on the principle of "commensurate deserts" as the basis for punishment in no way necessarily entails the emphasis on decarceration that accompanies it. Von Hirsch justifies the scaling down of prison sentences by asserting that incarceration is a severe penalty (in the sense of "being very unpleasant, given the prevailing tolerances for suffering") and hence should be restricted to serious crimes. But he

---

[1] Seriousness, as von Hirsch defines it, "depends both on the harm done (or risked) by the act and on the degree of the actor's culpability".

offers no clear standard for ascertaining what degree of severity properly corresponds to what degree of seriousness. The standard that first suggests itself, the *lex talionis*, according to which the suffering imposed on the criminal should insofar as possible equal in degree and kind the injury inflicted on his victims, is explicitly rejected by von Hirsch as unnecessarily severe. This traditional principle of "an eye for an eye" indeed seems excessively harsh and inhumane to modern sensibilities; yet difficult problems arise when one attempts—as von Hirsch does—to sever completely the link between the degree of suffering of the victim and that of the criminal. Let us take the example of a victim who is crippled for life as the result of a willful aggravated assault. Whatever von Hirsch may say about how unpleasant incarceration is, I doubt that most people would feel the demands of justice had been met if the assailant served only a two- or three-year sentence.

The Report's suggestion that crimes like burglary and auto theft not be punished by incarceration is also highly problematic. The rationale for this seems to be that nonviolent property crimes fail to "do or threaten sufficient injury" to warrant severe punishment. But harm done or threatened is not the only measure of the seriousness of a crime; one must also consider the profit gained by the criminal. For justice requires that a lawbreaker not benefit from his illegal acts—in other words, that crime not pay. A "professional" burglar or auto thief might well find intermittent confinement, when he is caught and convicted, a small price to pay compared to the profits of his illegal enterprise. In this case, the need for stiffer penalties, at least for repeat offenders, would be clear. That principle of justice which holds that crime should not pay would also enable a desert-based system of punishment to meet the needs of deterrence.

THAT punishment is necessary to make crime unprofitable and to "avoid cheating those who remained law-abiding" is a point clearly recognized by Ernest van den Haag. Many of the things that can be obtained through crime (e.g., money) are regarded by most of us as desirable. Hence the threat of punishment is needed to "offset the temptation to gratify individual wishes by unlawful means." Because van den Haag regards crime as rational in this sense, he opposes the view that most criminals are "sick," and rejects the rehabilitative model. He comes to the debate over how to deal with convicted offenders concerned primarily with the need to preserve the social fabric and to reduce crime. His conservatism has neither a libertarian nor a moralistic cast. The position he takes might best be described as a kind of hard-headed "realism," and he argues it with considerable learning and sophistication.

Although he emphasizes the utilitarian aspects of punishment, van den Haag is also sensitive to the importance of desert. He recognizes that justice and utility are closely intertwined in the institution of punishment—that considerations of justice almost always limit what we are willing to do for the sake of utility. He brings home this point with a particularly telling example:

> If laws aimed only at utility, they would threaten the most severe punishment for whatever causes the most serious and frequent injuries, wherever the threat might restrain people. We should then punish vehicular homicide (negligent manslaughter) by drunken drivers more severely than deliberate murder. The former victimizes more people by far than murder, is no less serious for the victims, and is not caused by passion or malevolence, which produces crimes hard to restrain. Homicidal drunken driving could probably be deterred more frequently than murder by the effective threat of severe punishment. Yet we punish murder more severely. Murderers have intentionally committed a wrong whereas the drunken driver did not intend to kill. We feel that he deserves less retribution because guilt depends on intent as well as on the effect produced.

Yet despite this insight, van den Haag insists on the practical importance of distinguishing the goal of defending the social order from the goal of doing justice to individuals, and stresses those instances in which punishment can legitimately serve the former goal at the expense of the latter. In this connection he cites the harsh, exemplary punishments which may be deemed necessary in an army at war, a ship threatened with mutiny, or a country suffering from a severe famine—punishments which far exceed our ordinary sense of what is deserved. The force of these examples cannot simply be denied. As Machiavelli delighted in pointing out, sometimes there do arise situations of extreme emergency in which the preservation of the political order—the precondition of justice for individuals—requires the abrogation of the ordinary rules of justice. What is disquieting about van den Haag's argument, however, is that he seeks to incorporate the suspension of justice that may be necessary in extreme situations into the everyday workings of the criminal justice system.

Thus, invoking the principle that "the preservation of society and the security and welfare of its members are legitimate political ends beyond justice," he advocates the preventive confinement of "dangerous" offenders *beyond* the terms of punishment deserved by their offenses. Van den Haag proposes that predictions of dangerousness be based on a "categorical method" taking into account such factors as prior convictions and age and sex of the offender, and suggests that "post-punishment incapacitation" be mandatory for violent criminals with "no less than a 60 per cent chance of recidivism." Now, it seems clear from van den Haag's discussion that prior convictions will be the chief determinant of whether additional preventive confinement will be imposed. But prior convictions, as it is argued in *Doing Justice*, can reasonably be viewed as increasing the offender's degree of culpability, and hence as making him *deserve* a lengthier sentence. Thus most of the protection for society that van den Haag is seeking can probably be achieved within a system that stays within the bounds of justice. And whatever additional safety benefits might be gained by post-punishment confinement on the basis of statistical factors like age or sex simply are not worth the price of bringing into the criminal justice system an element of blatant injustice to individuals. The crime problem is a serious one, but the situation is surely not desperate enough to justify such an expedient.

Von Hirsch and his colleagues would no doubt be horrified by van den Haag's willingness to override the rights of the convict in this way for the sake of protecting society at large. Yet the Committee for the Study of Incarceration also shows itself willing to allow the principle of post-punishment confinement, albeit for rather different reasons. The Committee admits an exception to its otherwise passionate opposition to predictive restraint in the case of "defendants who stand convicted of serious assault crimes and who have extensive records of violence." Given the public outcry that is likely if short sentences are applied in such cases, the Committee reasons that "unless express authority to invoke predictive restraint is granted here, the entire structure of 'deserved' sentences could become distorted upward." In short, rather than admit that someone handed a fourth conviction for violent crime might *deserve* a sentence of more than five years, the Committee prefers to countenance a direct violation of its own principle that imprisonment can be justified only on the basis of desert. So while van den Haag is ready to depart from justice for the sake of preserving social order, the Committee is ready to depart from justice in order to preserve a lower scale of prison sentences.

Whatever shortcomings *Punishing Criminals* and *Doing Justice* may have, however, should not be allowed to obscure their considerable virtues. Both van den Haag and von Hirsch clearly reject the two myths that have vitiated so much of the discussion about criminal justice—the view that criminals are "sick" individuals who are not morally responsible for their offenses, and the view that criminals are political rebels struggling against oppression. In place of these myths, both authors affirm the eminently sensible proposition that criminals are lawbreakers who deserve to be punished for their illegal actions. As the differences between these two books show, the acceptance of this proposition by no means provides unambiguous guidelines for reforming our system of dealing with convicted offenders. But it is an indispensable first step toward a just and rational response to the problem of crime.

The
great
American
gun war

B. BRUCE-BRIGGS

For over a decade there has been a powerful and vocal push for stricter government regulation of the private possession and use of firearms in the United States—for "gun control." The reader cannot help being aware of the vigorous, often vociferous debate on this issue. Indeed, judging from the amount of energy devoted to the gun issue—Congress has spent more time on the subject than on all other crime-related measures combined—one might conclude that gun control is the key to the crime problem. Yet it is startling to note that no policy research worthy of the name has been done on the issue of gun control. The few attempts at serious work are of marginal competence at best, and tainted by obvious bias. Indeed, the gun-control debate has been conducted at a level of propaganda more appropriate to social warfare than to democratic discourse.

No one disagrees that there is a real problem: Firearms are too often used for nefarious purposes in America. In 1974, according to the FBI's Uniform Crime Reports, 10,000 people were illegally put to death with guns, and firearms were reportedly used in 200,000 robberies and 120,000 assaults, as well as in a small number of rapes, prison escapes, and other crimes. There is universal agreement that it would be desirable, to say the least, that these numbers be substantially reduced. So everybody favors gun control. But there is wide disagreement about how it can be achieved. Two principal strategies are promoted. To use the military terminology now creeping into criminology, they can be called "interdiction" and "deterrence."

Advocates of deterrence recommend the establishment of stricter penalties to discourage individuals from using firearms in crimes. But "gun control" is usually identified with interdiction—that is, the reduction of the criminal use of firearms by controlling the access of all citizens to firearms. The interdictionist position is promoted by a growing lobby, supported by an impressive alliance of reputable organizations, and sympathetically publicized by most of the national media. Every commission or major study of crime and violence has advocated much stricter gun-control laws. The only reason that this pressure has failed to produce much tighter controls of firearms is a powerful and well-organized lobby of gun owners, most notably the National Rifle Association (NRA), which has maintained that improved interdiction will have no effect on crime, but will merely strip away the rights and privileges of Americans—and perhaps even irreparably damage the Republic. The organized gun owners advocate reliance on deterrence.

The debate between the "gun controllers" (as the interdictionists are generally identified) and the "gun lobby" (as the organized gun owners have been labeled by a hostile media) has been incredibly virulent. In addition to the usual political charges of self-interest and stupidity, participants in the gun-control struggle have resorted to implications or downright accusations of mental illness, moral turpitude, and sedition. The level of debate has been so debased that even the most elementary methods of cost-benefit analysis have not been employed. One expects advocates to disregard the costs of their programs, but in this case they have even failed to calculate the benefits.

The prevalence of firearms

While estimates vary widely, it can be credibly argued that there are at least 140 million firearms in private hands in the United States today. This number has been expanding rapidly in recent years.[1] Since 1968, 40 million firearms have been produced and

---

[1] One obvious reason for the growing gun sales is that the prices of firearms, like most mass-produced goods, have not risen as fast as incomes. The classic deer rifle, the Winchester 94, in production since 1894, cost 250 per cent of an average worker's weekly take-home salary in 1900, 91 per cent in 1960,

sold. And these counts do not include the millions of guns brought back from the wars and/or stolen from military stocks. These figures are usually cited by advocates of interdiction as demonstrative of the enormity of the problem and as implying the dire necessity for swift and positive action. But they also demonstrate the incredible difficulty of dealing with the problem.

In the gun-control debate, the most outlandishly paranoid theories of gun ownership have appeared. Some people seem to believe that private arsenals exist primarily for political purposes —to kill blacks, whites, or liberals. But of course, the majority of firearms in this country are rifles and shotguns used primarily for hunting. A secondary purpose of these "long guns" is target and skeet shooting. Millions of gun owners are also collectors, in the broad sense of gaining satisfaction from the mere possession of firearms, but even the serious collectors who hold them as historical or aesthetic artifacts number in the hundreds of thousands.

The above uses account for the majority of firearms owned by Americans. Weapons for those purposes are not intended for use against people. But there is another major purpose of firearms —self-defense. In poll data, some 35 per cent of gun owners, especially handgun owners, indicated that at least one reason they had for possessing their weapons was self-defense. A Harris poll found two thirds of these people willing to grant that they would, under certain circumstances, kill someone with their weapon. This sounds very ominous, but it is such a widespread phenomenon that interdictionists have felt obliged to conduct studies demonstrating that the chance of being hurt with one's own weapon is greater than the chance of inflicting harm upon an assailant. The studies making this point are so ingeniously specious that they are worth expanding upon.

For example, the calculation is made that within a given jurisdiction more people are killed by family and friends, accidents, and sometimes suicide, than burglars are killed by homeowners. In a Midwestern county it was found that dead gun owners outnumbered dead burglars by six to one. Both sides of that ratio are fallacious. People do not have "house guns" to kill burglars but to prevent burglaries. The measure of the effectiveness of self-defense is not in the number of bodies piled up on doorsteps, but in the property that is protected. We have no idea how many

---

and 75 per cent in 1970. The relationship to annual median family income has been even more favorable—from 2.8 per cent in 1900 to 1.4 per cent in 1960 and 1.0 per cent in 1970. More important, increased competition during the past decade has lowered the absolute price of handguns.

burglars are challenged and frightened off by armed householders. And, of course, there is no way to measure the deterrent effect on burglars who know that homeowners may be armed. Though the statistics by themselves are not particularly meaningful, it is true that the burglary rate is very low in Southern and Southwestern cities with high rates of gun ownership. Burglary in Texas would seem a risky business.

The calculation of family homicides and accidents as costs of gun ownership is equally false. The great majority of these killings are among poor, restless, alcoholic, troubled people, usually with long criminal records. Applying the domestic homicide rate of these people to the presumably upstanding citizens whom they prey upon is seriously misleading.

Other studies claim to indicate that there is little chance of defending oneself with a weapon against street crime or other assaults. But almost without exception, such studies have been held in cities with strict gun-control laws. My favorite study was the one purporting to show that it was very dangerous to attempt to defend yourself with a gun because the likelihood of suffering harm in a mugging was considerably higher if you resisted. But the data indicated only that you got hurt if you yelled, kicked, or screamed—but not if you used a gun.

Gun owners versus interdiction

All this, of course, is begging the question. Why do people feel it necessary to obtain firearms to defend themselves? The rising crime rates would suggest it is not lunacy. But the data are improperly understood. Despite the high crime rates, there is a very small chance of being attacked or robbed in one's home, or even during any given excursion into the highest crime area. But the average citizen does not make such calculations and certainly would not have much faith in them if he did. He is scared. The gun, if it does nothing else, gives the citizen reassurance.

This last is a reason for large numbers of guns being owned—not quite defense, but insurance. Many people have weapons tucked away with no explicit idea of how they might be used except "you never know when you might need one." No violent intent is implied, any more than a purchaser of life insurance intends to die that year. It is pure contingency.

Apparently most owners care little about their firearms *per se*, considering them as mere tools, to be properly cared for—and, because they are potentially deadly, to be handled with caution. Yet within the ranks of the gun owners is a hard core of "gun nuts" (they sometimes call themselves "gunnies") for whom firearms are a fanatic hobby. To them, the possession, handling, and use of guns are a central part of life. They not only accumulate guns, but also read books and magazines about firearms and socialize with kindred spirits in gun clubs and gun stores. Many such people combine business with pleasure as gun dealers, gunsmiths, soldiers, policemen, and officials of gun owners' organizations. All this is symptomatic of the earnest devotees of any hobby—there are similar ski nuts, car nuts, boat nuts, radio nuts, dog nuts, even book nuts. In this case, however, the "nuts" have political importance because they are the core of the organized gun owners, easily aroused and mobilized to thwart the enemies of their passion.

Polls are unreliable on this point, because internal inconsistencies in the data and common sense suggest that many respondents won't admit to gun ownership, but it appears that at least one half of all American households are armed. They own guns for recreation or self-protection. The principal form of recreation, hunting, has deep cultural roots. In rural areas and small towns, a boy's introduction to guns and hunting is an important rite of passage. The first gun at puberty is the *bar mitzvah* of the rural WASP. Possession of a gun for self-protection is based upon a perception of a real or potential threat to personal, family, or home security that is beyond the control of the police. Very rarely is there criminal or seditious intent. Yet these people are told by the interdictionists that their possession of weapons is a threat to public safety and order, that they must obtain permits, fill out forms, pay taxes and fees, and keep and bear arms only by leave of the state. Inevitably, some of them have organized themselves against such interdiction. With a million members, the NRA is the largest and most effective consumer lobby in America. It maintains its morale and membership by broadcasting the statements in favor of "domestic disarmament" by extreme and loose-mouthed interdictionists and by publicizing the legislative attempts to restrict gun ownership as merely part of a fabian strategy—to use the interdictionists' code words, a "step in the right direction"—toward liquidating the private ownership and use of firearms in America.

The interdictionist position rests on the self-evident proposition that if there were no guns, there would be no crimes committed with guns. But few are sanguine about achieving that situation. Instead, their argument is that if there were fewer guns and/or if gun ownership were better controlled by the government, there would be fewer crimes with guns.

Can interdiction work? Let us examine what is proposed. Guns and control are subdivided in several ways. Usually there is an attempt to distinguish between mere possession and use. Furthermore, different controls are suggested for different types of weapons—"heavy stuff" (machine guns and cannon); long guns (rifles and shotguns); handguns (revolvers and pistols); and "Saturday night specials" (cheap handguns). The levels of possible control can be roughly ranked by degree of severity: market restrictions, registration, permissive licensing, restrictive licensing, prohibition.

Market restrictions seek to limit the number of manufacturers, importers, or retailers of firearms, in order to keep better track of them. As in all areas of economic regulation, a principal effect is to promote the interests of the favored outlets, at the cost of the consumer. They do not deny anyone access to guns, but push up the cost—both the money cost and the personal inconvenience—thereby presumably discouraging some marginal purchasers, but surely few criminals, lunatics, and terrorists.

"Registration" is widely discussed, but no one is really advocating it. To register is merely to enroll, as a birth is registered. Merely to enroll weapons would be costly, to little or no purpose. What goes by the label of registration is actually "permissive licensing" whereby anyone may obtain a firearm except certain designated classes—minors, convicted criminals, certified lunatics.

"Restrictive licensing," such as New York's Sullivan Law, permits only people with a legitimate purpose to own a firearm. Police, security guards, hunters, target shooters, and collectors are obliged to demonstrate their bona fides to the licensing authorities. Typically, personal or home defense is not ordinarily considered a legitimate purpose for gaining a license.

Prohibition is self-defined. If there were no or few firearms already in circulation, a simple ban would be sufficient. But with tens of millions out there, prohibition would require buying or collecting existing weapons or some more complicated policy intended to make them useless.

The preferred program of most interdictionists today contains four elements, most of which have been attempted one way or another in one jurisdiction or another: 1) continuing and tightening all existing laws, 2) permissive licensing for long guns, 3) restrictive licensing for all handguns, and 4) prohibition of cheap handguns, the so-called "Saturday night specials."

The third element is currently considered most important. Because the great majority of gun crimes are committed with handguns, control of them would presumably promote domestic tran-
quility. Concentration on handguns is also politically useful. Relatively few of them are used for recreation, so this would seem to
outflank the objection of sportsmen to restrictions.

Existing gun control

There are reportedly some 20,000 gun-control ordinances in the
various jurisdictions of the United States. Most are prohibitions
against discharging a weapon in urban areas or against children
carrying weapons, and are trivial, reasonable, and uncontroversial.
Most states and large cities have laws against carrying concealed
weapons, the rationale being that no person has a legitimate reason
to do so. In a few large cities and states, particularly in the
Northeast, a license is required to buy or possess a handgun, and
in a very few but growing number of Northeastern cities and states
a permit or license is required to possess any sort of firearm.

At first sight, licensing seems eminently reasonable. Dangerous
criminals should not have weapons, nor should the mentally disturbed. But the administrative "details" of licensing become incredibly difficult. It is fairly easy to check out an applicant for
a criminal record, which can be a legitimate reason for denying
a license. But many criminals, judging from the comparison between reported crime and conviction rates, are not convicted of
crimes, especially violent crimes, so the difficulty exists of whether
to deny people the privilege of purchasing weapons if they have
merely been arrested, but then set free or acquitted. Civil libertarians should be taken aback by this prospect. The question of
mental competence is even nastier to handle. Is someone to be
denied a firearm because he sought psychiatric help when his wife
died?

From the point of view of the organized gun owners, licensing
is intolerable because of the way that it has been enforced in the
past. One of the peculiarities of most local licensing is the lack of
reciprocity; unlike marriage licensing, what is recognized in one
jurisdiction is not in another. In the Eastern states it is nearly impossible to travel with a firearm without committing a felony (not,
of course, that this troubles many people). Also many police
agencies, particularly in the Northeastern states with restrictive
licensing, have engaged in some extremely annoying practices. Not

only do they load up questionnaires with many superfluous personal questions, but they also require character witnesses to provide intimate information. When the police wish to restrict privately owned firearms, they resort to all manner of subterfuge. In a test of the local licensing procedure some years ago, the Hudson Institute sent several female staff members to try to make the necessary application. The forms were not available and the people responsible for the forms were absent.

Even when the applications are submitted, the waiting period is often deliberately and inordinately long. I have a friend on Long Island who spent three years getting a pistol permit for target shooting. Influence is useful, but even it is not necessarily sufficient. A staff aide to a leading New York politician who has frequently been threatened applied for a permit to carry a handgun as his boss's bodyguard. Even a letter to the Police Commissioner of New York City on the gentleman's stationery was inadequate; a personal phone call had to be made—and that has not speeded up the process very much. The system is not much better with long guns and sympathetic police. Immediately after New Jersey required the licensing of rifles, I happened to be in a police station in a suburb of Philadelphia when a young man came in to get his license. The process had taken six weeks. He commented bitterly, "It's a good thing that I planned well in advance for my Maine hunting trip." (By the way, if he had lost or damaged his weapon during a hunting trip, the Federal Gun Control Act of 1968 would have made it extremely difficult for him to get a replacement out of state).

This sort of anecdotal evidence can be continued almost indefinitely. It suggests to the organized gun owners that licensing systems are a screen not against criminals but against honest citizens, and that licensing authorities are not to be trusted with any sort of discretionary power. It is certainly an inefficient system that dribbles out gun permits and refuses to recognize self-defense as a legitimate reason for owning a gun, while muggers operate with impunity, illicit pistols are exchanged openly on the streets, and penalties for gun-law violations—even by people with criminal records—are very rarely imposed.[2]

Among the most unproductive local gun-control measures are

---

[2] The Police Foundation is currently engaged in a study of the details of local handgun-law enforcement. Unfortunately, because its head is known as a vocal interdictionist, the credibility of its results will necessarily be somewhat compromised.

the moratoria permitting individuals to surrender their firearms without fear of prosecution. The police will then investigate such people to make sure they are not wanted by some other agency, and they are then entered in police files. (Obviously, if you really wish to dispose of an illegal weapon, you merely disassemble it and throw the parts from a bridge.) The number of weapons delivered under such programs is infinitesimal. An extension of such programs is the buying of weapons by police departments. This was attempted in Baltimore and obtained a substantial number of guns. But the total collected is a matter of simple economics: Large numbers of guns worth much less than the price offered will be obtained. Few valuable weapons will be turned in—and it is perhaps needless to note that there has been no perceptible effect on the crime rate.

The latest innovation in local gun control is a sort of interdiction through deterrence. Massachusetts recently passed a law mandating a minimum jail term of one year for possession of an unlicensed weapon. This reflects an interesting set of social values, because there are no such mandated sentences for burglary, armed robbery, rape, or even murder in Massachusetts. Every hunter who passes through the state on the way to Maine is risking a year in prison. What is happening is predictable: The law is not enforced.

The Massachusetts experience is both a caution to the interdictionists and a reassurance to the organized gun owners. If restrictive gun legislation is passed, the police will be hesitant to arrest ordinary citizens, prosecutors will be loathe to prosecute, juries will be unwilling to convict, and judges will devise ingenious loopholes.

Most of the existing interdiction laws have been in effect for many years, yet it is not possible to make any sort of estimate as to whether they do any good in reducing crime. Attempts have been made to correlate gun ownership and/or gun-control laws with gun-related crimes, but they are singularly unconvincing for the very simple reason that the data are so miserable—we have no firm estimate even of the number of guns available nationwide, much less in any given community, and it seems that the gun laws now on the books are rarely enforced. Some ingenious attempts to use regression analyses are easy to demolish.

In any event, no serious student of the subject would disagree that regional, racial, and cultural factors completely swamp the effects of gun-control laws. It is true that places with gun-control laws tend to have lower violent crime rates, but it happens that these are Northern communities with a long tradition of relative nonviolence, and the existence of gun-control laws on the statute books is merely evidence of the same relative peaceableness that is also reflected in the low rates of violent crime. The gun-toting states are also the gun-using states and the violent states, mostly in the South. And where Southerners or ex-Southerners are in the North, there are high violence rates regardless of laws. In recent years a few Northern states have imposed stricter licensing and use laws, with no perceptible effect on the crime rate. As with so many things, the laws on the books don't matter as much as their application. People in these states claim that any effects of their laws are spoiled by the spillover of easily available weapons from outside the state, which certainly sounds eminently reasonable. But if the economists are right, the gun-control laws should at least increase the cost or the inconvenience of getting guns, and therefore discourage their use. Retail handgun price differentials between open sources in the South and the black market in New York prove that the Sullivan law does pass the cost of a less efficient transportation system onto the consumer. But we have no idea of the effect of these increased costs upon the demand for guns. Presumably, those who want to buy guns for illicit purposes are not likely to be much affected by an extra $25 or $100 on the price tag.

The spillover effect has led many public officials in the gun controlling states to advocate essentially the extension of their systems of licensing to the entire nation. It is easy to sneer at this approach as the characteristic reflex of failed government programs—X didn't work, so let's try 10X. But the thesis seems plausible. If one could cut off the supply of guns from, say, South Carolina, they would be more difficult to obtain in, say, New York; that is, they would be more difficult to obtain *casually*. So the principal interest of gun controllers is in national legislation.

Federal firearms control

National firearms control legislation is a relative innovation. The first important law passed was the Federal Firearms Act of 1934, which was allegedly a response to the wave of gangsterism that swept the country in the depths of the Depression. Originally the Roosevelt Administration attempted to require national licensing of all weapons, but it was thwarted by a previously quiescent organization, the NRA. The watered-down version that passed

Congress effectively prohibited (through punitive taxes) the private possession of submachine guns, silencers, sawed-off rifles and shotguns, and other weapons presumably of use only to gangsters. While there appears to be no information whatever on the effectiveness of this law, it seems to have been reasonably successful. Submachine guns are rarely used in crimes. That success, however, may simply reflect the fact that very few such weapons were in circulation, and their rarity gives them too much value to be risked in crime. (We know, of course, that there certainly are tens of thousands of unregistered automatic weapons in the United States, largely war souvenirs. Vietnam veterans brought back thousands of M-16's and Kalchnikov assault rifles in their duffel bags. But most of these gun owners have no criminal intent or any intention of selling such weapons to criminals.) Sawed-off shotguns and rifles may be made illegal, but they are impossible to prohibit; all that is needed is a hacksaw and a few minutes' time.

The second federal effort was the National Firearms Act of 1938. Again, this took the form of a revenue measure, requiring the licensing of firearms manufacturers and dealers. The law requires the firearms trade to keep records of the purchasers of weapons, and prohibits sales to known criminals. But only a simple declaration on the part of the buyer is required. These records are useful for tracing firearms. If a weapon needs checking, it is merely necessary to go back to the original manufacturer or importer and trace it through the serial number to the dealer. Although these records are not yet centralized, *in effect there has been registration of every new weapon sold in the United States since 1938.* How many crimes have been solved through this means, or how it has otherwise been effective to law enforcement, is by no means clear. It would not be difficult to find out, but no one has really tried to. Presumably, such registration is of some help to the police—though it seems to have had no effect on the crime rate or the conviction rates.

The most important national measure is the Gun Control Act of 1968, the immediate result of the disturbances in the 1960's and the assassinations of Robert Kennedy and Martin Luther King, Jr. The Act raised the taxes on firearms dealers, added cannon to the list of weapons subject to punitive taxes, prohibited the importation of surplus military firearms and "Saturday night specials," and prohibited the interstate retailing of all firearms. The last provision is the most important. The purpose was to prevent individuals like Lee Harvey Oswald from ordering weapons by mail under phony names. But it also has more annoying side effects. For example, if you live in Kansas City, Kansas, and wish to give your brother, who lives in Kansas City, Missouri, a .22 caliber rifle for his birthday, it is illegal for you to do so. If you are traveling in another state and see a weapon you wish to buy, you must go through the rigamarole of having it sent to a dealer in your own state. So far as one can determine, the law has had no perceptible effect in slowing down the interstate sale of arms.

Enforcement of federal firearms laws was given to what is now the Bureau of Alcohol, Tobacco, and Firearms (BATF) of the Department of the Treasury. These are the famous "revenuers" whose most important function was stamping out moonshining. But for economic and social reasons, the illicit liquor trade is fading and the BATF needs other things to do than break up stills. Since 1968 they have rapidly expanded their funding and activity in firearms control and now devote about half their personnel and budget to that function. BATF seems to be a crude and unsophisticated police agency, more like the Bureau of Narcotics and Dangerous Drugs or the Border Patrol than the FBI or the Secret Service. For example, it says it has no idea how many of the 250,000 licensed Title II firearms (i.e., machine guns, cannon, etc.) are held by police or other public agencies and how many by private citizens; nor has it any information on how many unlicensed Title II firearms were used for criminal purposes. Some of its methods of operating have been irritating to legitimate gun owners.[3] The Gun Control Act of 1968 says that BATF shall have access to the premises of a gun dealer during normal business hours, which BATF interprets to mean that there must be a business premises separate from, for example, a private residence, and that there shall be ordinary posted business hours. BATF also took upon itself the enforcement of local zoning laws. This problem arises because many gun owners have taken advantage of simple and cheap licensing procedures to obtain dealer licenses so they

---

[3] The BATF also made the grave error of providing the organized gun owners with their first martyr. In Maryland, in 1971, a local pillar of the community —a boy scout leader, volunteer fireman, and gun collector— was in his bathtub when a group of armed men in beards and rough clothes—BATF agents— broke through the door. Understandably, he reached for a handy antique cap-and-ball pistol and was shot four times and left on the floor while his wife, still in her underwear, was dragged screaming from the apartment. What had happened was that a local boy reported a hand grenade in the apartment. There was, but it was only the shell of a hand grenade. A simple records check would have been adequate to establish the resident's bona fides, and if there was an interest in following up the matter, someone might have come and knocked on his door. He is now crippled for life.

can buy firearms wholesale. The majority of the nearly 150,000 dealers operate from their homes.

The organized gun owners see the activities of the BATF as a plot against them, not realizing that its habits and state of mind are not much different from other regulatory agencies. Once an activity is licensed, it becomes a privilege; a citizen is obliged meekly to petition the regulator for the boon and to modify his behavior to suit the needs of the bureaucracy. At the present time, the Department of the Treasury is asking for a large increase in the licensing fee of gun dealers in order to reduce the number of license holders—not for any public benefit, but because it will make the job of regulation easier for BATF.

"Saturday night specials"

The "Saturday night special" is the latest target of the interdictionist. It is identified as a cheap, unreliable, inaccurate, and easily concealed handgun, allegedly employed for large numbers of "street crimes." Because it is impossible to define a "Saturday night special" precisely, the NRA claims that the concept is fraudulent —but any definition in practice or law is necessarily arbitrary. Concentration on the "Saturday night special" has definite political advantages. Firearms enthusiasts scorn it as sleazy junk quite unsuited for serious work. Nevertheless, the organized gun owners are making an effective fight against banning the "Saturday night special." They were unable to block prohibition of its importation in 1968, but have resisted attempts to ban domestic manufacture and the assembly of imported parts.

It has been said against the "Saturday night special" that it is employed to commit a disproportionately large number of street crimes, and that getting rid of it would cut substantially into those crimes. A BATF study claimed that 65 per cent of "crime guns" used for street crimes in 16 major cities were cheap "Saturday night specials." Unfortunately, the text of the report reveals that these weapons were *not* those used in crimes but all those handguns collected by police, and anyone who knows anything about how reliable the police are in handling contraband knows that the chances of a quality firearm like a good Smith and Wesson finding its way into the reporting system are infinitesimal. Because the principal sanction against the illegal carrying of guns is on-the-spot seizure by the police, it stands to reason that individuals would pack the cheapest effective gun.

But even if "Saturday night specials" are used for some half of crimes with handguns, their elimination is hardly likely to reduce handgun crime by that much. People buy them because they are cheap. If people want a weapon, and if their demand for handguns is highly inelastic, this only means that whatever guns fell outside of whatever arbitrary definition of a "Saturday night special" that was adopted would sell more. Perhaps this is recognized by the proponents of banning the "Saturday night special," because they have written bills to give the Secretary of the Treasury sufficient discretion to ban all handguns.

Actually, neither side cares much about the "Saturday night special" one way or another. The interdictionists advocate its regulation as a stepping stone toward tight licensing of handguns or the licensing of all guns, while the organized gun owners fear it as a camel's nose in the tent. It is difficult to escape the conclusion that the "Saturday night special" is emphasized because it is cheap and is being sold to a particular class of people. The name is sufficient evidence—the reference is to "nigger-town Saturday night."

Crackpot schemes

Some other suggestions for gun control are simply silly. One idea is to have all weapons locked up in armories of various sorts, to be drawn by hunters or target shooters when they are needed. But most hunters and gun owners perform ordinary maintenance on their own weapons, so that a storage facility would have to provide room for that. The most overwhelming drawback against the idea is the enormous cost of providing such facilities—no one has calculated how much, and they would, of course, be targets for anyone who wished to obtain illicit firearms.

Another crackpot scheme is to record the ballistics of all weapons, rather like finger prints. This would not be enormously expensive, costing only a few million a year for new weapons only. But it is physically impossible. The pattern that the rifling of a barrel imprints on a bullet is not consistent and can be simply modified by changing the barrel. Ballistics is excellent at a one-to-one comparison between bullets, but cannot be employed for a general identification search.

Perhaps the most peculiar gun-control proposal to date was made by the Department of Justice in 1975. It recommended that, when the "violent crime rate has reached the critical level," possession of handguns outside the home or place of business be banned altogether. This assumes that those areas where law enforcement is least efficient could enforce a handgun ban, and that where the forces of public order are weakest citizens should be denied the means to defend themselves. In almost all high-crime areas the carrying—or at least the concealed carrying—of handguns is already illegal. (Hard data are necessarily spotty, but it now appears likely that the widespread private ownership of handguns for self-protection among crime-liable populations leads to some transfer to criminals, principally by theft. If this is true, it would not seem unreasonable to dry up the demand for guns by providing security to these people.)

The limits to interdiction

So the utility of interdiction has not and perhaps cannot be demonstrated. While the lack of evidence that a policy can be effective should make prudent men wary of promoting it, that does not mean the policy is necessarily without merit. Nevertheless, in the case of gun control it is possible to identify some weaknesses in the principles behind the policy.

To begin with, gun control as a general anti-crime strategy is flawed because most crimes, including many of the crimes most feared, are not committed with guns. Firearms are rarely employed for rape, home burglary, or street muggings. On the other hand, a good portion of the most heinous crime, murder, is not a serious source of social fear. The majority of murders are the result of passionate argument, and although personal tragedies, are not a social concern—ditto for crimes committed by criminals against one another. Furthermore, the worst crimes, involving the most dangerous and vicious criminals, will not be affected by gun control. No serious person believes that an interdiction program will be effective enough to keep guns out of the hands of organized crime, professional criminals, or well connected terrorists and assassins. And almost all the widely publicized mass murderers were eligible for licensed guns.

Gun-control advocates grant this, and emphasize the need to limit spontaneous murders among "family and friends" that are made possible by the availability of firearms. But the commonly used phrase "family and friends" is misleading. The FBI's Uniform Crime Reports classify relationships between murderers and victims as "relative killings," "lovers' quarrels," and "other arguments." The last can be among criminal associates, as can the others. Nor can we necessarily conclude that such murders are spontaneous. The legal distinction between premeditated and non-premeditated murder prompts killers (and their lawyers) to present murders as unplanned.

The very nature of interdiction suggests other weakness. It is a military term used to describe attempts, usually by aerial bombing, to impede, not halt, the flow of enemy supplies to the battlefield. Interdiction has been the principal strategy used in drug control; it works only when pressure is being applied at the street level at the same time that imports and production are being squeezed. If there are 140 million privately owned firearms in the United States and guns can last centuries with minimum maintenance, merely cutting off the supply will have little or no effect for generations, and if the supply is not cut off entirely (which no serious person believes it can be), an interdiction policy is hardly likely to have a major effect even over the very long run. To my knowledge, no interdiction advocate has given a plausible answer to the very simple question of how to get 140 million firearms out of the hands of the American people.

Even more to the point, is it cost-effective to try to deal with 140 million weapons when you are presumably concerned with a maximum at the outside of 350,000 weapons used in violent crimes? The odds of any gun being criminally used are roughly on the order of one in 400. For handguns the rate is considerably higher; for rifles and shotguns considerably lower. I estimate that in 1974, roughly one of every 4,000 handguns was employed in a homicide, compared with one in 30,000 shotguns and one in 40,000 rifles. There are probably more privately owned guns in America than there are privately owned cars, and with the obvious exception of murder, the rate of criminal use of firearms is almost certainly less than the rate of criminal use of automobiles. How are we to control the 400 guns to prevent the one being used for crime? And if we decide the only way is to reduce the 400, to what must we reduce it? It must be assumed that the one gun used for crime will be the 400th.

Moreover, interdiction is a countermeasure against crime. Countermeasures provoke counter-countermeasures: Substitution is the most obvious strategy. If guns cannot be bought legally, they can be obtained illegally—organized crime is ready to cater to any illicit demand. If cheap handguns are unobtainable, expensive handguns will be used. If snub-nosed pistols and revolvers are banned, long-barreled weapons will be cut down. If the 40-million-odd handguns disappear, sawed-off rifles and shotguns are excellent substitutes. If all domestic production is halted, we will fall back on our tradition of smuggling. If all manufactured weapons vanish, anyone with a lathe and a hacksaw can make a serviceable firearm. In the 1950's, city punks produced zip guns from automobile aerials. A shotgun is easily made from a piece of pipe, a block of wood, several rubber bands, and a nail.

A more promising variation is to go after the ammunition rather than the gun. Whereas firearms are easily manufactured and last indefinitely, modern ammunition requires sophisticated manufacturing facilities and has a shorter shelf life. Recently the interdictionists attempted to get the Consumer Product Safety Commission (CPSC) to prohibit the sale of handguns on the basis of their being inherently unsafe. This was certainly the most intelligent gun-control tactic attempted so far; yet it failed because Congress explicitly prohibited CPSC from meddling in firearm matters. But a strategy directed against ammunition is also flawed. Hundreds of thousands of Americans "hand load" ammunition at home from commercially purchased shells, powder, and bullets in order to obtain substantial cost savings and to get precisely the sort of load they desire. Shell cartridges last forever and there are untold billions in circulation. Lead and steel bullets can be made by anyone with a stove or a file. So it would be necessary to close off powder sales as well. Smokeless powder would be extremely difficult to make at home, but the old-style black powder that fired weapons for 500 years can be manufactured by any kid with a chemistry set. Besides, any ammunition cutoff would be preceded by a long debate and bitter fight—during which time everyone would stock up. Also, thefts from the military, National Guard, and police would continue to be a major source of ammunition.

The costs of interdiction

Against the unconvincing or unsupported benefits of any interdiction law, one must count the costs; practically no attention has been paid to them. BATF is now expending $50 million per annum on enforcement of federal laws. Local police, court, and corrections expenditures are buried in budgets. The only serious accounting of costs was prepared for the Violence Commission of 1968 and was downplayed in the final report. New York's Sullivan Law licensing cost about $75 per permit in 1968; double that for current levels of expenditure; assume that a maximum of half the households in the country will register their weapons; the cost is therefore in excess of $5 billion—or more than one third of the present cost of the entire criminal justice system, from police to prisons. Simple "registration" on the model of auto registration would cost proportionately less, but the numbers are always in the hundreds of millions of dollars.

The financial costs do not exhaust the potential expense of gun-control laws. It is too much to expect government to count as a cost the time and trouble to a citizen of registering a gun, but we might look at the price of diverting police and other law-enforcement officials from potentially more rewarding activities.

But the worst cost is that of widespread flouting of the law. Existing gun controls are now being disobeyed by millions. More severe restrictions will be widely disregarded by tens of millions, including a huge group of stalwart citizens whose loyalty and lawfulness we now take for granted. Needless to say, the organized gun owners cite the Prohibition experience.

The limits to deterrence

Organized gun owners, on the other side of the issue, advocate enforcing the existing gun-control laws. I suggest that they do not take this recommendation seriously; the existing laws are not enforceable. Another suggestion would appear to be more credible at first glance—to employ deterrence by having add-on sentences for the use of guns in crime. But such laws are on the books in several states and are not enforced, for a fairly obvious reason: Americans are not concerned with the use of a gun in a crime, but with the crime itself. The murder or armed robbery is objectionable, not the gun. *Illegal gun ownership is a victimless crime.*

Several practical problems make a deterrence strategy extremely difficult. There is trouble putting anyone away these days, and enforcement of existing gun laws or of new laws would add to the overload of an already jammed criminal-justice system. Perhaps most important of all, when the effective sentence for premeditated murder is 7 or 8 years in a penitentiary,[4] how much leeway is there to add to sentences for lesser crimes? Given the advantages of a firearm to a robber, a few more weeks or months of jail is hardly likely to deter him from using it.

---

[4] The assassin of George Lincoln Rockwell was released from prison last year.

The organized gun owners also claim that the widespread possession of firearms in itself deters crime; criminals are likely to be restrained by an armed citizenry. Perhaps—but consideration of criminal tactics suggests the idea is limited in application. Take burglars—by definition they prefer stealth, choosing unoccupied houses. If the owner is at home it is unlikely that he will awaken. A noise that arouses him will also alert the burglar. Should the householder awake, the burglar will probably hear him—especially if he is fumbling for a gun that is, as it should be, secured. In a confrontation, the burglar is alert, while the householder is sleepy-eyed. It is far more likely that a gun will be stolen than that it could be used against a burglar.

In store robberies, the robber also has the advantage. Guns are clearly not a deterrent, since the armed stores are those most often hit—because, to use Willie Sutton's phrase, "that's where the money is." Arming stores will certainly dissuade non-gun robberies, obliging robbers to escalate to firearms. Street robberies offer a similar tactical imbalance: The mugger has the initiative. It is not unknown for even police to be disarmed by criminals. It is true that areas with high gun ownership tend to have less crime against property, but this is probably largely the result of cultural factors. In any event the low quality of data on crime rates and gun ownership makes rigorous examination impossible.

International experience

Many peripheral arguments used in the gun control debate have little relevance to the issue, but must be addressed. Both sides will deploy the testimony of police chiefs on the desirability or futility of gun-control laws. Liberal interdictionists often cite the testimony of those gentlemen who have most illiberal views on most other law-enforcement matters. Most, but not all, big-city chiefs favor interdiction, while small-town chiefs generally oppose it, both nicely reflecting the views of their political superiors. But, for what it is worth, one can cite the Sheriff of Los Angeles County staunchly demanding stricter gun control laws and the Chief of Police of Los Angeles City saying that public order has broken down so far that only a fool would not arm himself. The gun owners gained strong reinforcement when the Superintendent of Scotland Yard recently pointed out that the number of guns available in America makes an interdiction strategy impossible.

A surprising amount of attention has been paid in the gun-control debate to international experience. In the world of gun control there seem to be only three foreign countries: Great Britain, Japan, and Switzerland. British gun control is taken by the interdictionists as the model of a desirable system. Guns are tightly regulated in the United Kingdom, violent crime is trivial by United States standards, and even the police are unarmed. But, as James Q. Wilson recently pointed out in this journal, the English situation is slowly eroding. The key to the low rates of personal violence in England is not in rigorous gun-control laws (which only date from 1920), but in the generally deferential and docile character of the populace. Perhaps it is significant that interdictionists point to "Great Britain" as their model; gun-control laws are even stricter in the other part of the United Kingdom, Northern Ireland.

Japan is an even more gun-free country. Not only does it restrict the ownership of weapons, but it has prohibited the ownership of handguns altogether, and the rates of violent crime are so low as to be hardly credible to Americans. To which the organized gun owners reply that Japanese-Americans have even lower rates of violence than Japanese in Japan.

The third international comparison is used by the organized gun owners. Switzerland has a militia system: 600,000 assault rifles with two magazines of ammo each are sitting at this moment in Swiss homes. Yet Switzerland's murder rate is 15 per cent of ours. To which the interdictionists respond that the Swiss have strict licensing of weapons, though this would seem to have very little to do with the thesis that the mere availability of weapons provokes murder and other crimes with guns.

It is not entirely clear what these very different countries—with very different histories, politica. systems, and national character—have to do with the United States. Those interdictionists who defend civil liberties would be appalled at the suggestion that even the English system of justice be applied to the United States, much less the Swiss civil law or the authoritarian Japanese judicial system—none of which provides the criminal with the rights and privileges he has in the United States.

But let me muddy these waters by introducing two other countries of great interest. Israel is mostly inhabited by a people who have no tradition whatever of using firearms in self-defense and whose compatriots in America are for the most part unarmed and have little taste for hunting. But the objective political conditions of Israel have required them to arm in self-defense and the country bristles with public and private weapons. In addition to the armed

forces, soldiers on pass or in casual transit in border areas carry
their small arms with them. There is a civil guard in the tens of
thousands. Every settlement has an arsenal, and individual Israelis
are armed. The government requires registration of all weapons,
but the system is very lenient on handguns (for Jews, of course;
considerably tighter for Arabs) and very tough on rifles and shotguns, which might be used for military purposes. Israeli gun-control
policy is directed toward internal security, not against crime. But
despite these restrictions, the Israelis have accumulated huge
numbers of privately owned military weapons, including auto-
matics, in various wars and raids. These are held "just in case"
they may be needed. But strangely, hunting is on the increase in
Israel, as are target shooting and gun collecting, and there is talk
of forming an Israeli national rifle association. Needless to say, the
crime rate in Israel is much lower than in the United States.

The special conditions of Israel are too obvious to note, but
Canada is closer to home, and it is odd that so little attention has
been paid it. Since the early 1920's, Canada has registered all
pistols on what is essentially the same basis as New York's Sullivan
Law. Rifles and shotguns are sold freely, even through mail order.
Canada's crime rate is much lower than the United States'. Here,
too, cultural factors seem to predominate. It is not usually observed
that without the South and Southerners (black and white) trans-
planted to the North, the United States would have crime rates
comparable to other industrial nations. In fact, there is no appreciable difference in murder rates for "Yankee" whites in states
and provinces on either side of the 49th parallel.

The best point of the interdictionists is that America is an exception to the international system of strict restrictive licensing. To
which the "gunnies" reply that our ancestors came here to free
themselves and us from the tyrannies of the Old World.

The Second Amendment

One reason the organized gun owners have bad public relations
is that they take an absolutist position regarding the Constitution,
relying on the Second Amendment of the Bill of Rights: "A well
regulated Militia, being necessary to the security of a free State,
the right of the people to keep and bear Arms, shall not be in-
fringed."

To the NRA and other organizations this is an unqualified right,
like the freedom of the press, not to be compromised on any

grounds. To the interdictionists, the amendment merely guarantees the right of the states to maintain what is now called the National Guard. Actually, the status and meaning of the Second Amendment can be the subject of debate among reasonable men. It is certainly true that the original intention of the Second Amendment was that there be an armed citizenry. A "militia" as understood in the 18th century was indeed the people armed with their own weapons, and the inclusion of the Second Amendment in the Bill of Rights was meant to protect the independence of the states and the people against the threat of the central government's employing the standard instrument of baroque tyranny, the standing army. However, there was no intention of the Founding Fathers to guarantee the use of firearms for recreation, nor for self-defense against criminals (although of the 38 states that have similar "right to bear arms" provisions in their constitutions, 18 specifically provide for personal defense, and one, New Mexico, for recreation).

The supreme arbiter of the Constitution has never ruled directly on the matter. The four cases that have come before the Supreme Court have been decided on narrow technical issues. Three 19th-century cases seem to support the view that states have the right to regulate firearms, and the one 20th-century case, which rose out of the Federal Firearms Act of 1934, was decided on the very narrow ground of whether a sawed-off shotgun was a weapon suitable for a well regulated militia.

Gun-owning lawyers claim that the doctrine of "incorporation" to the states of Bill-of-Rights restraints protects gun owners from state controls. This is reasonable on the face of it. However, the Supreme Court, as it was intended to do, applies the standards of an enlightened public opinion to the law. If the dominant elements in the country favor gun control, it is to be expected that the courts will rule accordingly.

The organized gun owners also see the armed citizenry as a last line of defense against insurrection. This idea has roots in the disturbances of the 1960's. While many Americans viewed the urban riots as the inevitable outcome of centuries of repression, many more merely saw police standing aside while looters cleaned out stores and homes, then envisioned the same happening to *their* stores and homes, and armed themselves. They did not understand that the looting was permitted only so long as it was contained to black neighborhoods; any attempted "breakout" would have roused the forces of public order from their lethargy. Indeed, the contingency plans have been prepared.

The gun owners claim that any registration lists would be used by a conqueror or tyrant to disarm the potential resistance. A minor debate has grown up over what the Nazis did in occupied Europe, especially in Norway. A source in the Norwegian Defense Ministry says the Nazis did not make use of registration lists but rather offered to shoot anyone who failed to turn in his weapons.

But there are examples of the use of registration lists to disarm the public. All handguns were called in following the assassination of the Governor of Bermuda a few years ago. And the late, un-lamented regime of the Greek colonels ordered the registration of all hunting weapons, followed by their confiscation, in order to disarm the royalists. Although the guns were later returned by the colonels, the present republican regime is continuing the control apparatus, presumably "just in case." When the IRA began its offensive in Ulster earlier in the decade, the Irish Republic used registration lists to confiscate all privately owned firearms in the South.

Phallic narcissism

A common assertion in the dispute is that gun owners are some-how mentally disturbed. The weapon is said to be a phallic symbol substituting for real masculinity, for "machismo." The historian Arthur Schlesinger, Jr., has written of "the psychotic suspicion that men doubtful of their own virility cling to the gun as a symbolic phallus and unconsciously fear gun control as the equivalent of castration." When queried about the source of this suspicion, he responded that he thought it was a "cliché." Such statements never cite sources because there are no sources. Every mention of the phallic-narcissist theory assumes it is well known, but there is no study or even credible psychoanalytical theory making the point. The germ of the idea derives from the 10th lecture in Sigmund Freud's *General Introduction to Psychoanalysis,* where he main-tains that guns can symbolize the penis in dreams—as can sticks, umbrellas, trees, knives, sabers, water faucets, pencils, nail files, hammers, snakes, reptiles, fishes, hats and cloaks, hands, feet, balloons, aeroplanes, and Zeppelins. In other words, any long object can represent a phallus in a dream. Gun owners laugh at the thesis, or are infuriated. One said to me, "Anybody who asso-ciates the discharge of a deadly weapon with ejaculation has a *real* sexual problem."

Studies of hunters reveal that they are not much interested in guns or in killing but in the package of skills and camaraderie involved in the hunt. No one has studied the psychology of gun owners or even hard-core gun nuts, nor are there studies of gun phobia. Fortunately, there is a reasonable amount of sociological data available, in the form of public opinion polls, which are believable because they give support to ordinary observation. Gun ownership is more prevalent among men, rural and small-town residents, Southerners, veterans, and whites. Except for the lowest income groups (who may not be willing to admit ownership), guns are fairly evenly distributed by income. Education, occupation, and politics make little difference. Protestants are more likely to be armed than other religious groups. When asked why they own guns, most people respond that they hunt or target shoot. But most handgun owners have them for self-defense, and long-gun owners admit to defense as a secondary purpose of their firearms.

Two generations of good data show that substantial majorities of the populace support gun registration, and this is cited fervently by individuals who prefer not to cite similar data favoring, e.g., maintaining prohibitions on marijuana, having courts get tougher with criminals, and restoring capital punishment. Of course, questions on "registration" are considerably misleading, because no one is advocating the mere registration of weapons, but rather licensing. Most people live in places where there is no licensing and have no idea of the difficulty and expense this would impose upon public authorities and gun owners if the standards of New York or Connecticut were applied nationwide. Gun owners and people with knowledge of existing gun-control laws are considerably less enthusiastic for registration. Supporters of interdiction are more likely to be young, single, prosperous, well-educated, liberal, New England non-gun owners with little knowledge of existing gun-control laws.

The real issues

The main point that emerges from any serious analysis is that the gun-control issue, under conditions that exist in the United States today, has practically nothing to do with crime control. I think that there are other issues at stake.

In 1967, armed robbers with pistols killed two policemen in London. There was a wide outcry to "bring back the noose." The Labour government, opposed to capital punishment, responded by extending strict licensing requirements to small-bore shotguns used in rural areas for shooting birds and rodents. In Canada in 1974, there were two incidents of boys running amok with rifles in schools. There was wide agitation to restore capital punishment. The Liberal government, opposed to capital punishment, proposed a far-reaching program to eliminate registered pistols in private ownership and to register all rifles and shotguns. It is possible that gun control is, at least in part, a strategy to divert the mob away from the issue of capital punishment.

Political factors are clearly important. The assassinations of the 1960's and 1970's rather unnerved the politicians. But the wide social unrest of the 1960's probably had more impact. In 1939, George Orwell noted, "When I was a kid you could walk into a bicycle shop or ironmonger's [hardware store] and buy any firearm you pleased, short of a field gun, and it did not occur to most people that the Russian revolution and the Irish civil war would bring this state of affairs to an end." There is a remarkable coincidence between gun control agitation and periods of social upheaval. English and Canadian gun laws date from the "red scare" following the First World War, and the original United States national controls are the product of the violent days of the New Deal.

But underlying the gun control struggle is a fundamental division in our nation. The intensity of passion on this issue suggests to me that we are experiencing a sort of low-grade war going on between two alternative views of what America is and ought to be. On the one side are those who take bourgeois Europe as a model of a civilized society: a society just, equitable, and democratic; but well ordered, with the lines of responsibility and authority clearly drawn, and with decisions made rationally and correctly by intelligent men for the entire nation. To such people, hunting is atavistic, personal violence is shameful, and uncontrolled gun ownership is a blot upon civilization.

On the other side is a group of people who do not tend to be especially articulate or literate, and whose world view is rarely expressed in print. Their model is that of the independent frontiersman who takes care of himself and his family with no interference from the state. They are "conservative" in the sense that they cling to America's unique pre-modern tradition—a non-feudal society with a sort of medieval liberty writ large for everyman. To these people, "sociological" is an epithet. Life is tough and competitive. Manhood means responsibility and caring for your own.

This hard-core group is probably very small, not more than a few million people, but it is a dangerous group to cross. From the point of view of a right-wing threat to internal security, these are perhaps the people who should be disarmed first, but in practice they will be the last. As they say, to a man, "I'll bury my guns in the wall first." They ask, because they do not understand the other side, "Why do these people want to disarm us?" They consider themselves no threat to anyone; they are not criminals, not revolutionaries. But slowly, as they become politicized, they find an analysis that fits the phenomenon they experience: Someone fears their having guns, someone is afraid of their defending their families, property, and liberty. Nasty things may happen if these people begin to feel that they are cornered.

It would be useful, therefore, if some of the mindless passion, on both sides, could be drained out of the gun-control issue. Gun control is no solution to the crime problem, to the assassination problem, to the terrorist problem. Reasonable licensing laws, reasonably applied, might be marginally useful in preventing some individuals, on some occasions, from doing violent harm to others and to themselves. But so long as the issue is kept at white heat, with everyone having some ground to suspect everyone else's ultimate intentions, the rule of reasonableness has little chance to assert itself.

Age,
crime,
and
punishment

BARBARA BOLAND & JAMES Q. WILSON

IT is well known that young males commit a disproportionately large share of many serious crimes. Some persons think the solution to this problem is for juvenile courts to "get tough"; others think that if the penalties given to adult offenders by the courts were made sufficiently swift, certain, or severe, juvenile offenders would be dissuaded from becoming adult criminals. Still others doubt that anything the courts can do will affect juvenile crime. Until recently, however, it was almost impossible to say anything about the relationship between what courts of any kind do and a given individual's criminal career, in large part because the juvenile and adult courts are separate institutions with separate (or non-existent) records. In the real world, people grow older one year at a time, but as far as the criminal justice system is concerned, each person has two entirely separate lives— one as a juvenile (from birth to age 17 or 18), another as an adult (over age 17 or 18). And until recently, almost all analyses of the likely effect of sentencing policies on crime were confined to adult criminals, as if juvenile offenders did not exist.

Recent studies have shed new light on the criminal career and suggest that the problem of juvenile crime is even more serious than supposed, that adult and juvenile courts are often working at cross-purposes, that changes in how we handle adult offenders may have less effect on crime than once believed, and that a rational policy toward crime (if one is possible) may have to be based on institutional procedures that permit prosecutors and courts to make decisions based on the entire criminal career and not simply on the juvenile or adult component of it.

Juvenile crime

The general pattern is quite familiar. Persons under the age of 18 constitute about one fifth of the total population, but they account for one quarter of all persons arrested and nearly one half of all those arrested for one of the seven "index" crimes. Many of these index crimes, though serious, are nonviolent—burglary, auto theft, and larceny. Unfortunately, however, the rate at which juveniles are arrested for violent crimes—homicide, rape, robbery, and assault—has been growing faster than the rate at which they are arrested for nonviolent crimes, and faster even than the rate at which adults are arrested for violent crimes. Assuming, as seems likely, that changes in arrest rates bear a reasonably close relationship to changes in actual crime rates, we can conclude that juvenile violence has been increasing faster than crime generally.

This increase cannot wholly, or even primarily, be explained by the increased numbers of young persons in the population. Paul A. Strasburg, of the Vera Institute of Justice, has calculated that the rate at which youths aged seven to 17 were arrested for violent crime nearly tripled between 1960 and 1975; for property crime, it nearly doubled in the same period. Stated another way, the average juvenile between the ages of seven and 17 was almost three times as likely to be arrested for (and presumably to commit) a violent crime in 1975 as he was in 1960. The biggest increases were in robbery and assault; the increases in juvenile homicides and rapes were substantially less.

Some scholars challenge the validity of arrest rates as a measure of who is committing crimes. They suggest that arrest figures may exaggerate the increase in juvenile crime, perhaps because the police today are arresting juveniles for conduct they once would have ignored. But consider a crime such as homicide, which the police would never ignore and for which the guilty party is arrested in the great majority of cases. Richard Block and Franklin E. Zimring found that in Chicago the rate at which young (aged 15 to 24) black males committed homicides nearly tripled from 1965 to 1970, from 108 crimes per 100,000 population to 298 per 100,000.

The homicide rate for adult blacks (aged 25 and over) and for whites scarcely changed at all. Perhaps most disturbing, the number of homicides committed by young males where the motive was robbery (rather than a personal quarrel) increased the fastest—from 11 per 100,000 population during 1965 to 90 per 100,000 in 1970. In addition, killings by youth gangs increased far faster than those by lone assailants.

Far from overstating the amount of juvenile crime, arrest data actually *under*state it by a considerable margin. Several scholars have interviewed samples of teenagers to find out how many crimes they committed for which they were not arrested. There are difficulties with these "self-report" studies, as there are with arrest data, but the general pattern is quite clear: Young persons break a lot of laws.

Martin Gold's 1972 study of a national sample of young persons suggests that for juveniles aged 13 through 16, the rate at which crimes are committed is vastly higher than one would suspect from using official FBI data. This group claimed to have committed 12 times as many robberies, three times as many burglaries, and 60 times as many assaults as one would have concluded knowing only how often youths in this age bracket are arrested. We can probably assume, of course, that many of these self-reported offenses were minor: An "assault," for example, could be nothing more than a schoolyard fight. But even if the self-reports are discounted substantially, the admitted rate of robbery and other serious crimes remains impressive.

More important is the fact that the chances of being arrested for a crime are *lower* for a juvenile than for an adult, and especially low for chronic juvenile offenders, who account for a large portion of all serious crime. James J. Collins Jr. and Marvin Wolfgang, of the University of Pennsylvania, followed a group of boys in Philadelphia from birth in 1945 until age 30, tabulated the number of arrests, if any, and asked them periodically about the number of crimes they had committed. Overall, the young men admitted to having committed offenses twice as often as they were arrested. But the chronic offenders—those who committed five or more crimes —committed offenses *four* times as often as they were arrested. These "chronics" were 15 per cent of the boys born in 1945. By the time they were 30, they had committed nearly three fourths of all the crimes of the cohort. Equally important, the chronic offenders had the highest self-reported offense rate during their younger years: Between the ages of 14 and 17, they were committing more than four index crimes per year; by the time they turned 22, they were committing only three per year.

The same pattern was found by Joan Petersilia and her colleagues at RAND. She interviewed at length 49 serious adult criminals in California, all then serving prison terms for armed robbery and all having served at least one prior prison term. These 49 men reported having committed over 10,500 major crimes in their careers, or about 20 crimes a year while on the street. But the rate at which they broke the law declined with age: As juveniles, they committed more than three serious crimes *per month* of freedom; as adults, they committed only one serious crime every other month while free. (We do not know precisely why the Philadelphia data differ from the California findings concerning the absolute volume of crime committed by chronic offenders, though some difference is to be expected from the different groups studied: The California prisoners were among the most serious criminals in the state, while the Philadelphia group included, even among the chronics, offenders with relatively short records.)

Although the rate at which men commit crimes decreases with age, the chances of being caught and punished *increases* with age. In Philadelphia, a juvenile between the ages of 14 and 17 had only three chances in 100 of being convicted for a serious crime he committed during that period. An adult (aged 21 and over), on the other hand, had five chances in 100 of being convicted. Most of this difference is apparently the result of the fact that for any given crime, juveniles are less likely to be arrested than adults. In California, the odds of being arrested for a felony (other than selling drugs) rose from three chances in 100 for juveniles to 20 chances in 100 for adults. A juvenile is twice as likely to get away with a robbery as an adult, and two-and-a-half times as likely to get away with a burglary. But the differences do not end with arrest. Once arrested, a juvenile is less likely to be incarcerated than an adult for any given offense. And as offenders get older, their sentences get longer—the average length of the first prison term was 2.4 years, of the fifth term, 5.7 years.

In sum, the best evidence now available suggests rather strongly that juveniles, especially chronic juvenile offenders, commit a far larger proportion of serious crimes than arrest reports had previously led us to believe, that the rate at which they commit these crimes declines as they get older, but that the chances of being arrested, convicted, and incarcerated are higher not when they are young, active offenders, but when they are older and less active.

How age affects criminal justice

That young males commit more crimes than older males is a well-established criminological fact, and there are any number of theories—most quite plausible, and few mutually exclusive—as to why this should be so. Youth is a period when energy is abundant, adult authority is suspect, and peer-group reputation important. Young people develop passions and seek independence, expressing both in music, dress, sex, and occasionally crime.

Why youthful criminals are less likely to be arrested than adult offenders is less clear. To some degree, it is because many youthful crimes are so petty that they are beneath the notice or concern of the police—though this cannot explain the low arrest rates among serious, chronic juvenile offenders. Part of the explanation may be found in how juveniles commit crimes: They are less likely than adults to plan their offenses, to work with regular confederates, or to have a settled *modus operandi,* and the police are thus less able to stake out the scene of a planned crime and less likely to get a tip from an accomplice-informer. But legal constraints on the police also reduce their chances for making an arrest of a juvenile. In most jurisdictions, the police cannot fingerprint or photograph a juvenile or place him in a line-up for witness or victim identification; thus a valid arrest is often made impossible.

Juveniles may also have an advantage over some adult criminals in intimidating victims and witnesses. Most juveniles live in the neighborhoods where they commit crimes, whereas older burglars and bank robbers often travel several miles to find a suitable target. The dollar value of juvenile crime may be limited, since the neighborhoods in which they live and steal are often poor, but the chance of being arrested is also reduced, since those able to identify offenders may, rightly or wrongly, fear reprisals.

Prosecutors and judges may be less likely to punish juvenile offenders for a variety of reasons. Some believe that young persons, even those found to have committed serious crimes, deserve special consideration or are still amenable to rehabilitation. Others may wish to avoid further criminalizing the young and sending them to custodial institutions (though whether such criminalization occurs is not easily proved from available data). But we think that an equally important reason may be that those deciding what to do about a juvenile have quite incomplete information about their prior records. This is partly because so many of their offenses will be unknown to the police. Without fingerprints and mug shots, the police often cannot link an arrested juvenile to other previously unsolved crimes, and sometimes cannot get arrest data on a juvenile from other jurisdictions, or even from other precincts within their own jurisdiction.

Establishing a prior record is vital for the prosecutor and court. Though we hear much about using penalties to deter crime or incapacitate criminals, in fact the penalties actually reflect, more than anything, a retributive, social-debt theory of justice. By retributive, we mean that the penalty is based on, and roughly proportional to, the gravity of the offense. By social debt we mean that, after taking into account the gravity of the offense, the penalty is increased roughly in proportion to the criminal's prior record. If prior arrest information is missing or seriously incomplete (as it often will be for juveniles in big cities), even a tough-minded judge will often give, unintentionally, a lenient sentence to a repeat offender.

There are, no doubt, soft-hearted juvenile court judges, but it would be wrong to blame them and their tenderness for all the dispositions juvenile courts make. All judges, the tough and the tender, take into account prior record: If it is unknown, either because of low arrest rates or poor information systems, the apparent result will be leniency.

These two factors—differences in the value attached by judges to retribution and differences in the information providing the basis from which a social debt can be calculated—help explain why so few convicted juveniles are punished. The Strasburg study examined the disposition of 191 juveniles in three New York area counties (Westchester, Manhattan, and Mercer) who had committed a violent crime. Though all were guilty of violent offenses, only 17 (9 percent) were placed in any kind of facility. Even among the chronic offenders—those who had already committed five or more offenses—only 20.4 percent were placed in a facility. Most of the remainder were given probation or a suspended sentence, or released.

The Office of Children's Services of the New York State Division of Criminal Justice Services examined the court records of 3,892 persons under the age of 16 who had been arrested for robbery in New York City between July 1, 1973 and June 30, 1974. Only 118 were placed under close supervision or in a facility at the end of the process. Juveniles fall out of the family court system for many reasons and at many points, as Table I (on the next page) illustrates.

In short, only 3 percent of the juveniles arrested for robbery and only 7 percent of the juveniles actually tried in family court received any form of custodial care, whether with a relative, in a

TABLE I. *Disposition of Robbery Cases in Family Court**

Total number of juveniles charged with robbery	3,892
Number dismissed ("adjusted") at intake	2,165
Number referred to family court	1,727
Pending	134
Dismissed	1,010
Given probation	218
Placed in a foster home or juvenile home	113
Committed to a correctional facility	5
Other	128
"Not found"	119
Total referred to family court	1,727

*Source: Office of Children's Services of the New York State Division of Criminal Justice Services.

juvenile home or training school, or in an adult prison. It is hard to imagine anyone being satisfied with what now appears to be the case: Either far too many juveniles are arrested or far too few are punished.

Furthermore, dispositions are not quickly obtained. Fewer than one third of the New York City juvenile arrests studied by the Office of Children's Services were disposed of within three months, half took six months or longer, and 12 percent took over a year. These long delays were as likely to occur for juveniles charged with the most serious offenses as for those charged with relatively minor ones. Over a third of the murder cases, nearly a third of the rape cases, and over a quarter of the robbery cases took 10 months or more to resolve. Again, it is hard to see how society could benefit from such delays: If juveniles are detained awaiting disposition, they may unnecessarily spend months awaiting a decision that exonerates them; if juveniles are not detained and are guilty, then additional victims probably suffer.

Some changes are now underway in New York's juvenile-justice system. There is now a "designated felony" procedure that could make it easier for prosecutors and judges to distinguish procedurally between serious offenders and the large number of juveniles arrested for minor or "status" offenses. Juveniles arrested for certain offenses may now be fingerprinted. A centralized information system for juvenile records is being planned. It is too soon to tell what differences these changes will make.

Defects of the two-track approach

The specialized treatment given juveniles and the existence of a separate set of institutions (courts, probation workers, record systems) were based on the belief that special procedures for handling juveniles would serve their special needs, facilitate rehabilitation, and prevent premature criminalization. Of late, serious doubt has been cast on the accuracy of these predictions, especially concerning the possibility of rehabilitation, but it is not our purpose here to take sides in that argument. Suppose for the moment that there are good reasons for having special procedures for juvenile offenders. A two-track justice system—one for juveniles, one for adults—has serious costs in terms of both fairness and crime control that must be taken into account in evaluating its real or imagined benefits.

The two-track system means that the heaviest punishment will fall on offenders at or near the end of their criminal careers. Furthermore, there are good reasons to believe—though as yet there is no conclusive evidence—that some adults are punished too severely and some too leniently because of erroneous or incomplete information about their prior criminal records.

The first problem—imprisoning offenders when their criminal activity is low and falling rather than high and rising—is no problem at all, of course, if one believes simply in the social-debt rationale of punishment. Such offenders have, so to speak, used up society's hospitality: Forgiven as first offenders, forgiven as second offenders, they finally exhaust our patience and are sent away after the third, fifth or 10th offense. But a pure social-debt theory allows no room for crime-control objectives. This might be a manageable problem if every offender were equally likely to commit another offense in a given time period; we would then merely decide how many crimes we are willing to tolerate in exchange for indulging our preference for forgiving first or second offenders. But when crime commission declines with age, and does so without our being aware of it, our social-debt policy can have unexpectedly high costs in terms of crimes not prevented.

To make this clear, consider the data in Table II, from a sample of 3,688 adult offenders arrested for serious crimes in the District of Columbia in 1973. For each offender, we calculated the number of prior convictions and the annual rate at which offenders in each group commit crimes. (This calculation is based on past arrests, and thus overstates the true number of offenses, especially for older persons.) As Table II shows, younger offenders (aged 18 to 25) com-

mit many more felonies per year, on the average, than most criminals aged 30 and over, even after controlling for the number of
prior convictions. For example, among those with no prior convictions, younger offenders commit nearly 10 times as many felonies
per year as older ones.

TABLE II. *Annual Offense Rates by Prior-Conviction Record and Age**

	NUMBER OF OFFENDERS	ANNUAL OFFENSE RATES	
		INDEX CRIMES	ALL FELONIES
No previous felony convictions			
Ages 18-25	847	3.5	4.5
Ages 25-30	295	1.0	1.5
Ages 30 and over	561	.5	.5
One previous felony conviction			
Ages 18-25	434	4.0	5.5
Ages 25-30	242	2.0	2.5
Ages 30 and over	337	1.0	1.0
Two previous felony convictions			
Ages 18-25	139	8.0	10.5
Ages 25-30	88	2.5	4.0
Ages 30 and over	210	1.5	2.0
Three previous felony convictions			
Ages 18-25	32	8.0	15.0
Ages 25-30	56	5.0	7.0
Ages 30 and over	147	2.0	2.5
Four previous felony convictions			
Ages 18-25	19	8.0	17.5
Ages 25-30	43	6.0	8.5
Ages 30 and over	219	3.5	5.0
Total all ages	3,688	2.7	3.5

*Source: Federal Bureau of Investigation's computerized history file. The sample includes
all adults arrested in the District of Columbia in 1973 for an index crime (except larceny)
with at least one prior arrest. Offenders with one prior arrest represent 70 percent of all
adults arrested. An average annual offense rate was computed for each offender by divid-
ing all arrests (index or felony) before 1973 by the number of years between age 18 and
age just prior to the 1973 sampling arrest, less time in prison. Each arrest was presumed
to represent five crimes.

It is also true that, for any age group, the more prior convictions
an offender has, the more felonies he commits per year. But overall, the differences among criminals in their annual felony-commis-
sion rate by number of prior convictions is obscured by the decline in offense rates with age. Another problem is that the vast
majority of these offenders have no, or only one, prior conviction.

To see what that means in terms of crime control, suppose that
you are a judge who decides to send to prison every offender with
three or more prior convictions and to put on probation every
offender with two or fewer prior convictions. By incapacitating
those three-time losers, you will be imprisoning offenders who ac-

count for only about 20 percent of all crimes committed and assuring the freedom of those who commit the other 80 percent.

The conflict between the social-debt rationale of punishment and a rationale of crime-reduction-by-prison is clear. Unfortunately, for those who prefer the latter, its cost would be very great. Table II also shows that the number of offenders in the young (18-25) age group is quite large (1,471) while the number of offenders with three or more convictions, regardless of age, is much smaller (516). If we imprisoned young offenders, or more accurately (and fairly), offenders with the highest annual felony rates (who, as it happens, are mostly young), rather than those who have long records (who, as it happens, are mostly older), we might have to triple the size of the imprisoned population in the District.

The choice may not be quite that bleak, however. Suppose it were possible, before sentencing, to give prosecutors and judges accurate information about the prior record of convicted offenders. Then courts well might—in fact, almost surely would—send many more high-rate offenders to prison and perhaps far fewer low-rate offenders. Not everybody aged 18 has a high felony rate, and not everybody over 30 has a low rate. But the system is not well organized now to supply that information, in part because it is a two-track system.

In our District of Columbia study, we were unable to find out the juvenile records of our sample of arrested adults. There was no place where the two sets of records were merged. We think that is the case in many places. As a result, a judge sentencing an 18-year old convicted of robbery may not know whether he is sentencing a chronic or a first-time offender. As a result, he may sentence some too severely (in the mistaken view that they are troublemakers) and sentence others too leniently (in the mistaken view that they are novices). Even worse, some juvenile records may be made selectively available to the judge by a police officer, prosecutor, or probation officer who may know the offender and may have some special reason for putting in either a good word or a bad word for the accused, with possibly prejudicial effects.

At issue is not only some objective standard of fairness, but perceived fairness as well. Suppose you are a 35-year-old man serving a long sentence in prison. Suppose that you are one of those—who may be in the majority—for whom crime has lost its appeal; as a crook, you are almost burned out. For years, as an active criminal, you were allowed to stay on the street; now, about to retire, you find yourself facing the prospect of five or 10 years in prison. If nobody has explained the social-debt rationale of punishment to you, you might well feel unjustly treated. *Your* rationale for punishment may not be social debt but "current badness": People who are wicked *now* should be punished, people not wicked now should not be, or at least not severely.

Suppose instead that you are a 17-year-old who despises "straight" society, lives by his wits, and steals a lot. You notice that you are arrested from time to time, but not much happens even though you are an active criminal. Your record has not yet caught up with you. You do not feel unjustly treated; rather, you feel contemptuous of the system that claims to enforce the law. You feel you can beat that system and that, accordingly, it deserves no respect.

We think these are quite common reactions and help explain two disturbing facts—adult prisoners who feel the criminal-justice system is unjust and young offenders who find it irrelevant.

What to do

There is no easy answer to this problem. No one wants to throw all youthful, first- or second-time offenders in prison. Many of them have committed only trivial offenses, and in any event their numbers are vast. Wolfgang and his colleagues at the University of Pennsylvania estimated that a third of the boys who grew up in Philadelphia during the 1950's were arrested for some crime by age 18. To be sure, the vast majority of *serious* crimes were committed by a much smaller fraction of these boys—probably by the approximately 6 percent who are chronic offenders—but even 6 percent of all the boys under the age of 18 is a large number. In between the casual and the chronic offender are the recidivists arrested two, three, or four times in their careers. In an average year, these recidivists may commit only one or two offenses. This means that for every recidivist imprisoned for one year, only one or two crimes are prevented. To prevent a large number of crimes in this way would require a very large number of prison spaces.

We think two things can be done. One is to insure that some significant punishment befalls all offenders, especially young ones, who commit a serious crime. This could involve victim restitution, community service, or a weekend or two in jail, or more severe punishment in some cases. The object would be to heighten the credibility of the justice system and of the legal and moral code it is charged with enforcing, by establishing early in the prospective criminal career that some penalty (not "probation" or "case continued without a finding") follows any detected serious offense. Though studies of the process of deterrence have methodological problems and have not, so far as we know, been applied to sanctions other than imprisonment or fines, we are persuaded that sanctions do affect crime rates, other things being equal. (The other things that need to be equal are, of course, not unimportant: The presence or absence of job opportunities for young persons will affect, we think, the extent to which crime appears attractive and sanctions appear costly. We omit a consideration of such matters here only because we wish to draw attention to problems in the criminal justice system that should be solved under any labor market conditions.)

And second, we believe the criminal justice system should be organized so that there are not two independent tracks, based on age, for serious repeat offenders. There are probably good reasons for retaining a two-track approach for most offenders caught by the law. After all, the great majority of young men arrested in the Wolfgang study were never arrested again. Furthermore, juvenile courts handle many matters besides serious crime. But there should be a mechanism for identifying, compiling information about, and swiftly adjudicating serious repeat offenders, regardless of age.

In the RAND study, two kinds of career criminals were identified by the interviewers: intensive and intermittent offenders. The former committed more crimes per month on the street, committed more serious crimes, were more likely to think of themselves as criminals, and were somewhat more successful in avoiding arrest than the latter. To identify intensive offenders as early as possible, it will be necessary to photograph and fingerprint juveniles who commit serious crimes, especially violent ones; to allow them to be identified in line-ups; and to compile such information in some centralized manner, so that any criminal-justice agency (but not persons outside it) would have a complete record on intensive or violent offenders available at all points in the process, and in all nearby jurisdictions.

The current system is so badly organized that we have been unable to find anywhere the data that would permit us to measure more precisely the extent to which the two-track process produces inequities. Complete criminal (or arrest) records for offenders—juvenile and adult records combined—are needed, so that one can see whether an offender just entering the adult system (say, at age 19) is more or less likely to be punished than an offender with the same prior record who commits the same offense but is still in the juvenile system. We know enough to believe that some substantial inequities exist and that there may be many offenders who, as young adults (say, aged 18 to 22), get a "free ride" because their juvenile record is ignored. One fact should suggest that there is a "hole" in our system. In California, the average age of persons committed to a juvenile facility is 16; the average age of persons committed to an adult institution is 28. It is hard to believe that offenders between the ages of 17 and 27 do not tend to commit crimes deserving of punishment.

Perhaps there should be a two-track system, but with the tracks defined by the nature of the criminal career rather than by the age of the offender. One system would deal, largely by non-custodial means, with routine, intermittent offenders or those with short criminal records. The other would deal with serious, intensive offenders and would almost invariably employ close supervision or custody. The recent creation of major offense bureaus in various prosecutorial offices allows scarce court resources to focus sharply on serious repeat offenders, who are dealt with quickly and often severely. But these bureaus are limited to adult offenders; few comparable organizations exist for the serious young offender.

We make no recommendation concerning the exact dispositions such offenders should receive if convicted. The key would be close supervision, both to protect society and to make credible the costs of crime, as well as to insure justice. Such supervision can occur in many settings, and need not always or usually occur in conventional prisons. For some, this supervision can occur in the community, provided it is close; for others, separation from the community may be necessary.

All of these matters deserve to be debated. What needs to be understood in that debate is the extent to which the present two-track criminal justice system defeats the purposes of those who wish to protect society, as well as those who wish to protect the accused, and produces a distribution of penalties that is ultimately indefensible. Information about offenders is inadequate for purposes of calculating social debt, penalties are wrongly apportioned for purposes of crime reduction, and the system encourages young serious offenders to scoff, and older retired offenders to despair.

Fact, fancy, and organized crime

PETER REUTER & JONATHAN B. RUBINSTEIN

ORGANIZED crime has become firmly established on the agenda of national problems requiring Federal action for control. Since it was made a national issue by the Kefauver Committee's successful exploitation of the latent power of the emerging television networks, every President has been required to make a statement deploring the growth of organized crime and outlining a program to eliminate it. As an issue, its rise to prominence has not been slowed by the failure of any legislative or administrative body to define adequately what it is, or who is involved. Lacking such a definition, it is obviously difficult to determine whether the phenomenon is indeed growing or declining—but this has not prevented the continued, and successful, demand for increased authority and resources to fight it. The evident lack of any strategy behind these demands also has had a curiously small impact. Countless government reports are filled with "estimates" of the degree to which organized crime controls lucrative illegal activities, whose monopoly profits are then used to take over legitimate industries.

These analytic failures have had serious consequences. Unlike most bureaucratic puffery which results in inflated and wasteful expenditures, the threats posed by organized crime have been repeatedly cited to justify a significant expansion of police powers. Legal wire-tapping entered domestic life in order more effectively to pursue organized crime figures; for the same reason, immunity and conspiracy statutes have been greatly expanded, as have been the powers of investigative grand juries. Citing the threats of organized crime to legitimate business, governments are creating numerous licensing and regulatory agencies which permit public officials to meddle with all kinds of business activity. This threat has also been used to justify the creation of state-owned liquor and gambling monopolies, monopolies which would otherwise be deplored.

Each agency has its own definition, ranging from Frank Hogan's famous assertion that "organized crime is two or more persons engaged in criminal activity" to the FBI's careful (we have traced it through seven versions) and meaningless potpourri: "the sum aggregate of the more lucrative, continuing types of racketeering activities, involving some sort of formalized structure and generally requiring graft or corruption to conduct its operations without interference."

But despite strong differences about specifics, there is a consensus about the general characteristics of this social threat. Organized crime is viewed as a set of stable, hierarchically organized gangs which, through violence or its credible threat, have acquired monopoly control of certain major illegal markets. This control has produced enormous profits, which have been used to bribe public officials, thus further protecting the monopolies. These funds have also been invested in acquiring legitimate businesses in which the racketeers continue to use extortion and threats to minimize competition.

The "lifeline" theory

Ever since the Kefauver Committee asserted that racketeers from the larger cities had established a national monopoly in horse racing information, which gave them control over illegal gambling in America, gambling has been viewed as the fountainhead of criminal capital. Every government probe has come to the same conclusion. The absence of any concrete information did not stop the New York State Investigations Commission from concluding that the infamous meeting in November 1957 in Apalachin, New York, was a conclave of gambling operators. Joe Valachi, a long-time government informant and former numbers controller from Harlem, provided the McClellan Committee with "living proof" that the Mafia or La Cosa

Nostra, as he styled it, existed and that gambling and loansharking were the sources of its capital. This notion was raised to the level of orthodoxy by President Johnson's Crime Commission (1967), which estimated that organized crime netted a minimum of $7 billion annually from illegal gambling, a one-third profit from one of the lower estimates of total wagering made available to the Commission. In 1969 President Nixon asserted, using a confused metaphor, that "gambling income is the lifeline of organized crime. If we can cut it or constrict it, we will be striking close to the heart." Congress responded in 1970 by passing the Organized Crime Control Act, which enshrined this notion in statute. In 1974 the Department of Justice summarized government views of illegal gambling:

> It is the unanimous conclusion of the President, the Congress, and law enforcement officials that illegal organized gambling is the largest single source of revenue for organized crime. . . . [It] provides the initial investment for narcotic trafficking, hijacking operations, prostitution rings, and loan-shark schemes.

These are not just beliefs espoused by agencies and politicians in hearings or when they are asking for money. There is recent evidence that the police themselves hold these beliefs as firmly as Presidents and District Attorneys. In a 1976 survey of police departments throughout the country, some 73 percent of police agreed with the statement that "profits from illegal gambling operations are the main source of income for organized crime."

The belief in the dominance of stable criminal gangs and the centrality of gambling in their continuing control of the rackets extends beyond law enforcement circles. In addition to being continually restated in the daily press, which is almost completely dependent upon police sources for its crime news, these views are also espoused in academic circles—both by those friendly to the views of the police and those who argue for the revocation of prohibitory legislation on gambling, prostitution, and other so-called victimless crimes. Donald Cressey, who is the most respectable academic advocate of the official position, argued in his book *Theft of A Nation* that "the suppliers of illicit goods and services . . . accumulate vast wealth which can be used to attain even wider monopolies on illicit activities, and on legal businesses as well." Concerning illegal gambling, Cressey asserted, "the profits are huge enough to make understandable the fact that any given member of La Cosa Nostra is more likely to be a millionaire than not." Herbert Packer, whose book *The Limits of the Criminal Sanction* is the most widely quoted argument for decriminalization, made essentially the same argument as Cressey:

> In gross financial terms, the laws against gambling represent our most generous subsidy to organized crime. . . . By responding to the economic logic of the situation, criminal organizations have arisen that take enormous monopoly profits out of the gambling business. These monopoly profits then become available to sustain the activities of the criminal organization on a wide variety of fronts, including the penetration of legitimate and quasi-legitimate economic markets.

Many such statements from respectable academics could be found, but regardless of the policies they are arguing for, they all share one important feature: They all make assertions about the nature and organization of gambling based entirely on statements from the police, or on legislative reports that are themselves based on police statements.

A systematic analysis

For the last several years, we have been studying the structure and operation of the gambling rackets in metropolitan New York since 1965. With the cooperation of the New York City Police Department and several other departments in the area, as well as local prosecutors' offices, we have examined the financial records of many gambling operations raided by the police. We have been able to obtain numerous official records on gambling operations and investigations, some wiretap transcripts, and also information drawn from lengthy interviews with police gambling specialists and informants active in bookmaking and numbers. Enforcement agencies certainly have more access to all of these sources, but we are certain that no agency has ever analyzed the gambling rackets by the systematic use of such data.

The traditional account asserts that illegal gambling is dominated by a cartel of criminal gangs who are involved in many kinds of racketeering. Their domination of the gambling rackets is maintained by the use of violence and coercion when necessary, but whenever possible they use their corrupt relationships with local officials to make certain that independent operators do not enter the market. "Organized crime brooks no opposition," is a common refrain. The dominant position of these gangs allows them to extract monopoly profits from illegal gambling, further enhanced by the predatory pursuit of gambling debts by mob-licensed loansharks.

The evidence we have obtained makes it clear that illegal gambling in New York does not conform to this grim account. Our research has focused on bookmaking and numbers, the two most important forms of illegal gambling. These are, in fact, two quite distinct trades. They have entirely different operating routines and problems. Their customers come from different segments of society, in terms of both income and ethnic background. Given these fundamental differences, it is not surprising that there are few people who are active in both businesses. Most law and enforcement policy merges these forms of gambling in ways that can be quite misleading, although there is little more relationship between bookmaking and numbers than there is between the insurance industry and supermarkets.

The evidence we have obtained for each of these activities is sharply in conflict with the standard account. We begin with bookmaking. Most bookmakers are just that—bookmakers; perhaps not the worthiest of citizens but certainly not the terrifying mobsters of whom we are told. They have few involvements in other criminal activities such as narcotics trafficking or fencing. It is true that they are involved with loansharks—but as customers themselves, rather than as providers of customers. There is very little use of violence in bookmaking, either for purposes of restricting competition or for disciplining of recalcitrant customers. Given the extent to which bookmakers extend short-term credit, often totaling thousands of dollars for an individual customer, this is quite a striking finding indeed.

Moreover, there are many autonomous bookmaking organizations, all of them small when compared to legitimate firms. The very largest operations, of which there are perhaps five in New York, handle about $500,000 per week in bets. Such an operation would employ only five clerks to record the bets, although it will have as many as 50 commission agents, known as "sheetwriters," directing bets to the central office. The sheetwriters, however, are not employees and may work for several operations simultaneously. There are at least 50 bookmaking operations in the city and near suburbs, each with a high degree of autonomy. Many of them are quite ephemeral. Narrow profit margins, the high cost of credit, difficulty in collecting debts, law enforcement, and poor entrepreneurial judgment (which is characteristic of many bookmakers), all combine to ensure that most of even the largest operations have relatively short lifetimes, although most individual bookmakers stay in the business for many years.

There is nothing to suggest that bookmakers are part of a coercive cartel, and considerable evidence suggests that they are involved in a risky and highly competitive business. We are certain that there is no territoriality or control of entry into the business. Occasional efforts to raise prices have met with no success. Corruption is a minor and episodic feature now, in contrast to the situation prevailing in the 1950's at the time of the Kefauver Committee. While there is a lot of betting between New York and New Jersey, there is nothing to suggest a nationwide "layoff" network; New York bookmakers do not have regular dealings with bettors or bookmakers in other parts of the country.

The "sheetwriter"

Perhaps the easiest way to understand the extent and origins of the fluid nature of this market is through an examination of the role of the sheetwriter. In many instances it is he who brings the customer to the bookmaker in the first place. Because the bets are all telephone transactions, the bettor has very little information about the bookmaker. Generally, all he has is a telephone number, which is changed from time to time. This anonymity provides important security for the bookmaker and his clerks. The bookmaker rarely meets his customers, since it is the sheetwriter who moves money between them.

However, in the current system, it is also true that the customers are generally the "property" of the sheetwriter and not the bookmaker. The sheetwriter has the right, in most operations and under most circumstances, to move his customers to another bookmaker. It is a trivial matter for him to do so; all he has to do is to tell his customers to call a different number. Sheetwriters, in fact, frequently make these shifts and it is extremely rare for a bookmaker to take any effective retaliation against this, even though the shifts always cost him money.

Most shifting of customers by a sheetwriter occurs when he owes a bookmaker money. The sheetwriter is an uninvested partner with the bookmaker, sharing profits and losses. When the sheetwriter's customers, as a group, win money from the bookmaker, half of those winnings are charged against the sheetwriter, although he does not have to provide any of the money paid to the customers. Instead, this "red figure," as it is called, is charged against his future earnings, which are generally 50 percent of what his customers lose. When the red figure becomes large, the sheetwriter has little prospect of receiving any income from the bookmaker for some weeks. His response to this is to shift his customers to another book-maker with whom he has no red figure.

We want to stress that this is not a hypothetical problem. The reports of informants indicate that sheetwriters frequently move when they have accumulated large red figures. Financial records show that these debts owed to the bookmaker do get to be substantial; a red figure of $20,000 is not extraordinary. Indeed, the problem has become acute enough that at least two bookmakers, faced by the loss of sheetwriters with substantial red figures, have offered those particular sheetwriters alternative financial arrangements which give the writer a share of the total wagering, eliminating the red figure.

We take this arrangement to be a critical indicator of the lack of control by any individual or group in the bookmaking market in New York. No cartel would permit agents, such as sheetwriters, to play off one member against another. Indeed, while we find little centralization in the numbers business, it is apparently sufficiently organized so that the controller, who is in that business the equivalent of the sheetwriter, cannot shift to another operation while he owes money to his original employer.

Another important indication of the lack of coordinated control in bookmaking is the failure of occasional efforts to raise prices. The standard terms for betting football and basketball in New York involve the player risking $11 to win $10, giving an expected return to the bookmaker of 4.4 percent of the money wagered.[1] At the beginning of each football season some bookmakers try to persuade their colleagues to change the terms to six-for-five. These repeated efforts have never been successful, and the 11-for-10 bet has persisted for over a decade, despite a high rate of bankruptcy among bookmakers.

Though the expected margin of profit is 4.4 percent, records indicate that the actual gross margin is less than 1 percent. There are at least four factors that explain this difference. First, the bookmaker must share profits with his sheetwriters, who probably account for 80 percent of his wagering in a large operation. Second, sheetwriters may leave the operation when it has suffered losses through their accounts. Third, baseball betting, which may total nearly as much as football betting, works on a more complicated formula yielding an expected margin of less than 3 percent even

---

[1] If a bookmaker takes in one bet on each side of a game, he receives $22 in wagers. The winner receives $21, his $11 wager plus $10 in winnings, leaving the bookmaker with a $1 profit.

before the sheetwriters take their share. Finally, cheating by clerks is an endemic problem that has serious consequences for the bookmakers; clerks also make accounting errors which are not caught by any auditing system, and customers only point out errors that favor the bookmaker at their expense.

The fact that cheating is widely acknowledged but goes largely unpunished is frankly puzzling. It is certainly incompatible with the image of bookmakers who rule their organization and customers by the credible threat of violence. In a recent court case in New York, it emerged during pre-trial hearings that the tapes from a wiretap showed the clerks cheating their employer of some hundreds of thousands of dollars. In order to ensure that the tapes were played and that the bookmaker found out how much money was involved, he pleaded not guilty and ended up with a long jail sentence; if he had taken a guilty plea he would have received a shorter sentence, but he would not have found out how much money the clerks had taken. At this writing, some three years later, the clerks are still alive, although they have spent much of the intervening time in jail. And this particular bookmaker has a long-standing reputation for command of violence.

A fragmented market

Why, in fact, is this market fragmented? There are, after all, none of the usual legal constraints against cartel formation or domination through violence. We believe that a key element is the anonymity of everyone in the business. Because all the betting is done by telephone, often through call-back services that prevent the bettor from even knowing the telephone number of the operation, there is no way of determining who is in the business or the scale of their activities. Even bookmakers who command substantial resources and have ready access to "muscle," and there are several in the New York market, cannot prevent others from entering the business or control the terms on which they do business. Because members would have an interest in preserving anonymity, a bookmakers' cartel would have little more success in controlling the market.

This anonymity also bears directly on the role of police corruption. It is undoubtedly true that, at the time of the Kefauver Committee, bookmakers in New York systematically purchased police protection. At that time, though, they were primarily in the business of providing locations to which bettors came mainly to make horse bets; it was only at those "wire rooms" or "pool rooms" that bettors could hear the results of the races more or less immediately. With the shift to sports betting, an activity whose result can be heard over the radio, telephone betting became the dominant mode. The same difficulty facing a potential monopolist also hinders the corrupt policeman. It is not easy for him to locate the bookmakers for the purpose of extortion, and the bookmakers can move easily after the first contact. Bookmakers are still eager to purchase some degree of police cooperation, mainly for insurance (perhaps prior warning of a raid or a wiretap) we believe, but the relationships have become few and strained compared to the situation in earlier decades.

We have also been struck by the lack of violence and coercion in bookmaking.[2] It is a business that depends in large part on short-term credit. The bookmaker usually settles with his customers on a weekly basis in most operations, and the customer may owe several thousand dollars by that time. Yet it is extremely rare for violence to be used to collect that money. In case of any problem in making payment, the bookmaker will generally agree to some partial settlement and limit the betting of the customer until he pays the remainder of his debt. We have only isolated instances of a bookmaker turning over a delinquent account to a loanshark for collection. The bookmaker knows that an angry or frightened customer is the greatest threat to his anonymity and security.

Loansharks are, nonetheless, important to the functioning of the bookmaking business. They frequently provide capital for a bookmaker who is in financial difficulty. Since bookmakers are generally poor businessmen who often assume large risks voluntarily (being bettors themselves at heart), it is not uncommon for them to seek large sums at short notice, $50,000 being the upper end of the range of these loans. Only loansharks can supply this money. We are not in a position to estimate the importance of bookmakers' borrowing to the loansharking industry, but it is probable that a substantial segment of the industry specializes in lending to bookmakers.

The connection between loansharking and bookmaking is critical. Loansharking may well be an activity dominated by organized crime. Certainly a loanshark who does not have a well-established reputation for violence is at considerable risk from customers who believe they can defraud him; at a minimum he will have high collection costs. If it turns out that bookmakers account for a large

---

[2] To some extent this may be explained by the media's fascination with violence and organized crime. Many bookmaking customers, like citizens generally, probably have been convinced by the nightly news of the dire consequences of failing to meet their bookmaker's demands.

share of loanshark borrowing, then it will mean that bookmaking is important to organized crime for reasons almost exactly contrary to the conventional descriptions offered of the relationship between gambling and organized crime. In fact, this suggests that effective enforcement against bookmakers, by creating additional financial difficulties, may increase the market for loansharks—scarcely a blow to organized crime.

Whatever the exact relationship between bookmakers and loansharks, the police appear to be unaware of its importance. We have found no official documents that discuss the financing of gambling. Although the police have assembled much information about many bookmakers, they have almost no information about their financing. It is always assumed in law enforcement circles that gambling is the source of capital for other illegal activities, but our evidence indicates that the flow is in the other direction.

The numbers business

The numbers business, which we have also studied in great detail, is only slightly closer to the standard account of organized crime monopoly. Important racketeers, persons who are known to be involved in a variety of criminal activities and who have recognized status in the underworld, have a more direct involvement in the numbers than in bookmaking, though they are rarely involved in an operating capacity. Corruption also appears to be a more central feature, because numbers is still largely an activity involving face-to-face transactions between the customer and the seller. There is also some evidence of violence in the disciplining of sales agents, when, for example, they are believed to be withholding bets from the numbers "bank."

But it is important not to exaggerate these features. Although efforts have been made from time to time to establish a cartel, they have never had enduring success. Territoriality is slight. There are numbers banks with outlets in all five boroughs of the city. It is common for a single neighborhood to have several outlets, each representing a different bank. A "controller"—the intermediary between the collectors (who have almost exclusive access to customers) and the numbers "bank"—may set up his own bank with little threat of retaliation. Controllers also frequently maintain substantial interest-free balances, which the numbers banker has difficulty collecting.

There is considerably more stability among numbers banks than among bookmaking operations. It is not uncommon to find banks operating for a decade or longer. They also appear to generate larger and more stable flows of profits than bookmaking, but again far less than alleged in official accounts. We have found in New York that a bank doing $10 million annually is relatively large. On the average, we find that a gross profit of 4 percent can be reasonably expected—but from this must be deducted the not insignificant operating expenses of the bank.

It is useful to compare the retailing of illegal numbers in New York with the legal state monopolies that provide the same service in New Jersey and five other states. The state monopolies offer their retailers less than 10 percent of the wagers they process; the illegal operators in New York pay 25 percent and sometimes as much as 30 percent to their retailers. Similarly, the agents, who act in the same capacity as controllers, receive only about 2 percent from the state monopolies, while in New York controllers receive 10 percent of the wagers. The state monopolies restrict the number of outlets, so as to guarantee their agents total wagers of about $5,000 per week. In the illegal system retailers frequently handle less than $500 per week. The inability of numbers banks to coordinate their actions and to prevent new banks from entering or new retailers from starting with some existing bank has led to quite modest returns for the bank when compared to the cartel possibilities.

We can supplement our data in New York with some observations on numbers in the Miami area. Here we also find a large number of small banks, each bidding for the services of retailers and controllers. The recent influx of Cubans has led to a transfer in the control of banks, formerly operating in predominantly black areas but owned by native whites, and an increase in the share of wagering going to the retailers. In this case, despite the presence in Miami of major Italian and Jewish racketeers with a considerable interest in loansharking and narcotics, the Cuban numbers operators appear to have no relationship with any outside groups, though some individuals among them are involved in the drug business. Again, there is general agreement among our informants that violence and coercion are an unimportant part of the business.

The reforms instituted by the New York City Police Department after the Knapp Commission appear to have had a salutary effect on corruption. While there is undoubtedly still some corruption of street police, the systematic "pads," often involving quite senior commanders, appear to have come to an end. This reduction in corruption, which was accomplished essentially by ending aggressive enforcement, has been accompanied by a loosening up of the market. More controllers are branching out on their own, no longer needing to worry about arranging for protection from police they could not reach. The payout rate is rising, suggesting a growth in competition and a reduction in profits. Thus the reduction of enforcement has had three salutary effects. It has reduced police corruption, which may, in the long run, reduce overall access to police by criminals; it has reduced the concentration of the market (although it was not great prior to the reforms); and it has brought a better price to the customer.

It is possible that our findings apply only to New York. It is, after all, a larger metropolitan market than any other and anonymity is easier to achieve in such a large market than in areas served by only a few bookmakers. At this stage we have too little information about other areas, apart from Miami, to make any definite statement, but all of the scattered indications are consistent with our findings in New York. We note also that the Department of Justice estimated in 1974 that organized crime controlled over 50 percent of illegal gambling in New York City, compared to 42 percent in the nation as a whole. We are making our case in a city where the belief in organized crime's control of gambling is well-established.

Convenient errors

If our description of illegal gambling in New York is accurate and holds for other cities, then we must explain the rise and continued hold of the conventional wisdom, which has become the central doctrine of official statements on organized crime. It is not an easy task, for we have used no information or techniques that are not available to police agencies. Indeed, our analytic approach has been almost embarrassingly direct.

Two factors explain existing beliefs. First, these beliefs are bureaucratically and politically convenient. Second, they are produced by agencies whose unusually striking deficiencies in analytic work have gone largely unnoticed because, for a variety of reasons, they have been able to protect themselves from outside scrutiny with great success.

The police are the dominant source of information about organized crime in America. They collect almost all of the available information, do their own analyses of it, and then make the results available to the public and other government agencies. Government statements and legislative committee reports are mainly restatements of police views. The Kefauver Committee undertook no independent investigation or analysis; instead it provided a forum for information and theories advanced by local police and former FBI agents. The McClellan Committee did not "find" Joe Valachi; he was made available to them by the FBI on orders from the Attorney General. Valachi had been a Federal informant for several years and his testimony was the product of extensive debriefing by FBI agents. The President's Crime Commission acknowledged the lack of independent expertise available to it on organized crime.

The difficulty the government has had in obtaining accurate information on the reserves of energy-producing companies in the wake of the 1973 oil boycott should serve as a sober reminder of how difficult it is to collect accurate information even from legitimate organizations operating in a highly regulated environment. The challenges are immeasurably greater in collecting information about people who are consciously involved in illegal activities. The disproportionately large collections of photographs, tag numbers, and automobile descriptions in police files seem like an example of wasted effort until one realizes how difficult it is even to identify participants accurately. People on the street are frequently known only by nicknames, and often they use more than one.

One of our informants recalls being shown a surveillance photo of a suspect in a gambling investigation and being given a nickname for this person by an undercover police officer. On the basis of the nickname, which was familiar to him, he identified the suspect as a particular gambler. The police followed this person for several days before they learned that he was indeed a gambler, but not the person they thought they were following. This is not an uncommon occurrence nor is it evidence of the incompetence of the police. Rather it should be taken as a timely reminder of the difficulties involved in determining who is doing what, when the only sources of information are distant surveillances by people who are not familiar with the environment in which they are operating, informants who have no incentive to be accurate but considerable reason to provide information, and overheard snatches of converation whose meanings are frequently unclear.

The police are the only agents who have the authority and the necessary skills to collect information in this hostile environment. It would be very difficult for researchers to do a study of illegal gambling without the information obtained from police sources. In many areas of the city, people are simply unwilling to discuss these matters with strangers; other areas are too dangerous to wander about in. For some time we have been assembling information on the payout rate paid by numbers banks in various parts of New York and can attest to the difficulty of obtaining accurate, verified accounts from informants even about so simple a matter. It is striking, however, that not only are the police the exclusive suppliers of information to the entire system, they are also sovereign in interpreting what they collect.

Prosecutors are essentially passive receivers of the product of police work. They have almost no independent capacity to collect their own intelligence or to evaluate what the police are providing them. In New York City, under District Attorney Frank Hogan, any information about illegal gambling received by his office was turned over to the police department for investigation. He ordered his own investigators to do no work connected with gambling or narcotics. This division of labor between the police and their lawyers exists at Federal, state, and local levels of the criminal justice system. In responding to criticism over his unwillingness to allow the FBI to work under the direction of Justice Department lawyers in Strike Forces, J. Edgar Hoover wrote to an inquiring Congressman, ". . . as a general rule, we have found it to be true that greater efficiency results and responsibilities become more clearly established when investigators investigate and prosecutors prosecute."

This rigid separation of functions between police and prosecutors is another example of the deference for jurisdictional boundaries that is observable throughout the criminal justice system and is one of its defining characteristics. It is as common among units of the same organization as it is among separate agencies. One reason, certainly, why police and prosecutors are convinced that territoriality is an important characteristic of racketeering is because it is a defining feature of their own work routines. (As a matter of fact, we have found little evidence of territorial control of illegal gambling except where it is protected by the police.) In the processing of routine criminal cases, which is the majority of work done by prosecutors' offices, this separation is understandable; but in the area of organized crime enforcement it means that the police control the prosecutors' access to the critical facts on which decisions are made.

The police monopoly over information places prosecutors at a severe disadvantage in any discussion about tactics and strategy. The police are reluctant to tell a prosecutor very much about their sources of information, because he will most likely soon leave to enter private practice where he may defend people they are arresting. This is symptomatic of more fundamental differences between the police and their lawyers. The district attorney is elected, (that is, is inherently political) while the police view themselves as civil servants. Prosecutors are much better educated than police and have marketable skills, which means that most of them do enter private life after only a few years in public service, while the police, lacking alternative opportunities, tend to remain in their department for many years. The police, uniquely wedded to government, consider themselves to be more trustworthy. It is also true that the senior police involved in rackets investigations have many years of experience while most of the attorneys they deal with are relatively junior. The potential for conflict between them is substantial, and it is largely avoided by prosecutors deferring to the police in deciding how investigations are conducted.

Police sovereignty

The police are not unique in resisting the intrusion of experts into their domain, but they have been more successful than any other bureaucracy. The military resisted civilian control over their operations until the technological base, from which military doctrine and strategy were derived, compelled the inclusion of people in the decision-making process who possessed skills not available within the traditional military system. Although many military bureaucrats have resisted the expansion of civilian influences, the educational requirements of the officer corps have steadily expanded to the point where officers are routinely sent to traditional universities for higher degrees.

Using arguments about the need to keep from the underworld knowledge of informants and law-enforcement techniques, the police have managed to keep out everyone else as well. And since the police are ruled by a rigid civil service system which guarantees that anyone who has climbed high on the promotion ladder will be reluctant to express dissenting views, each force is insulated against external influences. They resist civilian intrusions even into nonsensitive areas such as communications control. This insularity makes it very difficult to have a discussion about organized crime, since the police can rightly claim they have most of the facts. Most discussions end up sounding like debates about UFO's: Those who have seen one are arrayed on one side, and all of those who have never seen one but dispute the validity or interpretation of the observations are on the other.

We know of no other area of public life where the sovereignty of the bureaucracy remains so strong. Like the rest of us, the police generalize from their own experience. Their policies are based primarily on the unanalyzed sum of their experiences, since even the few specialists who have been introduced to the policy-making process in recent years are rarely permitted to participate in the information-collection process, but are again passive recipients of what the street police bring them. A recent national survey of Rackets Bureaus by the Cornell Institute on Organized Crime found only one state or local agency among those sampled in their survey which was making an effort to analyze the information collected by its agents. The Institute concluded, "Put simply, intelligence activity continues essentially as a collection effort." Even the FBI, whose agents are much better educated than are the local police, has resisted outside specialists and sought to train its own people.

Gambling again provides an excellent example of the analytical limitations of the law enforcement community, even at the highest levels of government. The Department of Justice recognized that, since it frequently asserted that organized crime derived its major income from illegal gambling, it would be useful to have some notion of the absolute and relative scale of illegal gambling revenues. The President's Crime Commission, while endorsing the centrality of gambling, noted that estimates of revenues ranged from $7 to $50 billion per annum, and that, in 1967, there were no claims that any systematic study had been done.

In 1974, in testimony before the National Gambling Commission, the Justice Department announced that it had developed an estimate of the total volume of illegal gambling, which in 1973 lay somewhere between $29 and $39 billion. Details of the method used for producing the estimate were not made available for another two years, and even then in a most sketchy form. We cannot go through all the steps of the estimating procedure, but shall describe two of the critical steps which suggest that the estimate was exceptionally crude and designed to guarantee a very large result.

The basic data source was the wagering discovered by the Federal Strike Forces against Organized Crime during their program of intensive gambling enforcement in 1971 and 1972, known as Operation Anvil. It was assumed that all Strike Forces detected the same proportion of illegal wagering as had the Strike Force in New York City. No justification was offered for that assumption, which was unnecessary although it simplified the procedure. In fact, there is reason to believe that the Department had a higher sampling fraction in New York than elsewhere. Operation Anvil had been built around wiretapping, and the rate of surveillances per capita was higher in New York than in other major cities. This fact is by no means conclusive, but it is the only available piece of evidence on the reasonableness of the assumption—and it suggests an upward bias.

More important, the estimate required some measure of the percentage of illegal gambling sampled in each city by Operation Anvil. For this the Department used figures from a survey of gambling in New York carried out by the Oliver Quayle Company in 1973. The technique may be described as either ingenious or arcane.

The Quayle survey

Quayle found that, among *sports bettors who bet on horses,* betting with bookies accounted for 37.8 percent of their total off-track horse betting. The Department of Justice assumed that this was true for all persons who bet on horses, so that bookies accounted for 37.8 percent of all off-track horse betting. Since they had available the figures from the New York Off-Track Betting Corporation on its "handle," they could use this assumption to estimate total horse betting with bookies. They compared this figure with the total volume of illegal horse betting they had detected in New York through Anvil, and assumed that the same sampling fraction held for sports and numbers as well, in New York and all other cities.

There are many problems with this procedure. Most important is that it is unreasonable to assume that all horse bettors use bookmakers to the same extent as horse bettors who are also sports bettors. Because sports betting is the main service of bookmakers, any sports bettor who wants to bet on horses with a bookie is likely to have already established contact with one. Hence we might more reasonably expect that pure horse bettors—and the Quayle figures indicate that they account for most of the horse betting at the track and with OTB—do a smaller percentage of their off-track betting with bookies than does the subgroup on which Quayle obtained data.

It is interesting to compare the Department's estimate of illegal sports betting in New York with that obtained by Quayle—$2.8 billion for the Department, against $428 million for Quayle. It is difficult to see why the Department should have placed such faith in the survey's peculiar 37.8 percent figure, given the discrepancies in the two estimates of total betting.

In truth, we suspect that the real failing of the estimate was that no one really cared precisely how it was developed, but only that it produce a large number.[3] The assumption that the details of the calculations would not be subjected to any scrutiny led to a cavalier use of the available data. Also, the estimate had no possible consequences; it was produced for rhetorical purposes and has served those purposes very well.

This crude and cavalier treatment of information by police agencies is commonplace. It is important only because these agencies use the resulting estimates to provide legislatures with justification for passing statutes which define their tasks. In the case of organized crime, the tasks have been defined so that the police can continue their traditional fight against illegal gambling under a slightly altered rationale—the threat of national rather than local "mobs."

After years of concerted enforcement against gamblers, without any demonstrable results, it is difficult for the civil servants who direct the government's organized crime control program to conceal the fact that they have no policies. A recent study by the General Accounting Office of the Justice Department's Organized Crime Strike Forces elicited this appraisal, "The Chief, Organized Crime and Racketeering Section, does not believe that it is possible to establish overall program goals and then measure progress toward these goals." It is not often that a bureaucrat will admit this, although we suspect that more of them ought to. But the unembarrassed confession of the fact that there are no policies is symptomatic of the extent to which these particular civil servants have been free from outside scrutiny.

The Strike Forces, much heralded at the beginning of the decade as a bold new approach to the endless war on organized crime, are currently out of favor because of objections by U.S. Attorneys who feared the undermining of their autonomy. Despite all the ballyhoo about innovation, the Strike Forces mainly pursued gamblers. Between 1968 and 1974, 72 percent of Federal wiretaps were for gambling. Moreover, their attention was focused primarily on the traditional organized crime groups, the 24 crime families who are the national Mafia. In testimony before the National Gambling Commission, the Justice Department stressed its success in using antigambling statutes against senior members of the Mafia. Our interviews with former Strike Force prosecutors indicate that they

---

[3] Indeed, when the Department of Justice first announced the results of Operation Anvil, the range of estimates was far higher, $35-60 billion. No explanation for the later downward revision has ever been given.

felt a strong obligation to focus their efforts on Italian organized crime groups. Most of the press releases issued by the Strike Forces were about the activities of the Mafia.

It is not our intention to deny the existence of a Mafia. In this respect we differ from earlier critics who have had a splendid time demonstrating the inconsistencies of witnesses before legislative committees. Gordon Hawkins, some ten years ago in *The Public Interest*, showed how hard the McClellan and Kefauver Committees had to strain in using the evidence of their witnesses to show the existence of a national criminal conspiracy. Our own research does show that there is a Mafia, and probably more than one, although it is far less distinctive than is normally alleged and its relation to other criminal groups is not clearly defined.

The Mafia

All of our informants who are participants in gambling and other criminal activities firmly believe in the existence of the Mafia, although there are differences in terminology; alas, all have read *The Valachi Papers* or seen *The Godfather*. They also tend to agree about who is a member and who is not, and even about the relative seniority of various members. Though none of them claims to be a member, and no one alleges any of them is, several grew up in families associated with members and have friends they believe to be members. Curiously, none of them claims any knowledge of how members are "made" or what initiation actually involves.

It is clear that membership confers certain rights and obligations, but there is disagreement over whether it is better to be a member or a close associate; associates appear to enjoy most of the rights and incur none of the obligations. Which family one joins has relevance apparently only in case of disputes. There are no restrictions on whom one does business with, but if there is a dispute each member is required to align with his own family.

There may be a "national" Mafia Commission. If there is, it has very limited powers, perhaps only to mediate high-level disputes. The apparent intercity territoriality, whereby racketeers from Detroit are not active in Boston, is almost certainly a consequence of the local nature of the racketeer's power base, rather than any rulings by committees. A more important national function of the Mafia is that it provides a network of contacts in other cities that allows members, who tend to have a range of criminal interests, opportunities for intercity deals.

The Mafia is clearly only a part of the world of stable, hier-
archical criminal organizations. There are others, more or less eth-
nically homogenous (since most racketeering involves core groups
of persons who have known each other from childhood), which also
exert power in local criminal activities, have an established reputation for the use of violence, and use corrupt relations with public
officials to further their goals, as much as does the Mafia. Narcotics
trafficking is certainly one activity in which the Mafia exercises control over only a small part of the market. It is not merely a bow
to civil rights to suggest that public officials who focus so much
attention on one particular ethnic group, Italians, have an obligation
to provide some credible evidence that it is truly distinctive. Americans of other ethnic origins should be given their opportunities
to enter the pantheon of popular folk heroes, chased by equal opportunity prosecutors.

In fact, there is one distinctive service provided by the Italian
Mafia that is apparently not offered by any other group: arbitration.
In an economy without conventional written contracts, there is
obviously room for frequent disagreements. These are hard to resolve. Many bookmakers make payments to "wise guys" to ensure
that when disputes arise they have effective representation. Sometimes these disputes are resolved on their merits. Sometimes they are
resolved simply on the basis of the rank of the two arbitrators. It
is critical to note that this arbitration is used in only a very restricted set of circumstances.

It is *not* used to collect from delinquent customers who are unable to meet their commitments as a result of either poor planning
or over-indulgence. A legitimate bettor may be cut off and mildly
harassed, but he will receive no threats from "enforcers." If, however, the dispute is with a "wise guy" or a "connected" person, then
the arbitration system will be invoked. In particular, if it appears
that there is a deliberate intention by such persons to defraud the
bookmaker, then the Mafia man will be called in. This risk insurance is important to the bookmaker because people in the criminal
trades are among the largest bettors and are the customers most
likely to flout him. There is general, though only moderately well-
informed agreement among the police and our informants that no
such system of arbitrating disputes exists in other organized crime
groups.

These differences between Mafia groups and other racketeers do
not seem sufficiently threatening to justify the special attention they
receive either in the press or from law enforcement. But in order

to make that judgment we must consider the very basis for our concern with organized crime. Though it is true that organized crime control is a matter to which a relatively small percentage of police resources is devoted, certainly less than 5 percent, it has been used to justify giving the police and prosecutors special powers.

Two justifications

Two themes stand out in the legislative justification for organized crime laws. One is the predatory nature of racketeers. The FBI, in particular, is tireless in its reiteration of the notion that gambling is not a victimless crime, because homicides are committed as a result of gambling debts. Others point to the demoralizing nature of heroin addiction, or the inducement that "fences" provide for thieves. In fact, of course, all these are the function of supplying the service rather than of the existence of stable gangs. (By the same reasoning a case can be made for outlawing marriage since it is the principal "cause" of murder.) In other words, if bookies use violence against delinquent customers, it is unlikely that the destruction of the Mafia will reduce that violence. In fact, there is even a credible argument that, by reducing the customer's belief in the power of his bookie to enforce his demands, the actual use of violence will increase. One consequence of the proliferation of numbers banks in New York appears to be an increase in the robberies of runners and collectors by bandits who are not worried about retaliation from organized forces.

Corruption is the other evil that has been used to justify special legislation and action against organized crime. "The inevitable companion of flourishing gambling activity ... is the bribery and corruption of local law enforcement officials," asserted the preamble to the Organized Crime Control Act of 1970. It is certainly true that the historical record shows many cases of widespread and systematic corruption of major city police departments by gamblers. There are, however, two problems with this statement.

First, it assumes that the relation between illegal gambling and corruption is inevitable. Our own research indicates that it is a function of the particular environment and technology rather than inherent in gambling itself. Telephone bookmaking, during a period of low gambling enforcement, flourishes with little direct contact with the police.

Second, it is not clear that gambling does account for a particularly high percentage of police corruption, measured either in money or social impact. For example, narcotics dealing in recent years appears to have generated much larger bribery cases than gambling, as well as instances of police involvement in murder and other aspects of trafficking. And the Chicago Strike Force recently obtained numerous convictions against several networks of precinct police for "shaking down" tavern owners who had no connection with gambling.

More important, though, is the curious obsession with police gambling corruption without any accompanying concern to discover its causes or to find ways to eliminate it. Gambling enforcement has always posed dilemmas for police administrators. Most gambling statutes are designed to enforce prohibition, not to control the activity or to restrict it to certain places. But the police have never been given the political support necessary to achieve this dubious goal. Few judges have ever been willing to give convicted gamblers jail sentences and the fines imposed have usually been trivial. In New York City, gambling cases had so little importance to the District Attorneys' offices that they were used to train new assistants in the routines of criminal procedure.

In New York, at least, the police seem to be resolving this dilemma for themselves. They have abolished aggressive enforcement and replaced it with a policy which is directed at keeping gambling discreet and enforcement honest. There is a relatively small, specialized gambling unit which responds to complaints, maintains an intelligence-gathering apparatus, and conducts raids on those it considers major operators. This policy does not appear to have increased organized crime presence in illegal gambling, although gambling is somewhat more visible on the streets than it once was.

The costs of misinformation

The most important consequence of all the misinformation and inflammatory rhetoric put out by official agencies is to make impossible any realistic discussion about gambling policy. The possibility of legalizing bookmaking, as has been smoothly and successfully done in England, is never discussed. It seems to be assumed that because bookmakers are all working for organized crime, legalization would simply give the Mafia more money. When a state does lurch toward legalization of gambling, as New Jersey has just done with casinos in Atlantic City, there is obsessive concern about who will make money from it. Instead of asking whether there are any Italians who have ever played golf with executives of casino licensees, it would be more sensible to concern ourselves with the fact that one applicant hired as its lobbyists close relatives of the two legislators who chair the committees responsible for drafting casino regulations. Organized crime, in this instance, is clearly a diversion from a far more fundamental and familiar political problem.

It is clear that the campaign against organized crime has been based on myths and misinterpretations. These have led to bad law and even worse policy. We will continue to feel the consequences for a long time to come, as the government monopolies many states have created to regulate gambling become enveloped in the webs of special interests and collusion that afflict government regulation of the liquor and horse-racing industries. The remedies are easy to suggest, if difficult to implement. But a first step certainly is to develop a body of critical expertise based on access to more than statistical reports and conversations with law enforcement officials.

On
subway graffiti
in
New York

NATHAN GLAZER

F OR six years or so one of the
more astonishing sights of New York has been the graffiti on the
subway trains. The word "graffiti" scarcely suggests, to those who
have not seen them, the enormous graphics which decorate the
sides of subway cars—murals which march relentlessly over doors
and windows, and which may incorporate successive cars to provide the graffiti maker a larger surface on which to paint. They
are multicolored, and very difficult to read, but they all, in one way
or another, simply represent names. There are no "messages"—no
words aside from names, or rather simplified and reduced names,
nicknames, or indeed professional names, often with a number attached. (One will not see an Alfredo, Norman, or Patrick, but Taki
137, Kid 56, Nean.) There are no political messages or references
to sex—the two chief topics of traditional graffiti. Nor are there any
personal messages, or cries of distress, or offers of aid. There are
just large billboard-type presentations of the names of the graffiti-
makers, in an elaborate script which, with its typical balloon shapes,
covers as much surface as possible.

If that were all, then the view that this is art-as-personal-expres-
sion, that graffiti are controlled productions reflecting a canon of
aesthetic criteria that is beyond middle-class understanding or ap-

preciation, and to be welcomed and savored rather than suppressed, might make sense. Alas, there is more. The insides of the cars are also marked-up—generally with letters or shapes or scrawls like letters, made with thick black markers, and repeated everywhere there is space for the marks to be made, and many places where there is not. Thus the maps and signs inside the car are obscured, and the windows are also obscured so that passengers cannot see what station they have arrived at. The subway rider—whose blank demeanor, expressing an effort simply to pass through and survive what may be the shabbiest, noisiest, and generally most unpleasant mass-transportation experience in the developed world, has often been remarked upon—now has to suffer the knowledge that his subway car has recently seen the passage through it of the graffiti "artists" (as they call themselves and have come to be called by those, including the police, who know them best). He is assaulted continuously, not only by the evidence that every subway car has been vandalized, but by the inescapable knowledge that the environment he must endure for an hour or more a day is uncontrolled and uncontrollable, and that anyone can invade it to do whatever damage and mischief the mind suggests.

I have not interviewed the subway riders; but I am one myself, and while I do not find myself consciously making the connection between the graffiti-makers and the criminals who occasionally rob, rape, assault, and murder passengers, the sense that all are part of one world of uncontrollable predators seems inescapable. Even if the graffitists are the least dangerous of these, their ever-present markings serve to persuade the passenger that, indeed, the subway is a dangerous place—a mode of transportation to be used only when one has no alternative.

Of course the *sense* of a dangerous place is different from the *reality* of a dangerous place. The thoughtful head of the transit police, Sanford Garelik, will point out—and has statistics to prove—that the subway is less dangerous than the streets. It is well-patrolled, and the occasional sensational crime is no index to the everyday experience of the passenger. Yet the cars in which persons unknown to the passengers have at their leisure marked-up interiors, and obscured maps, informational signs, and windows, serve as a permanent reminder to the passenger that the authorities are incapable of controlling doers of mischief. One can see earlier graffiti underneath a fresh coat of paint that itself is beginning to be covered by new graffiti that mock, as it were, the hapless effort to obscure their predecessors. Thus the signs of official failure are everywhere. And the mind goes on, and makes a link between the graffiti and the broken signs—behind broken glass—that are supposed to tell passengers where the train is going, the damaged doors that only open halfway, and the other visible signs of damage in so many cars.

The graffiti artists, who have been celebrated by Norman Mailer and others, are to the subway rider, I would hazard, part of the story of "crime in the subway," which contributes to the decline of subway ridership, which in turn of course contributes to increasing the danger because of the paucity of passengers. (Official signs in stations warn passengers that between 8 P.M. and 4 A.M. they should congregate in the front cars of the trains, to give what protection numbers may provide against the marauders whose presence must always be assumed.) If this linkage is a common one, then the issue of controlling graffiti is not only one of protecting public property, reducing the damage of defacement, and maintaining the maps and signs the subway rider must depend on, but it is also one of reducing the ever-present sense of fear, of making the subway appear a less dangerous and unpleasant place to the possible user. And so one asks: Why can't graffiti be controlled?

A litany of proposals

Interestingly enough, as Chief Garelik points out, this is one crime whose perpetrator is known by the mere fact of the crime itself. The graffiti artist leaves his mark, his name, or a variant of it. Most of these names and marks are known to the police. Chief Garelik will show the visitor an astonishing "mug book," consisting of color photographs of the work of each graffitist, accompanied by a name and address. Almost every graffiti artist becomes known. Indeed, the police have invited graffiti artists up to police headquarters and engaged in "bull sessions" with them to try to figure out the best course of action. Nor is the number of graffiti artists so great—from one perspective—as to present too diffuse a target for police action. There are, at any given time, only 500 or so. They begin at about age 11, the mean age is 14, and they begin to graduate from graffiti after age 16—by then it is presumably "kid stuff." Or perhaps penalties rise as graffitists stop being considered juveniles. Young ones begin by marking the inside of cars, and later advance to the grand murals. There are aesthetic traditions. There are also rules, more or less observed, such as: One does not paint on another's graffiti.

Commonly, paints are stolen. The number of spray-paint cans

required to embellish the side of a subway car is prodigious and it
is hardly likely that young teenagers would have the money. In any
case, the police assure the visitor that most paint is stolen. Moreover,
Chief Garelik emphasizes—against the chic position that graffiti are
art and fun—that the graffiti artists do graduate to more serious
crime. The police studied the careers of 15-year-old graffiti artists
apprehended in 1974: Three years later, 40 percent had been arrested for more serious crimes—burglary and robbery. Graffiti may be
self-expression, but they are not only self-expression. For almost
half the graffiti artists there is evidence that graffiti-making is part
of an ordinary criminal career.

But if the police know most of them, and there are only 500, then
why can't graffiti be controlled? One can go through the litany of
proposals—only to end up baffled.

The first suggestion: Arrest them, punish them, make them clean
up the graffiti. Indeed, for a while the police were arresting them
(or giving out summonses) in very substantial numbers. There were
1,674 arrests in 1973; 1,658 in 1974; 1,208 in 1975; 853 in 1976; 414
in 1977; and 259 in the first half of 1978. As one can see, the arrests
dropped radically after 1975, but not because graffiti artists could
not be caught—rather because the effort seemed futile. The police
began to concentrate on the more determined graffitists and to un-
cover more serious crimes with which to charge them. For after all,
what could one do after arrest that could deter graffitists from going
back to graffiti? Put them in juvenile-detention centers? What judge
would do that when there were young muggers, assaulters, and
rapists to be dealt with, who were far more menacing to their fellow-
citizens—and who themselves could not be accommodated in the
various overcrowded institutions for juveniles?

But even if juvenile graffitists were not punished by detention,
could they not be required to clean-up graffiti? This was popular
with some judges for a while, but it turned out that it was expensive
to provide guidance and supervision (the cleaning usually had to
be done on weekends, requiring overtime payment for those who
taught and supervised the work), and the police believe that its
main effect was to teach the graffitists the technical knowledge
necessary to produce graffiti that effectively resist removal.

Could one, so to speak, "harden the target" by securing the yards
in which the cars are stored, and where, as is evident from observing
the graffiti, much of the work is done? (The large murals extend
below the surface of the subway platform, and clearly must be
done while the cars stand on sidings and the whole surface is ac-

cessible.) Chief Garelik points out that there are 6,000 cars, that one car-yard alone is 600 acres in extent, that many cars cannot be accommodated in the yards and stand in middle tracks, that there are 150 miles of lay-up track, and finally, that wire fences can be cut.

Is there a "technological fix"—a surface that resists graffiti and from which it can be easily washed off? Perhaps, but so far nothing has worked, though certainly the shiny surfaces of new cars put into service make it somewhat harder to apply dense graffiti to them. In time, however, the new surfacing wears off and will take paint. The more serious problem here is the fact that once graffiti gets on a car, it must be taken off immediately so as not to encourage other graffitists. This is the practice in Boston where, as in other cities, the mass-transit system does not have graffiti. But the New York system, so much huger, does not have enough maintenance men, and so the policy of immediately eliminating graffiti cannot be implemented.

One could give graffiti artists summer jobs, as a way of providing them with something else to do, and indeed the police have been instrumental in finding summer jobs for 175 of the young people involved. Well, it is worth a try. But one wonders whether most jobs available for unskilled youths would match the excitement of painting graffiti onto silent subway cars in deserted yards, watching for the police, stealing the paints, organizing the expeditions.

There are more imaginative proposals, such as hiring them to paint the cars in the first place. But one can imagine the technical problems involved in handing over such good (and well-paid) jobs to 11- to 16-year-olds.

One proposal after another has been considered, evaluated, tried. The police have not given up—far from it. Their favored approach, if it could be financed, would be intensive work, on a one-to-one basis, by youth workers (students in psychology and sociology), a "big brother" program that would involve young graffitists in other activities and introduce them to young adults who would help find other outlets for their energies. But one wonders whether the youth workers might not be converted by the graffiti artists, who do not believe they are doing anything wrong. They do see their graffiti as art and self-expression (and create albums in which fellow graffiti artists reproduce miniatures of their designs—the police have a few of these, which are quite beautiful examples of urban, vernacular art). They are not at this point in their lives engaged in the uglier crimes that are so common in New York. What arguments would the youth workers, who might themselves reflect the culture that has given approval to making graffiti (as to smoking marijuana, and other formally illegal activities), be able to present to convince the young graffiti artists to give up their work? What could they provide them in its place?

There have been some efforts to divert the energies of the young graffiti artists from the sides of subway cars to canvases. Some of the graffitists produce canvases for sale, with the assistance of the adults who work with them. Some have gone on to art school—have indeed gained fellowships because adults working with them saw talents that could be developed. But it is hard to imagine this kind of thing making much of an impact on the problem, though it may be a solution for a dozen or two a year. Indeed, these very opportunities might be attractive enough to serve as an incentive for others to try to develop and demonstrate their talents by working on subway cars!

As one learns more about the graffiti artists, realizes that most of them are known to the police, that their more serious crimes (if they move on to them) will take place after they have given up graffiti, and that among all the things urban youth gangs may specialize in this is not the worst—then, one's anger at the graffiti makers declines. One begins to accept graffiti as just one of those things that one has to live with in New York. But this tolerance should not lead us to forget the 3-million subway riders per day who do not have the opportunity to study the graffiti problem, who are daily assaulted by it, and who find it yet another of the awful indignities visited upon them by a city apparently out of control and incapable of humane management. Even if graffiti, understood properly, might be seen as among the more engaging of the annoyances of New York, I am convinced this is not the way the average subway rider will ever see them, and that they contribute to his sense of a menacing and uncontrollable city. The control of graffiti would thus be no minor contribution to the effort to change the city's image and reality.

Systematic deterrence?

But how? Chief Garelik suggests some food for thought. Why are there so few graffiti on trucks, he asks. Trucks provide great surfaces, without windows or doors. If one motive for making graffiti —as the kids tell us—is seeing one's name being sped through the four contiguous boroughs, and the thrill of the thought that one's name will be seen by people unknown, then trucks should offer an attractive opportunity. But truck drivers beat up the kids they find trying to deface their trucks! And there are no graffiti on trucks.

Why are there no graffiti on commuter railroad trains? Their car yards are as accessible as those in which subway cars are stored, and their trains run through low-income areas. Perhaps it is because the graffiti artists and their friends don't ride the commuter lines and don't care to advertise their skill and daring in unknown places. But Chief Garelik has a simpler answer: The maintenance men for those lines use buckshot. "They do?" I asked incredulously. Well, that is what the kids believe. Either there was such an experience, or rumor of it, and that seems enough to protect the commuter cars. Certainly here is a hint of something that might work. In fact, early in the graffiti plague, there was a proposal to use guard dogs in the subway yards. It might have been impractical for various reasons. But it might have worked, too. In any event, there was such an uproar at the prospect of juveniles being bitten or mauled that the idea was abandoned.

So it is possible, perhaps, to deter graffitists. But it is not possible to deter them through the regular juvenile-justice system, in which a weary judge, confronted by many difficult and intractable problems, can think of nothing better than asking Johnny to promise he won't do it again. Punishment at the scene of the crime seems to deter marvelously: being beaten up by a truck driver or facing a burst of buckshot if you are caught. The dogs also might have worked.

In other words, there are methods to deter graffiti artists. But are there any ways to institutionalize these methods in an orderly, rule-bound, and humane system of law enforcement? It is not possible to tell the transit police, "Don't bring the kids in, just beat them up." We would not want the transit police to do so, and the transit authorities would not want to encourage such uncontrolled and uncontrollable behavior: A transit police force of 3,000 members must be governed by rule and order rather than informal sanctions, informally applied. And rule and order mean that the graffiti artists are brought into a system of juvenile justice which has more important crimes to deal with, and in which punishment, if any, will be minimal.

Is it possible to apply deterrence in a systematic way in a large bureaucratic system? It should be. Chief Garelik points out that a natural experiment, comparing the treatment of those who avoid paying tokens in two boroughs, suggests that deterrence does reduce illegal acts. In one borough, for some reason, those given sum-

216

THE PUBLIC INTEREST ON CRIME AND PUNISHMENT

monses for trying to get into the subway without paying a fare were fined on the average 99 cents; in the other, during a comparable period, they were fined on the average $10.45. In the first borough, 20 percent of those caught were repeat offenders; in the second, only 3 percent. Obviously there are other plausible differences between the two boroughs that would have to be taken into account to explain why fare-avoiders in one are so much more commonly repeaters than in the other. But it is not unreasonable to take as a first possibility that in one borough this act is more severely punished.

Undoubtedly there is some form of deterrence that would reduce graffiti-writing. Some graffiti artists, we are told, inform on others when threatened by a term in a tough detention center. (Whether the police could deliver on such a threat is another matter.) Would a few days in the detention center have more effective results than a few weekend sentences to erase graffiti? What would be the problems in trying to test such an approach? In trying to institute it?

New approaches

Aside from deterrence approaches, there are what we might call "education" or "therapy" approaches. Trained juvenile officers, social workers, counselors, or other youth workers would work with the apprehended graffiti artist, either directly or by finding some social agency with which he would be required to maintain contact. Such programs have been begun on an experimental basis. Chief Garelik favors such approaches, has gotten some grants to institute them, and needs more such grants. It is certainly premature to evaluate these new programs, though certain considerations immediately come to mind. Unlike the case with some other crimes, it is difficult to enlist a youth's conscience or sense of right and wrong to combat his desire to make graffiti. There will be problems as well in getting youth workers to discourage graffiti-writing, both because it does not offend their sensibilities, and because they may view it as a comparatively insignificant offense. Nevertheless, these new programs constitute one of the few approaches that is available, and, in light of the proven ineffectiveness of other approaches, are certainly worth trying.

Graffiti raise the odd problem of a crime that is, compared to others, relatively trivial but whose aggregate effects on the environment of millions of people are massive. In the New York situation especially, it contributes to a prevailing sense of the incapacity of government, the uncontrollability of youthful criminal behavior, and a resultant uneasiness and fear. Minor infractions aggregate into something that reaches and affects every subway passenger. But six years of efforts have seen no solution. Graffiti of the New York style came out of nowhere, and strangely enough do not afflict other mass-public-transportation systems, except for that of Philadelphia. Maybe graffiti will go away just as unexpectedly, before we find a solution. But in the meantime, 500 youths are contributing one more element to the complex of apparently unmanageable problems amidst which New Yorkers live.

Elizabeth Kurshan assisted with the research for this article.

Crime
in
American
public schools

JACKSON TOBY

I N the early 1970's Senator Birch
Bayh's Subcommittee to Investigate Juvenile Delinquency heard
alarming reports of violence and vandalism in American public
schools—not just occasionally or in the central cities but chronically
and all over the United States. Partly in response to these hearings,
partly because of increasing preoccupation with school crime by
newspapers, magazines, and television, the 93rd Congress passed
an amendment to an education bill in 1974 requiring the Secretary
of the Department of Health, Education, and Welfare to conduct
a survey to determine the extent and seriousness of school crime.

The study was an elaborate one. Principals in 4,014 schools in
large cities, smaller cities, suburban areas, and rural areas filled out
questionnaires and returned them to Washington. Then 31,373 students and 23,895 teachers in 642 junior and senior high schools
throughout the country were questioned about their experiences
with school crime—in particular whether they themselves were victimized and, if so, how. From among the 31,373 students who filled
out anonymous questionnaires, 6,283 were selected randomly for
individual interviews on the same subject. Discrepancies between
questionnaire reports of victimization and interview reports of victimization were probed to find out exactly what respondents meant

when they answered that they had been attacked, robbed, or had property stolen from their desks or lockers. Finally, intensive field studies were conducted in 10 schools, schools that had had especially serious crime problems in the past and had made some progress in overcoming them.

In January 1978, the 350-page report to Congress, *Violent Schools —Safe Schools,* was published by the National Institute of Education. Though a scientific report, inevitably it had political overtones. Public schools with reputations for crime and violence tended to be located in the inner cities and to enroll high proportions of minority students from low-income families; average reading and mathematical levels were usually one or more grades behind national norms. Was there a causal relationship among high crime rates, low academic achievement, and a high proportion of minority students? Were parents with middle-class values enrolling their children in private or parochial schools out of fear of crime as well as out of desire for better academic instruction for their children? And, if so, did the problem of school crime explain an appreciable amount of middle-class flight from inner-city schools?

Perhaps because of the sensitivity of these issues, the report handled the data cautiously, drawing attention to some differences in the incidence of school crime and skipping lightly over others. The report showed that the crime problem was worse in junior high schools than in senior high schools, but it required careful examination of a table in an appendix to find statistics demonstrating that students in urban schools were robbed and assaulted more frequently than students in suburban or rural schools. (These statistics are reproduced in Tables I and II, below and on the next page, respectively.) But the differences are not as great as some of us might have expected. Statistics on the victimization of teachers, presented in Table III on page 22, were reported in an early chapter and showed unequivocally that urban teachers were more likely to be victimized than suburban or rural teachers—especially teachers in

TABLE I. *Percent of Students Who Reported Being Robbed within the Past Month*°

	URBAN SCHOOLS	SUBURBAN SCHOOLS	RURAL SCHOOLS
Junior High Schools	9.5%	7.5%	7.1%
Senior High Schools	3.9	2.4	3.5

° SOURCE: *Violent Schools — Safe Schools,* Appendix A, pp. A6–A7.

TABLE II. *Percent of Students Who Reported Being Assaulted within the Past Month* *

	URBAN SCHOOLS	SUBURBAN SCHOOLS	RURAL SCHOOLS
Junior High Schools	8.2%	7.2%	6.2%
Senior High Schools	4.0	3.0	3.4

* SOURCE: *Violent Schools – Safe Schools*, Appendix A, pp. A6–A7.

the largest cities. But the report tells us more than that, and we will present its findings in the form of answers to key questions on school crime.

Answered and unanswered questions

1. *How much real crime is there in the schools? Does it consist mostly of juvenile mischief given the alarming labels, "crime" and "violence," by exaggerated newspaper accounts, or is school crime mostly acts that adult perpetrators would be arrested and prosecuted for?*

Schools are plagued with real crime, according to the study. *Violent Schools—Safe Schools* was not mainly concerned with mischief or with foul language—although it mentioned in passing that a majority of American junior-high-school teachers were sworn at by their students or were the target of obscene gestures within the month preceding the survey. The report was concerned mainly with illegal *acts* and with the fear those acts aroused, not with language or gestures. Both on the questionnaires and in personal interviews, students were asked questions designed to provide an estimate of the amount of theft and violence in public secondary schools:

In [the previous month] did anyone steal things of yours from your desk, locker, or other place at school?

Did anyone take money or things directly from you by force, weapons, or threats at school in [the previous month]?

At school in [the previous month] did anyone physically attack and hurt you?

Eleven percent of secondary-school students reported in personal interviews having something worth more than a dollar stolen from them in the past month. A fifth of these thefts involved property worth $10 or more. One-half of one percent of secondary-school students reported being *robbed* in a month's time—that is, having property taken from them by force, weapons, or threats. One out of nine of these robberies resulted in physical injuries to the victims.

Students also told of being assaulted. One-and-a-third percent of secondary-school students reported being attacked over the course of a month, and two-fifths of these were physically injured. (However, only 14 percent of the assaults resulted in injuries serious enough to require medical attention.)

These percentages probably underestimated the true volume of student victimization. They were based on face-to-face *interviews* with students. The same questions asked of samples of students by means of anonymous *questionnaires* produced estimates of victimization about twice as high overall, and in the case of robbery four times as high. (Tables I and II are based on student questionnaires rather than on interviews.) Methodological studies conducted by the school-crime researchers convinced them that the interview results were more valid than the questionnaire results for estimating the extent of victimization; some students might have had difficulty reading and understanding the questionnaire. On the other hand, fear of crime kept some students from attending school. In reply to the question, "Did you stay at home any time in [the previous month] because someone might hurt you or bother you at school?" 8 percent of the students in big-city junior high schools said "yes," as compared with 4 percent in rural junior high schools and 5 percent in suburban and smaller-city junior high schools. Since the students who had an opportunity to reply to this question were those attending school on the day the questionnaire was administered (or on a subsequent make-up session), students in the sample who failed to fill out their questionnaires may have contained a higher proportion of victims of school crime and a higher percentage of those frightened into truancy.

The report also contained data on the victimization of teachers, data derived from questionnaires similar to those filled out by students. (There were no teacher interviews, perhaps because teachers were presumed more capable of understanding the questions and replying appropriately.) Table III on page 22 shows that an appreciable proportion of teachers reported property stolen, but that only a small proportion of teachers reported robberies and assaults. However, robberies were three times as common in inner-city schools as in rural schools, and assaults were nine times as common. Even in big-city secondary schools, less than 2 percent of the teachers surveyed cited assaults by students within the past month, but threats were more frequent. Thirty-six percent of inner-city junior-high-school teachers reported that students threatened to hurt them, as did 24 percent of inner-city high school teachers. Understandably,

TABLE III. *Percent of Teachers Who Reported Being Victimized within the Past Month: Thefts, Robberies, Assaults**

COMMUNITY SIZE	KIND OF VICTIMIZATION		
	THEFTS	ROBBERIES	PHYSICAL ATTACKS
Cities of 500,000 population or more	16.7%	1.3%	1.8%
Smaller Cities	15.8	0.6	0.7
Suburban Areas	12.0	0.5	0.4
Rural Areas	9.5	0.4	0.2

* SOURCE: *Violent Schools — Safe Schools*, p. 68.

many teachers said they were afraid of their students. Twenty-eight percent of big-city teachers reported hesitating to confront misbehaving students for fear of their own safety, as did 18 percent of smaller-city teachers, 11 percent of suburban teachers, and 7 percent of rural teachers.

Principals were questioned about a variety of crimes against the school as a community: trespassing, breaking and entering, theft of school property, vandalism, and the like. Based on these reports as well as on data collected by the National Center for Educational Statistics in a companion study, *Violent Schools—Safe Schools* estimated the monetary cost alone of replacing damaged or stolen property as $200 million per year.

2. *Are intruders from the outside community responsible for a major portion of school crime, or are the students themselves the main perpetrators of thefts, assaults, robberies, and vandalism? And, if the perpetrators are students, which students?*

According to the report, the notion that intruders are responsible for a great deal of school crime is a myth:

Preventive strategies designed to keep "intruders" from entering the school assume that offenses in the school are usually committed by outsiders; relative safety is believed to require keeping students inside the school and others who do not belong there outside.

Our data, however, suggest that rather than locking most offenders out, these strategies seem to lock the offenders in with their potential victims. Except for trespassing and break-ins, the great majority . . . of all reported offenses for which information about offenders is available were committed by current students at the school in question. . . . Even in the case of breaking and entering, slightly more than half (56 percent) of these offenses were committed by current students.

Another belief about perpetrators that the report called into question was that older students preyed on younger students. Although younger students were disproportionately victimized, three-quarters of those who attacked or robbed them were roughly the same age, according to estimates of the victims themselves.

Schools in which a majority of students were from minority backgrounds had rates of assault and robbery against both students and teachers twice as high as schools where white students predominated. But the data did not explain this finding. The issue is *what* characteristics of minorities make them more likely to engage in school crime. Here the report offered tantalizing hints that educational failure was causally implicated in school crime, but nothing conclusive. Teachers who said that they taught a majority of low-ability students were five times as likely to report being attacked and twice as likely to report being robbed as teachers who said that less than a third of their students were of low ability. Teachers who said that a majority of their students were "underachievers" were three times as likely to report being attacked and about 50 percent more likely to report being robbed than teachers who said that less than a third of their students were underachievers.

Staff members of the National Institute of Education had anticipated that students would prove to be the main perpetrators of school crime and had planned to include on the student questionnaire questions about crimes the students themselves had committed. This would have provided valuable information about the characteristics of student perpetrators and, inferentially, about perpetrators generally. But boards of education resisted; questioning students about their own crimes, even anonymously, was likely to arouse objections from parents, students, and perhaps from community groups. The plan was dropped.

The report did offer impressions about perpetrators based on its field studies in 10 schools—that is, on extensive observation over a period of at least two weeks in each school, and on intensive interviews with school counselors, school aides, security personnel, parents, and representatives of community organizations. Professor A. J. Ianni of Teachers College, Columbia University, the director of the field studies, had this impression of school-crime perpetrators:

> There was general agreement among respondents in many of the schools that a small percentage of students—the figure 10 percent was frequently cited—form a hard core of disruptive students who are responsible for most of the vandalism and violence in schools. While this troublesome group did not seem to be identifiable in terms of any specific racial, ethnic, or socioeconomic status background, school staff commonly described them as students who were also having difficulty

academically, were frequently in trouble in the community, and tended to come from troubled homes. These students were easily identifiable and generally seemed to be known both to staff and other students because of the frequency with which they were in trouble. These same respondents indicated that in their experience this group of troublesome students could find allies among the other students when specific issues, situations, or problems arose. Violence and disruptive behavior is thus described as interactive with a small group of students frequently causing problems and at times setting off a chain reaction among other student groups.

3. *Do attacks on and robberies of students occur mainly during classes or mainly before, after, and between classes?*

Not surprisingly, violence directed at other students was less likely to occur during classes than at other times. Thus, the presence of teachers seemed to protect students against violence. Apparently, hallways and stairs (where teacher supervision was weak) were the sites for about a third of the violent acts, and other poorly supervised places—toilets, cafeterias, and locker rooms—the sites for another third.

The report did not ask whether violence on the way to and from the school building was a special problem. If the trip to and from school were dangerous for students in the inner cities, such schools would continue to be perceived as dangerous even though violence might be adequately controlled inside the school building itself.

4. *Who are the main victims of school crime?*

Younger students and the youngest, least-experienced teachers were most likely to be attacked or robbed. However, *male* students were more than twice as likely to be victims of both forms of violence than *female* students. And male teachers were somewhat more likely to be attacked than female teachers, although less likely to be robbed. The most likely explanation for the fact that schools are more dangerous for males than for females is that since males are the main authors of violent crimes, their victims tend to be the other males with whom they associate. Propinquity, both physical and psychological, increases the likelihood of victimization.

Propinquity between perpetrators and victims also explains the higher rate of victimization of students and teachers from minority backgrounds than of white students and teachers. Minority students and teachers were more likely to be attacked and robbed because their schools tended to be urban schools with high crime rates.

5. *What are the causes of school crime?*

The word "cause" does not appear in the index of the report. This was not an oversight. The safe-schools study was designed to describe the crime problem in American public schools during a short period of time (1976 to 1977), not to probe causes. However, Congress expected that the study would show how school crime could be prevented. And this objective implied some knowledge of causes. The report waffled. It spoke of "potential contributions" to school crime and of "several factors that appear likely to have general explanatory value with respect to school crimes."

But more explicit concern with the causes of school crime would have made possible greater realism about what could be explained and what could be done. For example, even though the report suggested on the basis of other studies that levels of school crime had increased from the 1960's to the 1970's, the safe-schools study itself collected no data on trends in school crime; hence, it could not throw light on causes of the *increase* in school crime. Furthermore, it could not explain why some youngsters committed crimes and others in the same schools did not; it had not collected data from offenders, only from victims. All the study could do was to contrast the crime rates in some of the 642 schools of the sample with those of others and to attempt to identify characteristics of high-crime and low-crime schools. The report did this. Thus, high levels of violent crime occurred in schools with above-average proportions of children from families of low socioeconomic status and in schools located in high-crime neighborhoods. But its authors were extremely cautious in interpreting the associations in causal terms.

There are hints one can trace out. Among all the schools in the survey—urban, suburban, and rural—a strong relationship existed between laxness in enforcing school rules, as judged by teachers and students in the school, and rate of violent crime. But surrounding neighborhoods of low socioeconomic status and high crime resulted in lax rule enforcement only in urban schools, not in suburban or rural schools. Perhaps in high-crime communities of low socioeconomic status the enforcement of school rules was difficult for teachers and principals but not, as the rural and suburban data showed, impossible. Perhaps an urban school with sufficiently creative leadership could also enforce rules despite its adverse socioeconomic environment.

6. *Did the report suggest anything that the federal government can do to reduce crime in the schools?*

There *were* recommendations in the concluding chapter of the report, lots of them—but they were not recommendations for Congressional action nor indeed were they National Institute of Education recommendations. They were suggestions from school principals, teachers, and students, for controlling school crime. Principals and teachers were asked to write in their own words replies to the following question: "What measures would you recommend to schools having problems with vandalism, personal attacks, and theft?" Students were asked to make recommendations by means of a similar question: "If a school had a problem with personal attacks, theft, and property destruction, what could be done to make it safer?" The answers by principals, teachers, and students were grouped in the same eight categories: 1) security devices, 2) security personnel, 3) discipline and supervision, 4) curriculum and counseling, 5) training and organizational change, 6) physical-plant improvement, 7) parental involvement and community relations, and 8) improvement of school climate. Within each category, responses were carefully coded into subcategories to facilitate statistical tabulation. Although the victims and potential victims of school crime are not necessarily qualified to devise effective solutions, it may be worth noting that "discipline and supervision" [1] was the most popular recommendation of students and teachers as well as of principals.

The report also described—based on questionnaire responses from principals—efforts made by schools to cope with crime, and discussed the modest success (in the opinion of principals) of these different efforts to reduce "vandalism, personal attacks, and thefts." Big-city principals reported the highest proportion of successful practices, mostly in the areas of "security devices" and "discipline and supervision"; Table IV shows that, except for paddling—a measure more popular in rural and suburban schools and in smaller cities—schools in the big cities made the most serious disciplinary and control efforts. Aside from the impressionistic judgments of the principals, the report did not attempt to evaluate the effectiveness of these disciplinary efforts.

Social changes and school crime

The report described the current situation rather than attempting to explain how a less orderly school environment developed. The report did not consider social trends in American society that made it more difficult for public schools to control predatory, violent, or malicious student behavior.

---

[1] The responses classified under this heading included "enforcement of rules, suspensions, etc.," "restitution, payment," "special classes, expulsion," "monitoring, watching," "controlling student movement, I.D.," and others.

TABLE IV. *Percent of Schools Using Various Discipline and Control Procedures, by Location**

TYPE OF PROCEDURE	LARGE CITIES	SMALL CITIES	SUBURBAN AREAS	RURAL AREAS
Students must show I.D. card to authorized personnel when requested	6%	3%	3%	2%
Students must carry hall passes if out of class	41	23	20	18
Visitors must check in at the office	67	56	49	39
Suspension	47	36	33	27
Expulsion	6	3	4	4
Paddling	17	34	33	42
Assignment to special day-long class for disruptive students	10	7	7	5
Transfer to another regular school (social transfer)	35	19	7	3
Transfer to special school for disruptive students	10	7	4	2
Referral to community mental-health agency as disruptive student	40	29	20	17

* SOURCE: *Violent Schools — Safe Schools*, p. 147.

Historically, the development of American public education increasingly separated the school from the students' families and neighborhoods. Even the one-room schoolhouse of rural America represented separation of the educational process from the family. But the consolidated school districts in nonmetropolitan areas and the jumbo schools of the inner city carried separation much further. There were good reasons why large schools developed. The bigger the school, the lower the per-capita cost of education tended to be. The bigger the school, the more feasible it was to hire teachers with academic specialties like art, music, drama, and advanced mathematics. The bigger the school, the more likely that teachers and administrators could operate according to professional standards instead of in response to local sensitivities—for example, in teaching biological evolution or in designing a sex-education curriculum. But the unintended consequence of large schools that operated efficiently by bureaucratic and professional standards was to make them relatively independent of the local community. The advantages of autonomy were obvious. The disadvantages took longer to reveal themselves.

The main disadvantage was that students developed distinctive subcultures only tangentially related to education. Thus, in the 1950's Professor James S. Coleman showed in his book, *The Adolescent Society,* that American high school students seemed more preoccupied with athletics and personal popularity than with intellectual achievement. Students were "doing their own thing," and their thing was not what teachers and principals were mainly concerned about. Presumably, if parents had been more closely involved in the educational process, they would have strengthened the academic impact of teachers. Even in the 1950's, student subcultures at school facilitated misbehavior; in New York and other large cities, fights between members of street gangs from different neighborhoods sometimes broke out in secondary schools. However, Soviet achievements in space during the 1950's drew more attention to academic performance than to school crime and misbehavior. Insofar as community adults were brought into schools as teacher aides, they were introduced not to facilitate control over student misbehavior but to improve academic performance.

Until the 1960's and 1970's school administrators did not realize that order is chronically problematical when many hundreds of young people come together for congregate education. Principals did not like to call the police, preferring to organize their own disciplinary procedures. They did not believe in security guards, preferring to use teachers to monitor behavior in the halls and lunchrooms. They did not tell school architects about the need for what has come to be called "defensible space," and as a result schools were built with too many ways to gain entrance from the outside and too many rooms and corridors where surveillance was difficult. Above all, they did not consider that they had lost control over potential student misbehavior when parents were kept far away, where they could not see or know how their children were behaving. The focus of PTA's was the curriculum, and it was the bettereducated, middle-class parents who tended to join them. In short, isolation of the school from the local community always means that if a large enough proportion of students misbehave, teachers and principals cannot maintain order. It was not until the 1960's and 1970's, however, that this potentiality became a reality in many American schools, especially inner-city schools. The following paragraphs come from a case study of a particularly disorderly New York high school reported in *Violent Schools—Safe Schools:*

When the student turmoil in the late 1960's led to frequent fires started by students' dropping matches into other students' lockers, all the lockers, with the exception of those in the gyms, were closed and remain so. As a result, students must carry lunches and other belongings, and these are sometimes stolen when they are left out. Vandalism, while not nearly as dramatic or widespread as it was during the time of the disruptions, still presents problems. The cost to the school in 1976 for repainting or cleaning off graffiti was approximately $5,000. The principal explains that graffiti and the breaking of windows are a constant problem both because of the size of the school and the reduction in the custodial staff.

Another trend helping to explain how a less orderly school environment developed was the continuing pressure to keep children in school longer—on the assumption that children needed all the education they could get to cope with a complicated urban industrial society. The positive side of this development was rising educational levels. Greater proportions of the age cohort graduated from high school and went on to post-secondary education than ever before. The negative aspect of compulsory-school-attendance laws and of informal pressure to stay in school longer was that youngsters who didn't wish further education were compelled to remain in school. They were, in a sense, prisoners; understandably, some of them became troublemakers. When they became insolent, violent, or criminal, there was little the public schools could do about them. (The private schools simply expelled them—that is, sent them to public schools.) Since society now believes that public schools are ultimately responsible for primary and secondary education for all children—those with special physical, emotional, or behavior problems are diverted to special schools only as a last resort—public schools are less able to control their students than they used to be.

Discovering children's rights

A third trend indirectly affecting the school-crime-problem was the increasing sensitivity of public schools to the rights of children. A generation ago, it was possible for principals to rule schools autocratically, to suspend or expel students without much regard for procedural niceties. Injustices occurred; children were "pushed out" of schools because they were disliked by school officials. But this arbitrariness enabled school administrators to control the situation when real misbehavior occurred. Assaults on teachers were punished so swiftly that they were almost unthinkable. Even disrespectful language was unusual. Today school officials are required to observe due process in handling student discipline. Hearings are necessary. Witnesses must confirm suspicions. Appeals are provided for. Greater democratization of schools means that unruly students get better protection against school officials, and most students get less protection from their classmates.

Related to this third trend is a fourth: the decreased ability of schools to get help with discipline problems from the juvenile courts. Like the schools themselves, the juvenile courts have become more attentive to children's rights and less willing to exile children to a correctional Siberia. More than a decade ago the Supreme Court ruled in the *Gault* case that children could not be sent to juvenile prisons for "rehabilitation" unless proof existed that they had committed some crime for which imprisonment was appropriate.

The *Gault* decision set off a revolution in juvenile-court procedures and fostered a growing reluctance on the part of juvenile-court judges to send youngsters "away." Furthermore, a number of state legislatures restricted the discretion of juvenile-court judges. In New York and New Jersey, for example, juvenile-court judges may not commit a youngster to correctional institutions for "status offenses"—that is, for behavior that would not be a crime if done by adults. Thus truancy or ungovernable behavior in school or at home are not grounds for incarceration in New York and New Jersey. Many experts believe that the differentiation of juvenile delinquents from "Persons in Need of Supervision" is a progressive reform. But one consequence of this reform is that the public schools cannot easily persuade juvenile courts to act in school-problem cases. Student abuse of teachers, for example, is more difficult to cope with.

These social changes provide background for understanding the most important change of all: the erosion of the authority of the classroom teacher. If run-of-the-mill teachers could control effectively the behavior of students in their classes, in hallways, and in lunchrooms, there would be considerably less school violence—though theft and vandalism still might be problems. Nowadays some individual teachers can control their classes through personal charisma. But what has changed is that the *role* of teacher no longer has the prestige it once did for students and their parents, and so less forceful, less experienced, or less effective teachers cannot rely on the prestige of the role to maintain control. They are on their own in a sense that the previous generation of teachers was not. The most visible symptom of loss of automatic respect is assaults on teachers, mainly from students—but occasionally from parents themselves!

According to the report, somewhat more than 1 percent of American seventh-, eighth-, and ninth-grade teachers were assaulted by their students *every month*. Male teachers reported being attacked more frequently than female teachers, younger teachers more often than older teachers, inexperienced teachers more than experienced teachers, minority teachers more than white teachers.

What happened to erode the almost sacred status of teachers? This question was not dealt with in the report. Doubtless, lessened respect for teachers is related to fundamental cultural changes by which many authority figures—parents, police, government officials, military leaders, employers—have been removed from psychological pedestals. In the case of teachers, however, the general demythologizing process was amplified by special criticism. Best-selling books of the 1960's like John Holt's *Why Children Fail*, James Herndon's *The Way It Spozed to Be*, Jonathan Kozol's *Death at an Early Age: The Destruction of the Minds and Hearts of Negro Children in the Boston Public Schools*, and Herbert Kohl's *36 Children*, portrayed teachers, especially white middle-class teachers, as the villains of education—insensitive, authoritarian, and even racist. The failure of large numbers of children in inner-city schools to learn as much as they ought to have learned by national standards was interpreted as a responsibility of the schools and of the teachers. These books did not pretend to be quantitative surveys. They made no estimates of the percentages of American teachers who resembled the anecdotal examples the authors provided. But the consistency of the illustrations created an image of American teachers as, at best, inept and unfeeling.

The authors probably intended to exonerate youngsters for lack of academic success by portraying them as victims of failings in the educational system. *The effect on readers was to blame teachers for the poor results*. To be sure, few inner-city residents read these books. Yet the anti-establishment ideas that they contained percolated through American society as the clichés of television interviews and college education courses. Because the 1960's witnessed an enormous growth of enrollments in higher education, especially of minority community-college students, the notion that teachers could not be trusted spread from these books to college classrooms to American families, including minority families. Striking a teacher might almost appear to be a deserved punishment. Of course, only a tiny percentage of students and their parents subscribed to this ideologically extreme position. Even among parents and students who assaulted teachers, momentary anger rather than ideological conviction was probably the predominant motivation. Nevertheless, ideologically motivated attacks had symbolic impact. They suggested to children who witnessed them or heard about them that distrust of teachers must have *some* basis. Why else were people so angry? Thus ideological extremism fed on itself, increasing the mutual suspicions of students and teachers in inner-city schools and motivating some teachers to retire early and others to leave the teaching profession for other occupations.

Another indication of the erosion of teacher authority has been the decline of homework in secondary schools. When teachers could depend on all but a handful of students to turn in required written homework, they could assign homework and mean it. The slackers could be disciplined. But when teachers can no longer count on a majority of students doing their homework, the assignment of homework becomes a meaningless ritual, and many teachers give up. Of course, when homework is negligible, classroom instruction is less effective. The decline of homework also suggests that teachers lack authority to induce students to do *anything* they don't want to do: to attend school regularly, to keep quiet so an orderly recitation can proceed, to refrain from annoying a disliked classmate. Indeed, there are American public schools where one-third of the enrolled students are absent on an average school day. In the classrooms of such schools, teachers cannot build on information communicated and presumably learned during the previous lesson, because so many members of the class missed it.

To sum up: I believe school crime can best be understood in the context of social changes that separated secondary schools from effective family and neighborhood influences, that have kept older adolescents enrolled in school whether they craved education or not, that made it extremely difficult for schools to expel students guilty of intractable and even violent behavior, and that reduced the authority of classroom teachers.

Why care about school crime?

School crime receives attention mainly because individual teachers and students are assaulted and their property stolen or because the school's property is stolen or damaged. A more pernicious aspect of school crime, however, is that it reduces the effectiveness of public education, particularly in large cities.

Crime and the anticipation of crime in the past decade reduced teacher and student commitment to the educational process. Teachers in high-crime schools became less ready to demand from students in-class and out-of-class effort: Learning is work, and many teachers grew afraid to insist on what students regarded as unpleasant. They also became afraid to intervene when students fought or attacked another teacher. Some teachers found their role so different from what they had expected that they abandoned the teaching profession entirely or transferred to safer ("better") schools. Some older teachers chose to retire early. Most teachers—having invested too much in a professional career to quit—continued to serve, but with low morale. Students began to reject the educational process. They cut classes more than previous generations of students, and they took unauthorized absences of days and sometimes weeks. They complained that they weren't learning much in school—and they were right.

Those parents aware of the inadequate progress of their children in reading and arithmetic sometimes tried to correct the situation. For families with the economic resources to do so, the easiest way was to transfer their children to private or parochial schools or to move to suburban communities with reputations for good schools. Parents without the means to transfer their children could only attempt to make the local schools better, possibly by joining the PTA. But, in truth, parents could not have much impact, given the organizational and geographic isolation of the school from the local community.

The effect of this process of deterioration was to alter the role of the public school in underprivileged neighborhoods of big cities. American public schools have traditionally taught basic skills that all persons need to know in order to participate effectively in a complex industrial society. But they also served to select for post-secondary education youngsters whose native abilities and personal motivation prepared them for responsible and prestigious occupations. "Opportunity" was an incentive legitimizing the school in the eyes of the parents as well as students, and thereby justifying teacher authority. However, as crime grew more serious in big-city schools, they became less and less functional as a channel of social ascent for able students from disadvantaged backgrounds; they became traps instead of springboards. (The relentless support of the NAACP for busing to promote racial integration in public education should be understood against a background of disorder in big-city secondary schools that increasingly serve a minority clientele. Whatever else busing accomplishes, it promises to enroll minority students in safer and educationally more effective schools than they would otherwise attend and thus to return public education to its mobility-promoting function.)

Controlling violence in urban schools is thus not only desirable for its own sake, but also for the possibility of ameliorating two of the intractable problems of American education: 1) the draining away of better students and the consequent increase of racial segregation in the public schools of the largest central cities, and 2) educational ineffectiveness in those schools so serious as to prevent even intellectually able students from learning enough. To put the matter more dramatically, failure to control the violence problem in big-city schools means that urban public schools cannot propel youngsters from disadvantaged families toward successful occupational careers.

One way to avoid this conclusion is to assert that the causal order is not from violence to educational ineffectiveness to the flight from high-crime schools by better students, but rather that schools that arouse frustration and resentment in their students erupt in school crime. This is essentially the thesis of the Children's Defense Fund. According to the Fund, American schools are excessively arbitrary, especially with minority students, and suspend and expel students from school for trivial reasons unrelated to the educational process. The Children's Defense Fund refers to the "pushout problem" and argues that the disproportionate representation of black youngsters among those suspended or expelled is evidence at least of arbitrary standards and probably of racism on the part of school officials. The Fund's position is that schoolchildren need advocates to protect their legitimate interests against the oppressive authority of teachers and principals, and that more "due process" rather than less will reduce student frustration and therefore violence. Partisans of the youth-advocacy approach to crime reduction in the schools convinced the Senate Subcommittee to Investigate Juvenile Delinquency of the correctness of this approach. The Subcommittee's 1975 report, *Our Nation's Schools—A Report Card: "A" in School Violence and Vandalism,* put it this way:

> One common thread of particular interest to the Subcommittee running through many of the underlying causes of school violence and vandalism is what may be called the crisis of due process. Quite naturally schools, like other institutions, are compelled to issue rules and regulations concerning the conduct of persons within their jurisdiction. It is clear that without fair and meaningful control and discipline the schools would quickly lose their ability to educate students. Increasingly, though, educators and administrators are finding that the extent of stu-

dent conduct which is sought to be regulated, as well as the methods of regulation, are causing more problems than they are controlling. A 1975 NEA study interviewed a large number of students from different schools and found that "many students spoke of the need for consistent, fair discipline."

For example, the Subcommittee found that in numerous institutions across the country, students, administrators and teachers are embroiled in constant ongoing disputes over restrictions on hair style, smoking, hall passes, student newspapers and a myriad of other aspects of school life.

According to the Senate Subcommittee, the schools' failings in the area of due process incite students to violence, as do arbitrary expulsions and suspensions. The Subcommittee Report made the connections as follows:

At first glance it might appear that the expulsion, suspension, pushout, force out and truancy phenomenon [sic], although certainly tragic for those involved, might at least create a somewhat more orderly atmosphere for those remaining in school as a result of the absence of youngsters evidently experiencing problems adjusting to the school environment. The opposite, however, appears to be the case. The Syracuse study, for instance, found that in schools where the average daily attendance was lower, the disruptions, violence and vandalism rates were higher. This may be explained by the fact that the vast majority of students who are voluntarily or compulsively [sic] excluded from schools do, in time, return to those schools. In many instances their frustrations and inadequacies which caused their absence in the first place have only been heightened by their exclusion and the school community will likely find itself a convenient and meaningful object of revenge.

It is not possible to dismiss the arguments of the Children's Defense Fund, the Subcommittee on Juvenile Delinquency, and the various proponents of youth advocacy out of hand. Nonetheless, it seems more plausible that school violence lowers the effectiveness of the educational process through the fears that it arouses than that arbitrary school rules so enrage students that they rob and steal from each other and teachers, and perpetrate assaults and vandalism. Conceivably though, some students seek revenge on teachers, on the school building, and on their fellow students for perceived unjust treatment.

Violent-Schools—Safe-Schools asked students and teachers questions about their perception of the fairness of school rules; a scale of perceived school fairness was constructed. Did schools where students and teachers felt the rules were unfair have higher levels of violence than schools in which students and teachers thought the rules were fairer? Apparently not in the urban junior and senior high schools where the violence problem is most acute. The tendency for "less fair" schools to have higher violence rates virtually disappeared when other co-varying causal factors were statistically removed. Thus, in addition to being implausible, the hypothesis that student resentment of unfair rules contributes substantially to school violence did not stand up under empirical test.

How to reduce school crime

Reducing school crime requires a long-run strategy rather than a search for panaceas. Informal influences, such as greater parental involvement, might prove useful in controlling school crime. Informal social controls are a factor in human behavior generally—and certainly in adolescent behavior in schools. To fail to utilize informal controls is to throw the entire burden of preventing school crime on *formal* agencies of control: security guards, teachers, principals. But channeling informal influences is more complicated than hiring security guards or buying stronger locks. Time and effort must be devoted to developing practical programs.

Parents and other neighborhood adults are already employed in urban *elementary* schools as teacher aides; they are supposed to increase the effectiveness of classroom teachers. They may also contribute to a more orderly classroom atmosphere. But in *secondary* schools teacher aides are rare. (Paraprofessionals seem less useful for helping the teacher of specialized subjects.) If it could be arranged, the routine presence of parents in junior and senior high schools might have appreciable effects on crime rates and on the fear of crime, whether or not parents make a direct contribution to academic achievement.

But how can the presence of neighborhood adults in school buildings be justified? One possibility is to hire them to perform useful services that justify their being in lunchrooms, halls, stairways, offices, and even classrooms. Hiring parents for their indirect impact on school crime is expensive. And, indeed, the informal control resulting from a parental presence in secondary schools might be achieved more cheaply. Schools are already used for adult-education courses in evening hours. Such courses could be scheduled for the school day. If crime reduction were attained at the price of increased congestion and of reduced autonomy for teachers and principals, most people would consider the tradeoff worth it.

Greater efforts could be made to involve another informal influence, the peer group, in the control of school crime. This has already been done, reportedly with success, in vandalism control. The cost of vandalism for a previous year is calculated, and the student body collectively is given the monetary equivalent of the reduction in property damage for the current year. There have also been efforts to heighten the consciousness of students about school crime through public discussions. Although these steps are in the right direction, they do not seem to mobilize strong peer sanctions against more serious crime. What is needed is sustained thought and experimentation to discover the most effective way to motivate students to disapprove of predatory behavior. Again, a long view is required.

But along with a long-term perspective for school-crime reduction there must be a set of priorities. For not even the federal government can deal with *all* school crime in *all* of the urban, suburban, and rural areas of 50 states and the District of Columbia. Some types of school crime, while undesirable, are not major threats to public education. Marijuana and alcohol use on school premises probably belong in this category; perhaps vandalism and after-hours burglaries are also bearable costs in an affluent society. On the other hand, violent crimes at school are serious threats to the viability of public education. Controlling them should be the first priority of a safe-schools strategy.

School violence is most serious in big-city junior high schools, where assaults and robberies are more than twice as frequent as in senior high schools. Furthermore, a major factor in junior-high-school crime is that junior highs are pressed to keep troublesome students because of compulsory-school-attendance laws. Expulsion is theoretically possible, but difficult in practice. A junior-high-school student who attacks a teacher may be given a five-day suspension, whereas a high school student committing the same offense would be expelled. High schools have greater proportions of voluntary students. True, some high school students are trapped by the school-attendance laws in the ninth or tenth grades, but they are outnumbered by students legally free to drop out—and therefore possible candidates for expulsion for misbehavior. These considerations explain why the problem of coping with school violence is more difficult in junior high schools than in other public secondary schools.

Can violence be controlled in big-city junior high schools? "Youth advocates" believe that designing more intriguing curricula and selecting more stimulating teachers will reduce violence. Yet no curriculum is universally intriguing, and no teacher can be stimulating all the time. Public schools may not be responsive enough to their clienteles, as proponents of youth advocacy allege, but responsiveness or lack of it is only marginally relevant to the problem of violence. Rural schools are the least responsive and the safest; some of them paddle students and conduct strip-searches for drugs. *What makes violence likely is weak control.* Big-city junior high schools have high rates of assault and robbery because they contain a handful of violent students whom they cannot control and cannot extrude, and because they have not devised credible rewards and punishments for the larger group of potentially violent youngsters who are susceptible to deterrence. Addressing these two weaknesses of control will enable big-city junior high schools to reduce violence. But coping with these weaknesses involves painful measures, not the cost-free "solutions" suggested by youth advocates.

First, to rid the junior high schools of the small percentage of violent students who have proved that they cannot be controlled by anyone, the public schools should be allowed to use expulsion more freely. This means recognizing that the limits to the right of students to remain in school for educational purposes are reached when their presence jeopardizes the education of classmates. Expulsion is a drastic remedy. Though home instruction and alternative schools will be available for expelled students, the likelihood is that expelled students will not make much further academic progress. That is sad. Nevertheless, society must be permitted to give up on students who are threatening the educational opportunities of their classmates.

Milder sanctions

The second remedy is linked to the first. It may be possible to devise innovative lesser punishments for misbehavior provided that more drastic punishments (such as expulsion) are available should the lesser sanctions fail. Suppose, for example, that a student subject to expulsion for slapping a teacher is offered the option of working 14 hours every weekend at the school—painting, scrubbing, polishing—for three months. Supervision is given by paid college students from the local community working alongside the offender. The offender receives no pay; he is being punished, not rewarded by participation in an employment program. Perhaps the assaultive student prefers expulsion to hard work on his "free" weekends. (Experience with coerced community service in New Zealand—called "periodic detention"—demonstrated that some offenders preferred jailing for a period of time to labor-punishment on the installment plan.) On the other hand, his parents may prefer that he remain in school; they press him to accept the weekend penalty and, reluctantly, he agrees. But what happens if he does not show up for his weekend drudgery? In New Zealand the failure to report for weekend work without a medical excuse results in a bench warrant being issued, and the youngster goes to jail. Were magistrates unwilling to issue bench warrants, periodic detention could not succeed; periodic detention is not a Quaker work project. In order for coerced community service to be effective as a sanction for controlling school crime, boards of education would have to expel youngsters who dropped out of the program.

The parallel is not exact. Expulsion from school may be perceived by offenders as not wholly undesirable. The New Zealand experience is with jail, not with expulsion from school. Only experimentation can show whether expulsion is a sufficient threat to motivate the majority of offenders to abide by a lesser penalty. If not, the cooperation of juvenile courts would be necessary. Since school violence is delinquency, and legally subject to the juvenile or criminal courts, judges can stand behind school-imposed disciplinary measures with the more drastic threat of incarceration. To be sure, mention of expulsion or incarceration in relation to school crime horrifies "youth advocates," and the hope, of course, would be that these fairly severe sanctions need rarely be used. Experimentation is necessary to find out whether the threat of such sanctions is sufficient to ensure compliance.

Experimentation is also necessary with more palatable forms of influencing student behavior: rewards for good behavior rather than punishment for bad. Psychologists say that "positive reinforcement" is more effective than punishment, and positive reinforcement does not involve denying some students educational opportunities in order to preserve educational opportunities for others. Unfortunately, it is difficult to hook all students on the rewards offered by principals, teachers, and conforming students. According to sociologists, the basic social reward is approval, but teachers cannot easily bestow approval upon students who are uninterested in the curriculum and flout the behavioral rules of the classroom. Furthermore, such students are likely to receive approval for their disruptive behavior from close friends and to weigh this approval against the disapproval of teachers, principals, and the majority of the student body. Consequently, as desirable as it is to search experimentally for rewards that will help control violent crime in big-city junior high schools, the likelihood is that punishments will also be necessary, and that to protect the educational process the penalties of expulsion and referral to the juvenile-justice system will have to be used for the foreseeable future.

Americans are not patient or fatalistic. Given a national problem as unpleasant as school violence, our tendency is to attempt to do something about it—fast. Unfortunately, a crash program may not ameliorate the situation; it may even make the problem worse. School violence has not triggered our usual activist response. There have been stories in the mass media, hearings in the Congress, studies by the Department of Health, Education, and Welfare, but surprisingly little in the way of systematic national effort to reduce school crime. Part of the reason that school violence has been handled gingerly is the American tradition of local control over education. The main role for the federal government has been to supply funds for school programs that the Congress and the President deem worthy. Another reason is the concentration of the problem in big cities—where it is entangled with other difficult problems. So far about all that has happened is that urban school districts have improved control over entry to and exit from school buildings and have stationed security guards in the schools. *Violent Schools—Safe Schools* summarized the situation:

> More than one-third of all big-city schools employ trained security personnel; more than half of the big-city junior high schools have them, as do two-thirds of all big-city senior high schools. In suburban areas the proportion is much lower (7 percent), and in rural schools their use is negligible (1 percent).

Meanwhile, other efforts at control illuminate ironic twists of "children's rights" in practice, as when big-city school systems attempt to move violent students from one school to another. The rationale for such transfers is that youngsters may start fresh in a new school where they do not have a bad reputation. But the case study of one inner-city junior high school, called "Rogers" in the report, shows how this system of musical chairs works in practice:

> Since it is not legally possible to expel students considered disruptive, it is customary at Rogers as in other schools, to transfer students to other schools. By board regulation, the school is not permitted to inform the receiving school of the reason for the transfer or to provide any disciplinary records. "This can present some real problems," the dean says of the confidentiality requirement: "We had a kid last year who slashed another kid's throat with a razor blade and we finally had to transfer him to one of the intermediate schools, but we couldn't tell them officially what he had done or even that they should keep an eye on him because he was potentially violent."

No one knows whether transferring violent students from school to school reduces the total amount of violence in big-city school systems. Yet in any case humane considerations suggest that after a student has committed violent acts against students or teachers in a school, they ought not to have to encounter him in the corridors day after day. (In point of fact, it is at least as common for victims—both teachers and students—to transfer out voluntarily as it is for perpetrators to be compelled to transfer.)

What is being done?

On August 30, 1978, the Office of Juvenile Justice and Delinquency Prevention of the Law Enforcement Assistance Administration announced in the *Federal Register* a national initiative to combat school crime. Proposals were invited for a National School Resource Network; one grant of as much as $2,500,000 would be made for an initial 15-month period to finance the successful proposal. The presumption was that further grants would be made to maintain the School Resource Network if it seemed promising. Here is how the solicitation justified the new initiative:

> At the present time, there is no overall or resource strategy to assist schools in meeting the challenge of serious school crime. Resources are minimal and fragmented with little capacity to develop new resources to meet this challenge. The development of a nationwide school resource network dedicated to systematic advocacy, reform, and a safer environment on behalf of students and teachers is needed to provide overall direction and coordination of existing and new school resources. The promotion of due process, fairness and consistency in school security, and disciplinary policies and practices is important in assisting schools to develop and operate crime prevention and control programs.

The words have a pleasant sound, but it was not obvious what the School Resource Network was supposed to do. Later in the solicitation, the strategy of John M. Rector, then Administrator of the Office of Juvenile Justice and Delinquency Prevention, became clearer. Rector's approach was to move information from schools that had learned to cope with crime to schools that had not. Rector explained in a paragraph included under the heading, "technical assistance":

> The grantee shall produce technical assistance packages containing a variety of information materials on serious school violence and vandalism prevention. Sufficient copies of each package shall be produced to allow dissemination to appropriate technical assistance specialists in the national school resource network system. The information materials

to be included in each package shall include, but not be limited to, the Office of Juvenile Justice and Delinquency Prevention publications and materials such as the national evaluation reports, model school crime prevention programs and research reports, abstracts, bibliographies, grant project summaries, brochures, directories, and pamphlets. Materials developed and compiled should take into account regional, local and ethnic minority differences.

The dissemination of information about school violence will be helpful. But in order for improved communication to serve as the cornerstone of a national strategy for the control of school violence, some schools must be markedly more successful at coping with school violence than others. All that would then be necessary is to package the secret and send it around the country. But if, as is true especially in the inner cities, all schools are groping more or less ineffectively, a national strategy for coping with school crime should stress the systematic search for new approaches.[2]

The National School Resource Network is currently the main effort of the federal government, and local school systems are planning no new initiatives of their own. Nevertheless, school violence may diminish somewhat. The decline of births that began in the 1960's is likely to help. Junior-high-school enrollments have begun to fall. With smaller numbers of students, teachers and security guards are better able to defuse potentially explosive situations. Furthermore, teachers and principals have learned from their difficult experiences of the past decade; they know what to expect. They are less likely to become demoralized than the missionary-teachers who streamed into big-city schools in the 1960's—and streamed out again when they discovered that the role required less a guru than a policeman. Waiting passively for school violence to go away means relying on the happenstance of demography and other natural forces to cope with the problem. There is another possibility: that parents will become indignant enough about violent schools to make safer schools a political issue. Let's hope so.

---

[2] The failure of Mr. Rector's solicitation to include a research-and-development component was partly personal idiosyncracy. A lawyer by training, Rector was doubtful that social-science research could demonstrate the usefulness of an approach that practitioners were not already using—*somewhere*. This prejudice forced the School Resource Network to rely on what little was known about the control of school violence; Rector's strategy was to get the pamphlets in the mail. Rector was dismissed as Administrator in June 1979. Whether his successor will try to extricate the National School Resource Network from its presently-designed role is not yet known.

Torture
and
plea bargaining

JOHN H. LANGBEIN

T HE American system of plea
bargaining is becoming a subject of immense academic and public
attention. A dozen books have appeared in the last year or so describing plea bargaining as observed in one forum or another. The
law reviews are full of writing about the details; a special issue of
the *Law and Society Review* is now offering 20 more articles. The
general theme of much of the current writing is that although,
arguably, plea bargaining might be in need of various operational
reforms, the basic institution is natural, inevitable, universal, and
just.

In this essay I shall set forth some of the case against plea bargaining from a perspective that must appear bizarre, although I
hope to show that it is illuminating. I am going to contrast the
modern American system of plea bargaining with the medieval
European law of torture. My thesis is that there are remarkable
parallels in origin, in function, and even in specific points of doctrine, between the law of torture and the law of plea bargaining. I
shall suggest that these parallels expose some important truths about
how criminal justice systems respond when their trial procedures
fall into deep disorder.

The law of torture

For about half a millennium, from the middle of the thirteenth century to the middle of the eighteenth, a system of judicial torture lay at the heart of Continental criminal procedure. In our own day the very word "torture" is, gladly enough, a debased term. It has come to mean anything unpleasant, and we hear people speak of a tortured interpretation of a poem, or the torture of a dull dinner party. In discussions of contemporary criminal procedure we hear the word applied to describe illegal police practices or crowded prison conditions. But torture as the medieval European lawyers understood it had nothing to do with official misconduct or with criminal sanctions. Rather, the application of torture was a routine and judicially supervised feature of European criminal procedure. Under certain circumstances the law permitted the criminal courts to employ physical coercion against suspected criminals in order to induce them to confess. The law went to great lengths to limit this technique of extorting confessions to cases in which it was thought that the accused was highly likely to be guilty, and to surround the use of torture with other procedural safeguards that I shall discuss shortly.

This astonishing body of law grew up on the Continent as an adjunct to the law of proof—what we would call the system of trial—in cases of serious crime (for which the sanction was either death or severe physical maiming). The medieval law of proof was designed in the thirteenth century to replace an earlier system of proof, the ordeals, which the Roman Church effectively destroyed in the year 1215. The ordeals purported to achieve absolute certainty in criminal adjudication through the happy expedient of having the judgments rendered by God, who could not err. The replacement system of the thirteenth century aspired to achieve the same level of safeguard—absolute certainty—for human adjudication.

Although human judges were to replace God in the judgment seat, they would be governed by a law of proof so objective that it would make that dramatic substitution unobjectionable—a law of proof that would *eliminate human discretion* from the determination of guilt or innocence. Accordingly, the Italian Glossators who designed the system developed and entrenched the rule that conviction had to be based upon the testimony of two unimpeachable eyewitnesses to the gravamen of the crime—evidence that was, in the famous phrase, "clear as the noonday sun." Without these two eyewitnesses, a criminal court could not convict an accused who contested the charges against him. Only if the accused *voluntarily* confessed the offense could the court convict him without the eye-witness testimony.

Another way to appreciate the purpose of these rules is to understand their corollary: Conviction could not be based upon circumstantial evidence, because circumstantial evidence depends for its efficacy upon the subjective persuasion of the trier who decides whether to draw the inference of guilt from the evidence of circumstance. Thus, for example, it would not have mattered in this system that the suspect was seen running away from the murdered man's house and that the bloody dagger and the stolen loot were found in his possession. If no eyewitness saw him actually plunge the weapon into the victim, the court could not convict him.

In the history of Western culture no legal system has ever made a more valiant effort to perfect its safeguards and thereby to exclude completely the possibility of mistaken conviction. But the Europeans learned in due course the inevitable lesson. They had set the level of safeguard too high. They had constructed a system of proof that could as a practical matter be effective only in cases involving overt crime or repentant criminals. Because society cannot long tolerate a legal system that lacks the capacity to convict unrepentant persons who commit clandestine crimes, something had to be done to extend the system to those cases. The two-eyewitness rule was hard to compromise or evade, but the confession rule seemed to invite the subterfuge that in fact resulted. To go from accepting a voluntary confession to coercing a confession from someone against whom there was already strong suspicion was a step that began increasingly to be taken. The law of torture grew up to regulate this process of generating confessions.

The spirit of safeguard that had inspired the unworkable formal law of proof also permeated the subterfuge. The largest chapter of the European law of torture concerned the prerequisites for examination under torture. The European jurists devised what Anglo-American lawyers would today call a rule of probable cause, designed to assure that only persons highly likely to be guilty would be examined under torture. Thus, torture was permitted only when a so-called "half proof" had been established against the suspect. That meant either one eyewitness, or circumstantial evidence of sufficient gravity, according to a fairly elaborate tariff. In the example where a suspect was caught with the dagger and the loot, each of those indicia would be a quarter proof. Together they cumulated to a half proof, which was sufficient to permit the authorities to dispatch the suspect for a session in the local torture chamber.

In this way the prohibition against using circumstantial evidence was overcome. The law of torture found a place for circumstantial evidence, but a nominally subsidiary place. Circumstantial evidence was not consulted directly on the ultimate question, guilt or innocence, but on a question of interlocutory procedure—whether or not to examine the accused under torture. Even there the law attempted to limit judicial discretion by promulgating predetermined, ostensibly objective criteria for evaluating the indicia and assigning them numerical values (quarter proofs, half proofs, and the like). Vast legal treatises were compiled on this jurisprudence of torture to guide the examining magistrate in determining whether there was probable cause for torture.

In order to achieve a verbal or technical reconciliation with the requirement of the formal law of proof that the confession be voluntary, the medieval lawyers treated a confession extracted under torture as involuntary, hence ineffective, unless the accused repeated it free from torture at a hearing that was held a day or so later. Often enough the accused who had confessed under torture did recant when asked to confirm his confession. But seldom to avail: The examination under torture could thereupon be repeated. An accused who confessed under torture, recanted, and then found himself tortured anew, learned quickly enough that only a "voluntary" confession at the ratification hearing would save him from further agony in the torture chamber.

Fortunately, more substantial safeguards were devised to govern the actual application of torture. These were rules designed to enhance the reliability of the resulting confession. Torture was not supposed to be used to elicit an abject, unsubstantiated confession of guilt. Rather, torture was supposed to be employed in such a way that the accused would disclose the factual detail of the crime—information which, in the words of a celebrated German statute of the year 1532, "no innocent person can know." The examining magistrate was forbidden to engage in so-called suggestive questioning, in which the examiner supplied the accused with the detail he wanted to hear from him. Moreover, the information admitted under torture was supposed to be investigated and verified to the extent feasible. If the accused confessed to the slaying, he was supposed to be asked where he put the dagger. If he said he buried it under the old oak tree, the magistrate was supposed to send someone to dig it up.

Alas, these safeguards never proved adequate to overcome the basic flaw in the system. Because torture tests the capacity of the accused to endure pain, rather than his veracity, the innocent might (as one sixteenth-century commentator put it) yield to "the pain and torment and confess things that they never did." If the examining magistrate engaged in suggestive questioning, even accidentally, his lapse could not always be detected or prevented. If the accused knew something about the crime, but was still innocent of it, what he did know might be enough to give his confession verisimilitude. In some jurisdictions the requirement of verification was not enforced, or was enforced indifferently.

These shortcomings in the law of torture were identified even in the Middle Ages and were the subject of emphatic complaint in Renaissance and early modern times. The Europeans looked ever more admiringly at England, where the jury system—operating without the two-eyewitness rule—had never needed the law of torture. In the eighteenth century, as the law of torture was finally about to be abolished along with the system of proof that had required it, Beccaria and Voltaire became famous as critics of judicial torture; but they were latecomers to a critical legal literature nearly as old as the law of torture itself. Judicial torture survived the centuries not because its defects had been concealed, but in spite of their having been long revealed. The two-eyewitness rule had left European criminal procedure without a tolerable alternative. Having entrenched this unattainable level of safeguard in their formal trial procedure, the Europeans found themselves obliged to evade it through a subterfuge that they knew was defective. The coerced confession had to replace proof of guilt.

The law of plea bargaining

I am now going to cross the centuries and cross the Atlantic in order to speak of the rise of plea bargaining in twentieth-century America. The account of the European law of torture that I have just presented (which is based upon my monograph *Torture and the Law of Proof*, 1977), should stir among American readers an unpleasant sensation of the familiar, for the parallels between our modern plea bargaining system and the ancient system of judicial torture are many and chilling.

Let us begin by recollecting the rudiments of the American system of plea bargaining in cases of serious crime. Plea bargaining occurs when the prosecutor induces an accused criminal to confess guilt and to waive his right to trial in exchange for a more lenient criminal sanction than would be imposed if the accused were adjudicated guilty following trial. The prosecutor offers leniency either directly, in the form of a charge reduction, or indirectly, through the connivance of the judge, in the form of a recommendation for reduced sentence that the judge will follow. In exchange for procuring this leniency for the accused, the prosecutor is relieved of the need to prove the accused's guilt, and the court is spared having to adjudicate it. The court condemns the accused on the basis of his confession, without independent adjudication.

Plea bargaining is, therefore, a nontrial procedure for convicting and condemning the accused criminal. If you turn to the American Constitution in search of authority for plea bargaining, you will look in vain. Instead, you will find—in no less hallowed a place than the Bill of Rights—an opposite guarantee, a guarantee of trial. The Sixth Amendment provides: "In *all* criminal prosecutions, the accused shall enjoy the right to . . . trial . . . by an impartial jury . . ." (emphasis added).

In our day, jury trial continues to occupy its central place both in the formal law and in the mythology of the law. The Constitution has not changed, the courts pretend to enforce the defendant's right to jury trial, and television transmits a steady flow of dramas in which a courtroom contest for the verdict of the jury leads inexorably to the disclosure of the true culprit. In truth, criminal jury trial has largely disappeared in America. The criminal justice system now disposes of virtually all cases of serious crime through plea bargaining. In the major cities between 95 and 99 percent of felony convictions are by plea. This nontrial procedure has become the ordinary dispositive procedure of American law.

Why has our formal system of proof been set out of force and this nontrial system substituted for the trial procedure envisaged by the Framers? Scholars are only beginning to investigate the history of plea bargaining, but enough is known to permit us to speak with some confidence about the broad outline. In the two centuries from the mid-eighteenth to the mid-twentieth, a vast transformation overcame the Anglo-American institution of criminal jury trial, rendering it absolutely unworkable as an ordinary dispositive procedure and requiring the development of an alternative procedure, which we now recognize to be the plea bargaining system.

In eighteenth-century England jury trial was still a *summary proceeding*. In the Old Bailey in the 1730's we know that the court routinely processed between 12 and 20 jury trials for felony in a single day. A single jury would be impaneled and would hear evidence in numerous unrelated cases before retiring to formulate verdicts in all. Lawyers were not employed in the conduct of ordinary criminal trials, either for the prosecution or the defense. The trial judge called the witnesses (whom the local justice of the peace had bound over to appear), and the proceeding transpired as a relatively unstructured altercation between the witnesses and the accused. Plea bargaining was unknown—indeed, judges actively discouraged pleas of guilty even from defendants who tendered them voluntarily and without hope of sentencing concessions. In the 1790's, when the Americans were constitutionalizing English jury trial, it was still rapid and efficient. The trial of Hardy for high treason in 1794 was the first that ever lasted more than one day, and the court seriously considered whether it had any power to adjourn. By contrast, we may note that the trial of Patricia Hearst for bank robbery in 1976 lasted 40 days and that the average felony jury trial in Los Angeles in 1968 required 7.2 days of trial time. In the eighteenth century the most characteristic (and time-consuming) features of modern jury trial, namely adversary procedure and the exclusionary rules of the law of criminal evidence, were still primitive and uncharacteristic. The accused's right to representation by retained counsel was not generalized to all felonies until the end of the eighteenth century in America and the nineteenth century in England. Appellate review was very restricted into the twentieth century; counsel for indigent accused was not required until the middle of this century. The practices that so protract modern American jury trials—extended *voir dire* (pretrial probing of the views and backgrounds of individual jurors for juror challenges), exclusionary rules and other evidentiary barriers, motions designed to provoke and preserve issues for appeal, maneuvers and speeches of counsel, intricate and often incomprehensible instructions to the jury—all are late growths in the long history of common-law criminal procedure. No wonder, then, that plea bargaining appears to have been a late-nineteenth-century growth that was scarcely acknowledged to exist in the United States before the 1920's. (The English are only now facing up to the fact of their dependence on plea bargaining.)

Nobody should be surprised that jury trial has undergone great changes over the last two centuries. It desperately needed reform. The level of safeguard against mistaken conviction was in several respects below what civilized peoples now require. What we will not understand until there has been research directed to the question, is why the pressure for greater safeguards led in the Anglo-American procedure to the law of evidence and the lawyerization of the trial, reforms that ultimately destroyed the system in the sense that they made jury trial so complicated and time-consuming as to be unworkable as the routine dispositive procedure.

Similar pressures for safeguards were being felt on the Continent in the same period, but they led to reforms in nonadversarial procedure that preserved the institution of trial. In the middle of the nineteenth century, when Continental criminal procedure was being given its modern shape, the draftsmen of the European codes routinely studied Anglo-American procedure as a reform model. They found much to admire and to borrow, but they resisted the temptation to adversary domination. Their experience with the way that their medieval rules of evidence had led to the law of torture also left them unwilling to imitate the nascent Anglo-American law of evidence. And they were unanimous in rejecting the institution of the guilty plea. As early as the 1850's German writers were saying that it was wrong for a court to sentence an accused on mere confession, without satisfying itself of his guilt.

Parallels to the law of torture

Let me now turn to my main theme—the parallels in function and doctrine between the medieval European system of judicial torture and our plea bargaining system. The starting point, which will be obvious from what I have thus far said, is that each of these substitute procedural systems arose in response to the breakdown of the formal system of trial that it subverted. Both the medieval European law of proof and the modern Anglo-American law of jury trial set out to safeguard the accused by circumscribing the discretion of the trier in criminal adjudication. The medieval Europeans were trying to eliminate the discretion of the professional judge by requiring him to adhere to objective criteria of proof. The Anglo-American trial system has been caught up over the last two centuries in an effort to protect the accused against the dangers of the jury system, in which laymen ignorant of the law return a one- or two-word verdict that they do not explain or justify. Each system found itself unable to recant directly on the unrealistic level of safeguard to which it had committed itself, and each then concentrated on inducing the accused to tender a confession that would waive his right to the safeguards.

The European law of torture preserved the medieval law of proof undisturbed for those easy cases in which there were two eyewitnesses or voluntary confession. But in the more difficult cases (where, I might add, safeguard was more important), the law of torture worked an absolutely fundamental change within the system of proof: It largely *eliminated the adjudicative function.* Once probable cause had been determined, the accused was made to concede his guilt rather than his accusers to prove it.

In twentieth-century America we have duplicated the central experience of medieval European criminal procedure. We have moved from an adjudicatory to a concessionary system. We coerce the accused against whom we find probable cause to confess his guilt. To be sure, our means are much more polite; we use no rack, no thumbscrew, no Spanish boot to mash his legs. But like the Europeans of distant centuries who did employ those machines, we make it terribly costly for an accused to claim his right to the constitutional safeguard of trial. We threaten him with a materially increased sanction if he avails himself of his right and is thereafter convicted. This sentencing differential is what makes plea bargaining coercive. There is, of course, a difference between having your limbs crushed if you refuse to confess, or suffering some extra years of imprisonment if you refuse to confess, but the difference is of degree, not kind. Plea bargaining, like torture, is coercive. Like the medieval Europeans, the Americans are now operating a procedural system that engages in condemnation without adjudication. The maxim of the medieval Glossators, no longer applicable to European law, now aptly describes American law: *Confessio est regina probationum,* confession is the queen of proof.

Supporters of plea bargaining typically maintain that a "mere" sentencing differential is not sufficiently coercive to pressure an innocent accused to convict himself. That point can be tested in the abstract simply by imagining a differential so great—for example, death versus a 50-cent fine—that any rational defendant would waive even the strongest defenses. The question of whether significant numbers of innocent people do plead guilty is not, of course, susceptible to empirical testing. It has been established that many of those who plead guilty claim that they are innocent. More importantly, prosecutors widely admit to bargaining hardest when the case is weakest, which is why the leading article on the subject, by Albert Alschuler ("The Prosecutor's Role in Plea Bargaining," University of Chicago Law Review, 1968), concluded that "the greatest pressures to plead guilty are brought to bear on defendants who may be innocent." Alschuler recounted one such case:

San Francisco defense attorney Benjamin M. Davis recently represented a man charged with kidnapping and forcible rape. The defendant was innocent, Davis says, and after investigating the case Davis was confident of an acquittal. The prosecutor, who seems to have shared the defense attorney's opinion on this point, offered to permit a guilty plea to simple battery. Conviction on this charge would not have led to a greater sentence than 30 days' imprisonment, and there was every likelihood that the defendant would be granted probation. When Davis informed his client of this offer, he emphasized that conviction at trial seemed highly improbable. The defendant's reply was simple: "I can't take the chance."

I do not think that great numbers of Americans plead guilty to offenses committed by strangers. (The European law of torture was also not supposed to apply in the easy cases where the accused could forthrightly explain away the evidence that might otherwise have given cause to examine him under torture.) I do believe that plea bargaining is used to coerce the waiver of tenable defenses, as in attorney Davis's example, and in cases where the offense has a complicated conceptual basis, as in tax and other white-collar crimes. Like the medieval law of torture, the sentencing differential in plea bargaining elicits confessions of guilt that would not be freely tendered, and some of the confessions are false. Plea bargaining is therefore coercive in the same sense as torture, although surely not in the same degree.

I do not mean to say that excesses of the plea bargaining system affect only the innocent who is coerced to plead guilty or the convict whose sentence is made more severe because he insisted on his right to trial. In other circumstances plea bargaining has been practiced in ways that result in unjustified leniency. Many observers have been struck by the extent of the concessions that prosecutors have been prepared to make in serious criminal cases in order to avoid having to go to trial. One Alaskan prosecutor told Alschuler in 1976 that "prosecutors can get rid of everything if they just go low enough. The police complained that we were giving cases away, and they were right."

I have said that European law attempted to devise safeguards for the use of torture that proved illusory; these measures bear an eerie resemblance to the supposed safeguards of the American law of plea bargaining. Foremost among the illusory safeguards of both systems is the doctrinal preoccupation with characterizing the induced waivers as voluntary. The Europeans made the torture victim repeat his confession "voluntarily," but under the threat of being tortured anew if he recanted. The American counterpart is Rule 11(d) of the Federal Rules of Criminal Procedure, which forbids the court from accepting a guilty plea without first "addressing the defendant personally in open court, determining that the plea is voluntary and not the result of force or threats or of promises *apart from a plea agreement*." Of course, the plea agreement is the *source* of the coercion and already embodies the involuntariness.

The architects of the European law of torture sought to enhance the reliability of a torture-induced confession with other safeguards designed to substantiate its factual basis. We have said that they required a probable-cause determination for investigation under torture and that they directed the court to take steps to verify the accuracy of the confession by investigating some of its detail. We have explained why these measures were inadequate to protect many innocent suspects from torture, confession, and condemnation. Probable cause is not the same as guilt, and verification, even if undertaken in good faith, could easily fail as a safeguard, either because the matters confessed were not susceptible of physical or testimonial corroboration, or because the accused might know enough about the crime to lend verisimilitude to his confession even though he was not in fact the culprit.

The American law of plea bargaining has pursued a similar chimera: the requirement of "adequate factual basis for the plea." Federal Rule 11(f) provides that "the court should not enter judgment upon [a guilty] plea without making such inquiry as shall satisfy it that there is a factual basis for the plea." As with the tortured confession, so with the negotiated plea: Any case that has resisted dismissal for want of probable cause at the preliminary hearing will rest upon enough inculpating evidence to cast suspicion upon the accused. The function of trial, which plea bargaining eliminates, is to require the court to adjudicate whether the facts proven support an inference of guilt beyond a reasonable doubt. Consider, however, the case of *North Carolina v. Alford,* decided in this decade, in which the U.S. Supreme Court found it permissible to condemn without trial a defendant who had told the sentencing court: "I pleaded guilty on second degree murder because they said there is too much evidence, but I ain't shot no man.... I just pleaded guilty because they said if I didn't they would gas me for it.... I'm not guilty but I plead guilty." I invite you to compare Alford's statement with the explanation of one Johannes Julius, seventeenth-century burgomaster of Bamberg, who wrote from his dungeon cell where he was awaiting execution, in order to tell his daughter why he had confessed to witchcraft "for which I must die. It is all falsehood and invention, so help me God.... They never cease to torture until one says something."

The tortured confession is, of course, markedly less reliable than the negotiated plea, because the degree of coercion is greater. An accused is more likely to bear false witness against himself in order to escape further hours on the rack than to avoid risking a longer prison term. But the resulting moral quandary is the same. Judge Levin of Michigan was speaking of the negotiated guilty plea, but he could as well have been describing the tortured confession when he said, "there is no way of knowing whether a particular guilty plea was given because the accused believed he was guilty, or because of the promised concession." Beccaria might as well have been speaking of the coercion of plea bargaining when he said of the violence of torture that it "confounds and obliterates those minute differences between things which enable us at times to know truth from falsehood." The doctrine of adequate factual basis for the plea is no better substitute for proof beyond reasonable doubt than was the analogous doctrine in the law of torture.

The factual unreliability of the negotiated plea has further consequences, quite apart from the increased danger of condemning an innocent man. In the plea bargaining that takes the form of charge bargaining (as opposed to sentence bargaining), the culprit is convicted not for what he did, but for something less opprobrious. When people who have murdered are said to be convicted of wounding, or when those caught stealing are nominally convicted of attempt or possession, cynicism about the processes of criminal justice is inevitably reinforced. This willful mislabelling plays havoc with our crime statistics, which explains in part why Americans—uniquely among Western peoples—attach so much importance to arrest records rather than to records of conviction. I think that the unreliability of the plea, the mislabelling of the offense, and the underlying want of adjudication all combine to weaken the moral force of the criminal law, and to increase the public's unease about the administration of criminal justice. The case of James Earl Ray is perhaps the best example of public dissatisfaction over the intrinsic failure of the plea bargaining system to establish the facts about crime and guilt in the forum of a public trial. Of course, not every trial resolves the question of guilt or innocence to public satisfaction. The Sacco-Vanzetti and Rosenberg cases continue to be relitigated in the forum of popular opinion. But plea bargaining leaves the public with what I believe to be a more pronounced sense of unease about the justness of results, because it avoids the open ventilation and critical evaluation of evidence that characterize public trial. (Just this concern appears to have motivated the gov-

ernment in the plea-bargained bribery case of Vice President Agnew
to take extraordinary steps to assure the disclosure of the substance
of the prosecution case.) It is interesting to remember that in Europe in the age of Beccaria and Voltaire, the want of adjudication
and the unreliability of the law of torture had bred a strangely
similar cynicism towards the criminal justice system of that day.

The moral blunder

Because plea bargaining involves condemnation without adjudication, it undermines a moral postulate of the criminal justice system so basic and elementary that in past centuries Anglo-American
writers seldom bothered to express it: Serious criminal sanctions
should only be imposed when the trier has examined the relevant
evidence and found the accused guilty beyond reasonable doubt.

Why have we been able to construct a nontrial procedure that is
irreconcilable with this fundamental proposition? A major reason is
that we have been beguiled by the similarities between civil and
criminal litigation in our lawyer-dominated procedural system.
"What's wrong with settling cases?" the argument runs. "Surely
society is correct not to insist on full-scale adjudication of every
private grievance. If the parties are satisfied with their deal, there
is no social interest in adjudication. Likewise in criminal adjudication: If the prosecutor and the accused can reach agreement about
the sanction, hasn't the matter been satisfactorily concluded?"

The answer is that because the social interest in criminal adjudication differs importantly from that in civil cases, the deeply
embedded policy in favor of negotiated (nontrial) settlement of
civil disputes is misapplied when transposed to the criminal setting.
There is good reason for treating adjudication as the norm in the
criminal law, but as a last and exceptional resort in private law. Ken-
neth Kipnis has provided a wry illustration of the distinction with
an example drawn from neither. Kipnis asks us to imagine a system of "grade bargaining," in which the teacher would offer a student a favorable grade in exchange for a waiver of the student's
right to have the teacher read his examination paper. The teacher
would save time, thus conserve his resources, and the student would
not accept the teacher's grade offer unless he calculated it to be in
his interest by comparison with his expected results from conventional grading.

We see instantly what is wrong with grade bargaining. Because
third parties rely upon grades in admissions and hiring decisions,

the grade bargain would adversely affect the legitimate interests of these outsiders. And because the grade is meant to inform the student about the teacher's perception of the comparative quality of his performance, the grade bargain would disserve the larger interests of the student.

Quite analogous objections apply to plea bargaining. Criminal sanctions are imposed for public purposes: certainly in order to deter future crime, probably still with the object of reforming at least some offenders, and perhaps still in the interest of retribution. Sentences that satisfy the accused's wish to minimize the sanction and the prosecutor's need to reduce his trial caseload are arrived at with only passing attention to these social interests. In particular, the enormous sentence differential needed to sustain the plea bargaining system is repugnant to any tenable theory of sentencing. We can scarcely claim to be tailoring the sentence to the crime when one of the largest aggravating factors we consult is whether the accused had the temerity to ask for his right to trial. The truth is that when an accused is convicted following jury trial, we customarily punish him twice: once for the crime, and then more severely for what the Constitution calls "enjoy[ing] the right to . . . trial . . . by an impartial jury."

Twenty years ago in a celebrated article the late Henry Hart compared so-called "civil commitment" for mental or contagious disease with imprisonment for criminal conviction. Many a prison is more pleasant than a nearby asylum. Why, then, do we treat the decision to imprison as the more serious and surround it with safeguards that, at least in theory, are more substantial than those for the civil-commitment process? Notwithstanding the operational similarity between civil and criminal sanctions, said Hart, there is a profound difference in purpose. "The core of the difference is that the patient has not incurred the moral condemnation of his community, whereas the convict has." The very stigma of criminal conviction is the source of much of the deterrent and retributive power of the criminal sanction. I believe that this moral force of the criminal sanction is partially dependent on the sanction having been imposed after rational inquiry and decision on the facts. Adjudication alone legitimates the infliction of serious criminal sanctions, because it alone is adequate to separate the innocent from the guilty and to establish the basis for proportioning punishment to the degree of culpability. To assert (as a defender of plea bargaining must) the equivalency of waiver and of adjudication is to overlook the distinctive characteristic of the criminal law.

The prosecutor

Our law of plea bargaining has not only recapitulated much of the doctrinal folly of the law of torture, complete with the pathetic safeguards of voluntariness and factual basis, but it has also repeated the main institutional blunder of the law of torture. Plea bargaining concentrates effective control of criminal procedure in the hands of a single officer. Our formal law of trial envisages a division of responsibility. We expect the prosecutor to make the charging decision, the judge and especially the jury to adjudicate, and the judge to set the sentence. Plea bargaining merges these accusatory, determinative, and sanctional phases of the procedure in the hands of the prosecutor. Students of the history of the law of torture are reminded that the great psychological fallacy of the European inquisitorial procedure of that time was that it concentrated in the investigating magistrate the powers of accusation, investigation, torture, and condemnation. The single inquisitor who wielded those powers needed to have what one recent historian has called "superhuman capabilities [in order to] . . . keep himself in his decisional function free from the predisposing influences of his own instigating and investigating activity."

The dominant version of American plea bargaining makes similar demands: It requires the prosecutor to usurp the determinative and sentencing functions, hence to make himself judge in his own cause. There are dangers in this concentration of prosecutorial power. One need not necessarily accept Jimmy Hoffa's view that Robert Kennedy was conducting a personal and political vendetta against him in order to appreciate the danger that he might have been. The power to prosecute as we know it carries within itself the power to persecute. The modern public prosecutor commands the vast resources of the state for gathering and generating accusing evidence. We allowed him this power in large part because the criminal trial interposed the safeguard of adjudication against the danger that he might bring those resources to bear against an innocent citizen —whether on account of honest error, arbitrariness, or worse. But the plea bargaining system has largely dissolved that safeguard.

While on the subject of institutional factors, I have one last comparison to advance. The point has been made, most recently by the Attorney General of Alaska, that preparing and taking cases to trial is much harder work than plea bargaining—for police, prosecutors, judges, and defense counsel. In short, convenience—or worse, sloth —is a factor that sustains plea bargaining. We suppose that this factor had a little to do with torture as well. As somone in India re-

marked to Sir James Fitzjames Stephen in 1872 about the proclivity
of the native policemen for torturing suspects, "It is far pleasanter
to sit comfortably in the shade rubbing red pepper into a poor dev-
il's eyes than to go about in the sun hunting up evidence." If we
were to generalize about this point, we might say that concessionary
criminal-procedural systems like the plea bargaining system and the
system of judicial torture may develop their own bureaucracies and
constituencies. Here as elsewhere the old adage may apply that if
necessity is the mother of invention, laziness is the father.

The jurisprudence of concession

Having developed these parallels between torture and plea bargaining, I want to draw some conclusions about what I regard as the
lessons of the exercise. The most important is this: A legal system
will do almost anything, tolerate almost anything, before it will
admit the need for reform in its system of proof and trial. The law
of torture endured for half a millennium although its dangers and
defects had been understood virtually from the outset; and plea
bargaining lives on although its evils are quite familiar to us all.
What makes such shoddy subterfuges so tenacious is that they shield
their legal systems from having to face up to the fact of breakdown
in the formal law of proof and trial.

Why is it so hard for a legal system to reform a decadent system
of proof? I think that there are two main reasons, one in a sense
practical, the other ideological. From the standpoint of the practical, nothing seems quite so embedded in a legal system as the
procedures for proof and trial, because most of what a legal system
does is to decide matters of proof—what we call "fact finding." (Was
the traffic light green or red? Was this accused the man who fired
the shot or robbed the bank?) Blackstone emphasized this point in
speaking of civil litigation, and it is even more true of criminal litigation. He said: "Experience will abundantly shew, that above a
hundred of our lawsuits arise from disputed facts, for one where the
law is doubted of." Every institution of the legal system is geared
to the system of proof; forthright reconstruction would disturb, at
one level or another, virtually every vested interest.

The inertia, the resistance to change that is associated with such
deep-seated interests, is inevitably reinforced by the powerful ideological component that underlies a system of proof and trial. Adjudication, especially criminal adjudication, involves a profound intrusion into the lives of affected citizens. Consequently, in any

society the adjudicative power must be rested on a theoretical basis that makes it palatable to the populace. Because the theory of proof purports to govern and explain the application of the adjudicative power, it plays a central role in legitimating the entire legal system. The medieval European law of proof assured people that the legal system would achieve certainty. The Anglo-American jury system invoked the inscrutable wisdom of the folk to justify its results. Each of these theories was ultimately untenable—the European theory virtually from its inception, the Anglo-American theory after a centuries-long transformation of jury procedure. Yet the ideological importance of these theories prevented either legal system from recanting them. For example, I have elsewhere pointed out how in the nineteenth century the ideological attachment to the jury retarded experimentation with juryless trial—that is, what we now call bench trial—while the plea bargaining system of juryless nontrial procedure was taking shape out of public sight. Like the medieval European lawyers before us, we have been unable to admit that our theory of proof has resulted in a level of procedural complexity and safeguard that renders our trial procedure unworkable in all but exceptional cases. We have responded to the breakdown of our formal system of proof by taking steps to perpetuate the ideology of the failed system, steps that closely resemble those taken by the architects of the law of torture. *Like the medieval Europeans, we have preserved an unworkable trial procedure in form, we have devised a substitute nontrial procedure to subvert the formal procedure, and we have arranged to place defendants under fierce pressure to "choose" the substitute.*

That this script could have been played out in a pair of legal cultures so remote from each other in time and place invites some suggestions about the adaptive processes of criminal procedural systems. First, there are intrinsic limits to the level of complexity and safeguard that even a civilized people can tolerate. If those limits are exceeded and the repressive capacity of the criminal justice system is thereby endangered, the system will respond by developing subterfuges that overcome the formal law. But subterfuges are intrinsically overbroad, precisely because they are not framed in a careful, explicit, and principled manner directed to achieving a proper balance between repression and safeguard. The upshot is that the criminal justice system is saddled with a lower level of safeguard than it could and would have achieved if it had not pretended to retain the unworkable formal system.

The medieval Europeans insisted on two eyewitnesses and wound

up with a law of torture that allowed condemnation with no witnesses at all. American plea bargaining, in like fashion, sacrifices
just those values that the unworkable system of adversary jury trial
is meant to serve: lay participation in criminal adjudication, the
presumption of innocence, the prosecutorial burden of proof beyond
reasonable doubt, the right to confront and cross-examine accusers,
the privilege against self-incrimination. Especially in its handling
of the privilege against self-incrimination does American criminal
procedure reach the outer bounds of incoherence. We have exaggerated the privilege to senseless lengths in formal doctrine, while
in the plea bargaining system—which is our routine procedure for
processing cases of serious crime—we have eliminated practically
every trace of the privilege.

Furthermore, the sacrifice of our fundamental values through plea
bargaining is needless. In its sad plea bargaining opinions of the
1970's, the Supreme Court has effectively admitted that for reasons
of expediency American criminal justice cannot honor its promise
of routine adversary criminal trial, but the Court has simply assumed
that the present nontrial plea bargaining procedure is the inevitable
alternative. There is, however, a middle path between the impossible system of routine adversary jury trial and the disgraceful nontrial system of plea bargaining. That path is a streamlined nonadversarial trial procedure.

Routine nonadversarial trials

The contemporary nonadversarial criminal justice systems of
countries like West Germany have long demonstrated that advanced
industrial societies can institute efficient criminal procedures that
nevertheless provide for lay participation and for full adjudication
in every case of serious crime. I have described the German system
in detail in my *Comparative Criminal Procedure: Germany* (1977),
and I have made no secret of my admiration for the brilliant balance that it strikes between safeguard and procedural effectiveness.
Not the least of its achievements is that in cases of serious crime it
functions with no plea bargaining whatsoever. Confessions are still
tendered in many cases (41 percent in one sample), but they are
not and cannot be bargained for; nor does a confession excuse the
trial court from hearing sufficient evidence for conviction on what
amounts to a beyond-reasonable-doubt standard of proof. In a trial
procedure shorn of all the excesses of adversary procedure and the
law of evidence, the time difference between trial without confes-

sion and trial with confession is not all that great. Because an accused will be put to trial whether he confesses or not, he cannot
inflict significant costs upon the prosecution by contesting an overwhelming case. Confessions are tendered at trial not because they
are rewarded, but because there is no advantage to be wrung from
the procedural system by withholding them.

Plea bargaining is all but incomprehensible to the Europeans,
whose ordinary dispositive procedure is workable without such
evasions. In the German press, the judicial procedure surrounding
the criminal conviction and resignation of Vice President Agnew was
viewed with the sort of wonder normally inspired by reports of the
customs of primitive tribes. The *Badische Zeitung* reported as the
story unfolded in October 1973: "The resignation occurred as part
of a 'cowtrade,' as it can only in the United States be imagined."

I hope that over the coming decades we who still live under criminal justice systems that engage in condemnation without adjudication will face up to the failure of adversary criminal procedure. I
believe that we will find in modern Continental criminal procedure
an irresistible model for reform. For the moment, however, I am left
to conclude with a paradox. Today in lands where the law of torture
once governed, peoples who live in contentment with their criminal
justice systems look out across the sea in disbelief to the spectacle
of plea bargaining in America, while American tourists come by the
thousands each year to gawk in disbelief at the decaying torture
chambers of medieval castles.

"To serve and protect": learning from police history

MARK H. MOORE & GEORGE L. KELLING

Over the last three decades, American police departments have pursued a strategy of policing that narrowed their goals to "crime fighting," relied heavily on cars and radios to create a sense of police omnipresence, and found its justification in politically neutral professional competence. The traditional tasks of the constable—maintaining public order, regulating economic activity, and providing emergency services—have been deemphasized, and those of the professional "crime fighter" have increased. Joe Friday's polite but frosty professionalism ("Just the facts, Ma'am") is a perfect expression of the modern image.

In many ways, this strategy has been remarkably successful. Thirty years ago, the idea that the police could arrive at a crime scene anywhere in a large city in less than five minutes would have been idle dreaming, yet we now have that capability. Similarly, the idea that the police would have moved out from under the shadow of political influence and flagrant abuses of individual rights would also have seemed unrealistic, yet most people now think of the police as much more honest and professional than in the past. In fact, in many ways the current strategy of policing is the apotheosis of a reform spirit that has guided police executives for over eighty years.

It is ironic, then, that precisely at the moment of its greatest triumph, the limits of this strategy have also become apparent. The concrete experience of citizens exposed to this strategy of policing is different from what the reformers had imagined. Officers stare suspiciously at the community from automobiles, careen through city streets with sirens wailing, and arrive at a "crime scene" to comfort the victim of an offense that occurred twenty minutes earlier. They reject citizen requests for simple assistance so that they can get back "in service"—that is, back to the business of staring at the community from their cars. No wonder so many citizens find the police unresponsive. Officers treat problems which citizens take seriously—unsafe parks, loud neighbors—as unimportant. And when a group of citizens wants to talk about current police policies and procedures, they are met by a "community relations specialist" or, at best, a precinct patrol commander, neither of whom can respond to their problems without calling headquarters.

This situation would not be so bad if the police were succeeding in their crime-fighting role. But the fact of the matter is that they are not. Crime rates continue to increase, and the chance that a violent crime among strangers will be solved to the satisfaction of the police (let alone the prosecutors and the courts) is still less than 20 percent. The reason for this poor performance, research now tells us, is that the police get less help than they need from victims and witnesses in the community.

How has this peculiar situation come about? How is it that the one public body that promises "to serve and protect" today seems incapable of doing either satisfactorily? And how might police procedures be reformed to allow officers to control crime effectively *and* give citizens the kind of service they need to feel safe and comfortable in their communities? A useful way to begin answering these questions is to review the history of American policing and note some of the paths abandoned along the way. While much of this history is well known to some, what is less well understood is how the pursuit of a professionalized, politically neutral police force—narrowly focused on "serious crime" and relying on new technologies—eventually weakened the bonds between private citizens and the police, and shifted the burdens of enforcement to a public agency that could not succeed by itself.

Private and public policing

It is easy to forget that publicly-supported police agencies were only recently created in the United States. Throughout the colonial period and up until the mid-nineteenth century, everyday policing was performed by night watchmen who also lit lamps, reported fires, managed runaway animals, and stood ready to help in family emergencies. Their role as "crime fighters" was restricted to raising a general alarm whenever they saw criminal misconduct—an event that must have been rare, given the small numbers of watchmen and the haphazard methods of patrol. Apprehension of the fleeing felons then depended on vigorous pursuit by private citizens. The investigation of past criminal offenses also depended on private initiative. When sufficient evidence was gathered, a victim could enlist the aid of a constable to regain his property or make an arrest, but the constable would ordinarily rely on the victim to locate the suspect.[1]

By the 1840s, this informal arrangement became insufficient to deal with the increasing lawlessness of American cities, so city governments began experimenting with new forms of policing. The most important model for these changes was England, which was also debating about and experimenting with new forms of policing. The old English system, which had served as the model for the American, also placed heavy reliance on private individuals for crime prevention, apprehension, and investigation; beyond that, there was only a loose network of publicly supported watchmen, constables, and courts. Publicly supported policing was, however, supplemented by commercial "thief catching" firms, the "Bow Street Runners" being the most famous. These firms depended on informants and undercover operations, as well as more traditional investigative techniques. While these methods seemed to give commercial firms a competitive advantage in solving crime, the potential for corruption and abuses was quite high. (Some of their success seems to have depended on arranging for the crimes to occur in the first place!)[2]

Despite the traditional authority of the constables, and the vitality and ingenuity of private commercial policing, the English forces of public order tottered before the social challenges of the 1830s. As in the United States, the problem lay in the growing cities, where authorities not only had to cope with street crime, but also with riots, demonstrations, and increasing assaults on public decency (i.e., drunkenness and "juvenile delinquency"). And the street lights still had to be lit.

Much as the American "crime wave" and riots of the 1960s led to the creation of federal commissions and independent research centers to study the prevention of crime, the English social disturbances of the early-nineteenth century led to a fundamental re-evaluation of policing. Jeremy Bentham and Patrick Colquhoun proposed a form of "preventative policing" and drafted legislation mandating the regular supervision of known criminals, people in "dangerous" occupations (e.g., minstrels), and even specific ethnic groups (e.g., Jews).[3] The English also looked across the Channel at the "continental model" of policing based on informants and covert surveillance rather than overt patrols.[4]

In the end, neither "detective policing," as suggested by the Bow Street Runners and the French, nor "preventative policing," as conceived by Colquhoun, was adopted as a strategy for English policing in the mid-1800s. Instead, Parliament chose a model of policing based on the success of the Thames River Police. Originally established as an experiment funded privately by insurance companies to reduce property losses, the Thames River Police were so successful that they became the first police organization in England to be financed entirely by public revenues. Publicly-supported policing was then mandated throughout England in 1829 by the Metropolitan Police Act, and the Metropolitan Police began patrolling the streets of London shortly thereafter.[5]

The British approach to policing consolidated older traditions. The strategy was still based on overt, reactive patrol, and the patrol force, armed only with concealed truncheons, was trained to be civil in confronting citizens. The only major changes were that the patrol force became larger, trained, and were deployed more carefully, and were organized in chains of command that would allow operations in large units as well as small. Investigation was still privately supported, and no use of informants or covert police was explicitly sanctioned to gather prior information about crimes.

The transformation of British policing in the early-nineteenth century had a tremendous impact on American thinking and practice. New York City established a municipal police force based on the British model in 1845, followed quickly by Boston and Philadelphia; by 1855, cities as far west as Milwaukee had police departments. As in England, these departments consisted of overt, reactive patrol forces capable of operating in large or small units. And because the forces were accessible to citizens at all hours, they retained their constabulary functions, providing emergency service as well as controlling crime and maintaining public order.

The establishment of publicly-supported police departments patrolling city streets was clearly a major event shaping the institutional development of police departments. Indeed, current strategies of policing are the direct descendants of these innovations. As important as these events were, however, the innovations of the mid-1800s were a less decisive resolution of basic issues in the design of police strategies than is often supposed.

The reforms did not mean, for example, that the responsibility for crime control had passed irrevocably from private to public hands. Private police forces, in the form of railroad police, "Pinkertons," and private detectives, played a major role in controlling crime and disorder well into the twentieth century. And though these private police forces were less prominent through the 1960s, they are now reappearing in the form of commercial security guards and volunteer citizen block-watches. (And the police remain dependent, as they always have been, on the willingness of citizens to alert them to crime and aid them in the identification, apprehension, and conviction of suspects.)

Nor did the American reforms of the mid-1800s focus the attention of the police exclusively on crime, demonstrations, and riots. The scope of police responsibilities remained very broad: They were responsible for discouraging lesser forms of public disorder (e.g., drunkenness, vandalism, obscenities, harassment, lewdness), for regulating economic activity (e.g., enforcing traffic laws, coping with unlicensed peddlers, inspecting facilities), and for handling everyday medical and social emergencies (e.g., traffic accidents, fires, lost children).

Similarly, although the adopted strategy seemed to emphasize overt, reactive patrols, other strategies did not entirely disappear. By the late 1800s, most metropolitan police departments had developed detective divisions as well as patrol divisions. These units not only conducted investigations of past crimes at public expense (a major change from the earliest traditions), but also began using informants and covert methods that allowed them to prevent future crimes, as well as solve past ones.[6] And while no explicit authorization was given for "preventative policing" as it existed on the Continent, the police were able to use their authority to enforce public order and regulate commerce to accomplish the same purpose.

Perhaps the most significant question left unresolved by the innovations of the 1850s, however, was the basis of the new institution's legitimacy. What gave the new police force the right to interfere in private matters? Were they to be considered agents of the state, allies of current political figures, neutral instruments of the law, or specialized as professionals? In England, the police were able to draw on the traditional authority of the crown and explicit parliamentary authorization, and even so the legitimacy of the police was suspect. (Upper class people reportedly whipped the police as they passed in carriages, and the press commented favorably whenever· a policeman was killed in a crowd.)[7] In the United States, the police had even less on which to rely. Local political support would always be fickle in a democratically-spirited country ever skeptical of authority and claims to "expertise," so it should come as no surprise that the new police forces would be suspect and considered potentially dangerous.

From constable to crime fighter

The tension between the need to maintain order in a growing country and the inherent distrust of authority profoundly shaped the development of the American police between 1870 to 1970. The first phase began immediately when the new municipal police forces became allied with local politicians. In the words of Robert Fogelson, police departments in the 1800s became "adjuncts to the political machine," and a major source of jobs and upward mobility for newly-arrived immigrants.[8] Their duties ran from maintaining public order, economic regulation, and crime and riot control, to providing lodging and soup kitchens for vagrants. Of course, since their legitimacy rested on local political support, rather than an abstract notion of full and impartial enforcement of the laws, their enforcement efforts were far from even-handed. By accommodating differences among ethnic neighborhoods and the purposes of local politicians, the police were more a central cog than a mere adjunct of the big city machines.

By the end of the 1800s the police became a favorite target of reformers in the Progressive movement, who despised both the established power of the political machines and the "disorder" that characterized those parts of the cities where police had stopped enforcing vice laws. Ending the "corruption" of the police became a central feature of the Progressive program, as was the transfer of social welfare functions from the police to the new social work professionals. The Progressive conception of the police was one radically different from the practices which had developed over the previous century, and consisted of several significant departures: The police were to become a highly disciplined, paramilitary organization independent of local political parties; to ensure that independence, the force would be organized along functional rather than geographic lines; personnel procedures would be strictly meritocratic rather than political; and police duties would be limited to the strict enforcement of existing laws.

The first wave of reform did not succeed completely, mainly due to Prohibition. Popular opposition to the liquor control laws was so widespread that "equal enforcement of the laws" was out of the question, and "corruption" reappeared to accommodate the unwillingness of responsible citizens to comply with the law. This experience taught a significant new lesson to the reformers: Not all laws command equal respect, so only those laws that are widely supported should be enforced. (Later, this idea was expanded to cover so-called "victimless" crimes.)

This "lesson," whatever its flaws and whatever its unforeseen consequences, laid the basis for the next phase of American policing, in which the police became primarily concerned with serious crime: murder, assault, robbery, rape, burglary, and theft. "Victimless" crimes, disorderliness, economic regulation, and social services became less important after the 1930s because, it was argued, police activity in these aroused citizen opposition, encouraged unequal enforcement, and spawned corruption. The clean, bureaucratic model of policing put forward by the reformers could be sustained only if the scope of police responsibility was narrowed to "crime fighting."

Several other developments reinforced the notion of police officer as "crime fighter." One was the improvement of communication and transportation technologies. With cars, telephones, and radios, all of which became widely available to the police in the 1940s and 1950s, it seemed that an omnipresent patrol force could be created.[9] Moreover, the new technology complemented the objective of creating centralized, tightly disciplined police organizations. The second influence was the development of the Uniform Crime Reports which publish rates of homicide, rape, robbery, aggravated assault, burglary, larceny, and motor vehicle theft for every city in the country. These data inevitably became important indicators of police performance, and encouraged police administrators to focus on these crimes as the most important targets of police work.

The net result of these recent developments—cars, radios, and statistics—has been a new reform strategy that resembles the old in its commitment to equal enforcement of the laws and its emphasis on a disciplined police bureaucracy, but differs in that it focuses narrowly on property crimes and violent crimes rather than

the enforcement of all laws—especially those regarding public order and economic regulation. To a great extent, the professionalized "crime fighting" strategy of policing that emerged after World
War II is the current dominant police strategy. Its explicit goal is
the control of crime, not maintaining public order or providing
constabulary services. It depends on even-handed, non-intrusive
enforcement of the laws, but only those laws with widespread
public support. Its basic mode of operation includes motorized patrol, rapid responses to calls for service, and retrospective investigation of offenses, not high-profile foot patrol or "preventative
policing."

The consequences of reform

By now, the goal of "professionalizing" police forces—of making
them conform to the reform strategy—has become an orthodoxy.
Police executives, experts on policing, the police themselves, even
mayors and legal philosophers, are all eager to trade constables
and cops on the beat for professional crime fighters—to transform
their "street corner politicians" into Joe Fridays and then into SWAT
teams. The irony is that this orthodoxy has become powerful in
shaping police aspirations and practices at about the same time
that embarrassing weaknesses are beginning to appear.

It is now clear, for example, that there is a limit to the deployment of police resources (squad cars, rapid-response police teams,
investigators) beyond which the rate of violent crime is very insensitive. The most recent research convincingly establishes three
points. First, neither crime nor fear of crime are importantly affected by major changes in the number of officers patrolling in
marked cars.[10] Apparently, within broad ranges, neither criminals
nor citizens can tell whether an area is heavily or superficially pa-
trolled when the patrolling is done in cars. Second, rapid responses
to calls for service do not dramatically increase the apprehension
of criminals.[11] The reason is that citizens do not call the police
until long after a crime has been completed, and the attacker has
fled the scene. Given these delays, even instantaneous police responses would do little good. Third, police investigators are unable
to solve crimes without major assistance from victims and witnesses.[12] Indeed, unless they can identify the offender, chances are
overwhelming that the crime will not be solved. On the other hand,
if citizens can identify the offender, it is difficult to see what modern detectives add to what the local constables used to do. And,

at any rate, the capacity of the police to solve crimes—particularly those involving violence among strangers—remains shockingly low. Fewer than 20 percent of robberies are solved, and an even smaller fraction of burglaries.[13] All this suggests that the orthodox police strategy provides neither general deterrence, nor successful apprehension of individual offenders.

Besides running up against limits to professionalized crime fighting, it is now clear that contemporary police strategies ignore a large number of tasks which the police have traditionally performed. There are no streetlamps to light anymore, but there are a large number of constabulary functions—maintaining order in public places (parks, buses, subway platforms), resolving marital disputes, disciplining non-criminal but harmful juvenile behavior, preventing public drug and alcohol use—which no other public organizations have taken up since they were abandoned by the police. These jobs simply are not done, and what is worse, they have come to be seen as illegitimate functions of *any* public body or private citizen. The role of modern legal philosophy is very important here, for it has been most responsible for making many of these once implicitly-sanctioned practices explicitly illegal for the police, and without that implicit support individual private citizens have become unwilling to take matters into their own hands.

The bitter irony of this development is that it is probably these constabulary functions, properly performed, that make people feel safer in their neighborhoods than a drop in the "crime rate" as measured in the Uniform Crime Reports. Seeing a cop on the beat, allowing one's children to play unsupervised in the park, not being offered drugs on the street, taking the bus or subway late at night without being approached by vagrants—all these things probably make citizens feel safer than a drop in average police response time from five to three minutes. The sort of infringements on public order we are describing are often "unlawful," but they are not serious crime. As a result, the police neglect these offenses and escape the charge of discriminatory enforcement. Yet such offenses may matter more to citizen security than relatively rare "crime" as the police now define it.

Perhaps the most significant and least obvious limitation of the current police orthodoxy is the loss of a political base for police organizations. This is obscure largely because the current orthodoxy claims an opposite virtue: Once freed from corrupting political influence, the police become legitimate, neutral instruments of the law. Yet the weakness of politically neutral police depart-

ments was evident in the mid-1960s when local police confronted
the peaceful civil rights movement, large-scale student demonstrations, inner-city riots, and political terrorist groups. These activities challenged orthodox police strategy—since none is ordinary
"crime"—and the police simply could not respond effectively. Zeal-
ously pursuing ordinary street crime, they were accused of exac-
erbating rather than controlling riots. Dealing with terrorism required proactive policing, and the police found themselves without
local political allies in conducting these operations. The strategy
of professionalized crime fighting simply could not deal effectively
with the political attack on city governance in the 1960s; and rather
than fundamentally rethink their strategy, local forces made lame
gestures toward improving "police-community relations"—a phrase
that only highlights the false distinction at the heart of modern
policing.

There is a common element in each of these areas of weakness:
an insufficient link between the aspirations and interests of local
communities, and the operations of the police. In professionalizing
crime fighting, the "volunteers," citizens on whom so much used
to depend, have been removed from the fight. The effect has not
been increased security, but impotence in apprehending offenders,
widespread fear triggered by disorder, and a sense that things must
really be bad if police departments with all their capabilities cannot seem to cope with the problem.

Reforming the reforms

If there is anything to be learned from the relatively short history of the American police it is that, whatever the real benefits
of professionalization (e.g., reduced corruption, due process, serious
police training), the reforms have ignored, even attacked, some
features that once made the police powerful institutions in maintaining a sense of community security. Of course, it would be hopelessly romantic to think that modern police could immediately
reclaim an intimate relationship with well defined communities in
today's cities, or resume their broad social functions. And, indeed,
there is much in the modern conception and operations of police
departments that is worth preserving.

But still, within bounds, it may now be possible for imaginative
police executives and those who supervise their operations to make
changes that could reclaim some of the old virtues while sacrificing
little of value in the modern reforms. We offer ideas in four dis-

tinct areas: police dealings with private self-defense efforts; scope of police responsibility; police deployment; and the organizational structure of the force. In each case, the proposals are designed to link the police more surely to the communities in which they now operate.

Private and public enforcement. Private citizens inevitably play an important role in controlling crime. By limiting their exposure to risk, investing in locks and guns, banding together to patrol their own streets, or financing a private security force, private citizens affect the overall level of crime, and the distribution of the benefits and burdens of policing. Police strategists should encourage those private mobilizations, provide guidance and technical assistance, and position the police as back-ups to private efforts.

To a degree, of course, police forces now do this. They pass out police whistles, urge people to mark their property so that it can be more easily identified when stolen, help to organize block watches, and set up emergency call systems tied to rapid responses to calls to service. Yet, apart from responding to calls for service, one has the feeling that the police do not really take such activities seriously; and when the private efforts become powerful, the police often attack them as a danger to liberty (though their greater concern might well be the economic security that comes from monopolizing crime control efforts).

Nowhere is this ambivalence more obvious than in the general response to the growth of the Guardian Angels, a private paramilitary group that began in New York City and spread across the country. Many consider the Guardian Angels a useful auxiliary patrol force that reminds private citizens of their public responsibilities, and dignifies the young men and women who join; opponents (often including the police) see the Angels as vigilantes threatening the rights of citizens with undisciplined enforcement. Neither view is quite appropriate. Those who welcome the Angels as a novelty forget that private policing was the only form of policing for centuries, and that the creation of a public police force was conceived as a great reform.

Those who think of the Angels as dangerous vigilantes forget the value of private crime-control efforts, and the crucial difference between vigilantes and responsible citizens playing their traditional role in crime control. The Guardian Angels limit their functions to deterrence and, occasionally, apprehension; they neither judge guilt nor mete out punishment. And the Angels do not take offense or intervene easily; they respond only to serious crimes that they observe. In so doing, they assume nothing more than the rights and responsibilities of good democratic citizens. It is somewhat ironic that the appearance of several thousand Guardian Angels attracts such great public interest and worry, when the emergence of a *commercial* private security force numbering in the millions has attracted almost no notice at all.

In sum, the Guardian Angels serve as a reminder that, while private policing entails some risks, it remains a useful part of overall crime control efforts. Each increase in public policing may be offset by some reduction in private policing, and it is not uncommon for citizens to refuse involvement, saying, "Let the police do it, they get paid for it." But if the public is made to understand that public policing *complements* private efforts, private individuals will take more public responsibility. They will call the police when they see offenses, agree to act as witnesses, and even intervene themselves precisely because public police are available to support them. To the extent possible, the local police must encourage, rather than resist, these private efforts.

The scope of police responsibility. If the police are going to ask for more help from their communities, it seems likely that they will have to produce more of what communities want. As we have seen, police agencies have narrowed their purposes to combatting serious crime. This narrowing is applauded by a general citizenry that thinks "serious crime" is what it fears, by legal philosophers who think the enduring social interest in non-intrusive and fair policing can best be served by focusing attention on a few serious and visible crimes, by professional police administrators who want to allocate scarce resources to the most urgent areas, and by the police themselves who prefer the imagery of "combating bad guys" to the more complex, mundane tasks. This is a strategic error. The error comes not in emphasizing the importance of controlling violent crime—no one looking at U.S. crime statistics could possibly propose not taking violent crime seriously—but rather in imagining that effective control can be gained simply by complaining about court decisions that "handcuff" the police. More effective control of violent crime depends on an increased willingness on the part of communities to help the police identify and prosecute offenders, but the police miss many opportunities to establish closer relationships with the community, relationships that would encourage such assistance.

Take, for example, the current police response to victims of violent crime. When a violent crime occurs, the police dispatch a patrol car. The officer takes a statement from the victim and identifies witnesses; occasionally an arrest is made at the scene. The officer disappears, and the case is turned over to a detective who may, or may not, interview the victim. The offender is taken to court and often released on bail. The terrified victim may well be intimidated by the offender, yet when he or she calls the police, the call is given a low priority. Neither the arresting officer nor the detective is likely to hear of, or allay, the victim's fear. Surely there is more that can be done by the police to reassure victims: They could be given a name and number of another to call, and the police might even arrange to visit periodically, in unusual cases, or to stake out the home of the victim. Note that the *police* should do this, not some social work agency. Police involvement is important, not only because they have a plausible capacity to protect, but also because they can simultaneously earn credit with the community and strengthen their case against the offender.

In a similar vein, the police could take more seriously their responsibilities to maintain public order. If, as an accumulating body of evidence suggests, it is public disorder and incivility—not violent crime—that increases fear, and if the police wish to reassure citizens, they must maintain public order—in parks, on busy street corners, at bus stops—as well as fight crime. Similarly, commercial regulation such as traffic and parking control, which is now performed mechanically, should be explicitly organized to support local commerce. Finally, police departments should *welcome* their role in providing emergency services—coping with traffic accidents, fires, health emergencies, domestic disputes, etc. Officers will inevitably perform these services, so they might as well incorporate them in their mission, perform them well, and get credit for them. After all, it is an important and popular function which the police typically do well.

Deployment and organization

Deployment. Current police deployment strategy is based heavily on overt, reactive patrol: About 60 percent of the resources of most police departments are committed to patrol, and most of that to uniformed officers riding the streets in clearly marked cars. In addition, most police departments devote 10 percent of the resources to a detective unit engaged in retrospective investigations of criminal offenses. The rest of the resources are devoted to other tasks such as vice squads, juvenile units, narcotics division, and so on.[14]

This strategy is consistent with a focus on serious crime and a strong interest in evenhanded, non-intrusive policing. The capacity of patrol to thwart crimes through general deterrence, and their capacity to respond quickly to calls for service, are assumed to control crime; when deterrence fails and the police force arrives too late to catch the offender, the detectives take over to solve the crime. The enforcement effort is even-handed because patrol surveillance is general, and because anyone, for the price of a phone call, can claim services. And modern policing is non-intrusive in that intensive investigation begins only after a crime has been committed and focuses narrowly on the solution of that crime. Thus, the decision made in the mid-1800s to make public policing a patrol and detective activity, rather than a system of preventive policing, carries on until today: The police skim the surface of social life.

Given the success of this deployment in protecting important social values, it is not surprising that it has been widely utilized. Still, this deployment has internal contradictions as a crime-fighting strategy, to say nothing of the limitations as a device to draw the community into a closer relationship with the police. One basic contradiction has already been noted: In the vast, anonymous cities of today, this deployment apparently fails to deter crime or apprehend offenders. A second difficulty is that once an overt patrol force is made available to citizens at the price of a phone call, officers will be involved in much more than crime fighting. The commitment to "accessibility" then conspires to defeat the narrow focus on crime fighting: We end up with police forces that invite more citizens' requests than can be handled, then frustrate them by failing to take some calls seriously, and finally fail to control crime.

It is now time for police executives to reconsider their deployment strategies. The enormous investment in telephones, radios, and cars that now allow the police to respond to crime calls in under five minutes (often with more than one car) has bought little crime control, no greater sense of security, and has prevented the police from taking order maintenance and service functions seriously. To the extent that victim services, order maintenance, and a general community presence are valuable not only in themselves, but also as devices for strengthening crime control and building the police as a popular community institution, it is crucial that police executives get some of their officers out of cars and away from dispatchers at least some of the time. Some recent evidence suggests that foot patrol *does* promote a sense of security, and also reduces calls for service. Apparently cops on the beat can deal effectively with many citizen complaints.[15]

For "crime fighting," other tactics may be appropriate and effective. Special decoys or stake-outs targeted at muggers and robbers may be more effective in controlling such offenses than random patrol. Similarly, if current evidence about the large number of offenses committed by a small number of offenders turns out to be correct, it may make sense for the police to develop intelligence systems for "street crimes" similar to those used in combatting organized crime and narcotics traffic. It is even possible that expanded use of informants would be possible. Obviously these methods are more intrusive and proactive than the current deployment, but they may be tolerable if they prove to be effective, and if they enjoy the support of local communities.

Departmental organization. Most police departments are currently organized along functional lines: There is a patrol division, a narcotics bureau, a youth division and so on. This structure is consistent with many reform ambitions: It allows for convenient reallocation of resources across the city to respond to changing circumstances; it promotes the development of specialized expertise; and, most importantly, it strengthens the control police chiefs have over their subordinates. The alternative scheme is to organize along geographic lines, giving area commanders responsibility for all police operations within a given geographic area. This geographic organization would also make the police department policy-making and operations more accessible to citizens in the community because the area commander would have both the interest and the capacity to respond to local requests.

Geographic organization was the traditional form attacked by the reformers because precinct-level politicians had become too powerful and had bent the police to their corrupt purposes. It was preferable, the reformers thought, to organize in a way that moved power towards the chief (and those who influenced him) rather than leave it in the hands of precinct captains vulnerable to local political machines. The functional organization served these purposes; but there was a price to be paid. Local community groups such as PTA's, merchants associations, block associations, churches, and individual citizens frightened by crimes—all no longer organized in political machines—now have no one to turn to in the local precinct. There is the precinct commander, but his direct authority typically extends only to the patrol division, and he feels more

responsible to those "downtown" than the citizens of the community. There may also be a "community relations officer," but his
authority usually extends nowhere. It is no wonder, then, that citizens who have interests and problems different from those of the
city as a whole feel abandoned by the police. If police executives
wish to cultivate stronger political support from local neighborhoods, they should consider a more geographic division of responsibilities, shifting more power to local precinct commanders, or
even to lower levels in the department such as lieutenants or ser-
geants who could serve as lenders for "team policing" units. Again,
the point is that the police must become more visible and active
in neighborhood affairs.

A post-Dragnet era?

Police strategies do not exist in a vacuum. They are shaped by
important legal, political, and attitudinal factors, as well as by local
resources and capabilities, all factors which now sustain the modern conception of policing. So there may be little leeway for modern
police executives. But the modern conception of policing *is* in serious trouble, and a review of the nature of that trouble against
the background of the American history of policing gives a clear
direction to police forces that wish to improve their performance
as crime fighters *and* public servants.

The two fundamental features of a new police strategy must be
these: that the role of private citizens in the control of crime and
maintenance of public order be established and encouraged, not
derided and thwarted, and that the police become more active,
accessible participants in community affairs. The police will have
to do little to encourage citizens to participate in community policing, for Americans are well practiced at undertaking private, voluntary efforts; all they need to know is that the police force wel-
comes and supports such activity. Being more visible and accessible
is slightly more difficult, but hiring more "community relations"
specialists is surely *not* the answer. Instead, the police must get
out of their cars, and spend more time in public spaces such as
parks and plazas, confronting and assisting citizens with their private troubles. This is mundane, prosaic work but it probably beats
driving around in cars waiting for a radio call. Citizens would
surely feel safer and, perhaps, might even be safer.

ENDNOTES

1 See T.A. Critchley, *A History of Police in England and Wales,* (London: Constable and Company, Ltd., 1967).

2 Critchley, pp. 19-20; Sir Leon Radzinowicz, *A History of English Law,* Vol. 2, (London: Stevens and Sons Ltd., 1956), p. 289.

3 Radzinowicz, Vol. 2, pp. 271-273.

4 Radzinowicz, Vol. 3 (1956), p. 539.

5 Critchley, p. 51.

6 David R. Johnson, *Policing the Urban Underworld,* (Philadelphia: Temple University Press, 1979).

7 Critchley, p. 54.

8 Robert Fogelson, *Big City Police,* (Cambridge MA: Harvard University Press, 1977), Chapter 1.

9 O. W. Wilson and Roy Clinton McLaren, *Police Administration,* Third Edition, (New York: McGraw-Hill, 1983).

10 G. L. Kelling, T. Pate, C. Dieckman and C. E. Brown, *The Kansas City Preventive Patrol Experiment,* (Washington, D.C.: Police Foundation, 1974); J. F. Schnelle, et al. "Patrol Evaluation Research: A Multiple-Baseline Analysis of Saturation Police Patrolling During Day and Night Hours," *Journal of Applied Behavior Analysis* 10, no. 1.

11 William Bieck, *Response Time Analysis,* (Kansas City Police Department).

12 Peter W. Greenwood, Jan M. Chaiken, Joan Petersilia, *The Criminal Investigation Process,* (Lexington MA: D.C. Heath and Company, 1977).

13 *Uniform Crime Report for the United States, 1980,* (Washington, D.C.: U.S. Department of Justice, 1981), p. 180.

14 *Survey of Police Operational and Administrative Practices—1981* (Washington, D.C.: Police Executive Research Forum and Police Foundation), pp. 22-24.

15 *Newark Foot Patrol Experiment,* (Washington, D.C.: Police Foundation, 1981); Robert C. Trojanowicz, "An Evaluation Report: The Flint Neighborhood Foot Patrol," unpublished; Dato Steenhuis, paper presented at American Society of Criminology Annual Meeting, November 5, 1982, Toronto, Canada.

Contributors

David H. Bayley is a Professor in the Graduate School of International Studies at the University of Denver and author of *Forces of Order: Police Behavior in Japan and the United States*.

Barbara Boland is Senior Research Associate at INSLAW, Inc., Washington, DC.

B. Bruce-Briggs is with the Hudson Institute. He is not a member of the National Rifle Association.

Edward Epstein is the author of several books including *News From Nowhere*, and writes frequently for *The New Yorker*.

Nathan Glazer is Professor of Education and Social Structure at Harvard University. He is editor of *The Public Interest*.

George Kelling is Adjunct Lecturer and Director of the Program in Criminal Justice Policy and Management at the Kennedy School of Government at Harvard University.

John H. Langbein is Professor of Law at the University of Chicago.

Jess Marcum is a consultant in the fields of investment and legalized gambling with R&D Associates, Santa Monica, CA.

Robert Martinson, the former chair of the Department of Sociology, City College of New York, died in 1979.

Mark Moore is Professor of Government at Harvard University.

Marc F. Plattner is a Fellow at the National Humanities Center in North Carolina.

Peter Reuter is Senior Economist with the Rand Corporation in Washington, DC.

Henry Rowen is Professor of Public Management at Stanford University.

Jonathan B. Rubinstein is Research Director for the Center for Research on Institutions and Social Policy in New York, NY.

Jackson Toby is Professor of Sociology and Director of the Institute for Criminological Research at Rutgers University.

Gordon Tullock is University Distinguished Professor at the Center for the Study of Public Choice at George Mason University. He is the editor of *Public Choice*.

James Q. Wilson is Professor of Government at Harvard University.